IBM InfoSphere Replication Server and Data Event Publisher

Design, implement, and monitor a successful
Q replication and Event Publishing project

Pav Kumar-Chatterjee

[PACKT] enterprise

PUBLISHING

professional expertise distilled

BIRMINGHAM - MUMBAI

IBM InfoSphere Replication Server and Data Event Publisher

First published: August 2010

Production Reference: 1120810

Published by Packt Publishing Ltd.
32 Lincoln Road
Olton
Birmingham, B27 6PA, UK.

ISBN 978-1-849681-54-4

www.packtpub.com

Cover Image by Sandeep Babu (sandyjb@gmail.com)

Credits

Author
Pav Kumar-Chatterjee

Reviewer
Rich Briddell

Acquisition Editor
Rashmi Phadnis

Development Editor
Akash Johari

Technical Editors
Ishita Dhabalia

Aditi Suvarna

Indexer
Monica Ajmera Mehta

Editorial Team Leader
Gagandeep Singh

Project Team Leader
Lata Basantani

Project Coordinator
Poorvi Nair

Proofreader
Lesley Harrison

Graphics
Nilesh Mohite

Production Coordinator
Alwin Roy

Cover Work
Alwin Roy

About the Author

Pav Kumar-Chatterjee (Eur Ing, CENG, MBCS) has been involved in DB2 support on the mainframe platform since 1991, and on midrange platforms since 2000. Before joining IBM, he worked as a database administrator in the airline industry as well as various financial institutions in the UK and Europe. He has held various positions during his time at IBM, including in the Software Business Services team and the global BetaWorks organization. His current position is a DB2 technical specialist in the Software Business. He has been involved with Information Integrator (the forerunner of Replication Server) since its inception, and has helped numerous customers design and implement Q replication solutions, as well as speaking about Q replication at various conferences.

Pav Kumar-Chatterjee has co-authored the *DB2 pureXML Cookbook*, published in August 2009.

This book would not have been possible without the help that the following people have given us over the years:

Anuradha I Pariti (IBM US), Beth Hamel (IBM US), David Tolleson (IBM US), Jayanti Mahapatra (IBM US), Kevin Lau (IBM US), Neale Armstrong (IBM UK), Nikola Slavicic (IBM Slovenia), Ray Houle (Canada), Sean Byrd (IBM US).

Any mistakes or omissions in this book are the sole responsibility of the author.

About the Reviewer

Rich Briddell is a Senior Managing Consultant with IBM Software Group, Replication Center of Competency, specializing in Q Replication on z/OS, and Distributed platforms. He works in the St. Louis, MO area and has 19 years of experience in the DBMS field. He has been an application development team lead and independent consultant. He holds a Master of Arts degree in Operations Management from the University of Arkansas and a Master of Science from Webster University in Computer Resources and Information Management. He is an IBM Certified Solutions Expert for Informix Dynamic Server V10, V9, and V7, an IBM Certified Advanced Database Administrator for DB2 UDB database systems, and an IBM Certified Application. Developer for DB2 UDB Family, and an IBM Certified Specialist for WebSphere Application Server. He is co-author of the IBM Redbook *DB2 Information Integrator Q Replication: Fast Track Implementation Scenarios*.

I would like to dedicate this book to Carrie and Scott – you never know where life's journey will take you, but you will always be in the thoughts of those who love you

Table of Contents

Preface

Business planning is no longer just about defining goals, analyzing critical issues, and then creating strategies. You must aid business integration by linking changed-data events in DB2 databases on Linux, UNIX, and Windows with EAI solutions, message brokers, data transformation tools, and more.

This book will accompany you throughout your Q replication journey. It will bring you some of the best practices to implement your project smoothly and within time scales. The book has in-depth coverage of Event Publisher, which publishes changed-data events that can run updated data into crucial applications, assisting your business integration processes. Event Publisher also eliminates the hand coding typically required to detect DB2 data changes that are made by operational applications.

In this book, we start with a brief discussion on what replication is and the Q replication release currently available in the market. We then go on to explore the world of Q replication in more depth. The latter chapters cover all the Q replication components and then talk about the different layers that need to be implemented — the DB2 database layer, the WebSphere MQ layer, and the Q replication layer. We conclude with a chapter on how to troubleshoot a problem. The Appendix (available online) demonstrates the implementation of 13 real-time Q replication scenarios with step-by-step instructions.

What this book covers

Chapter 1, Q Replication Overview, describes why we want to replicate data and what is available today in the IBM world of data replication. It introduces the architecture of Q replication and different types of Q replication available and discusses various DB2 replication sources including XML data and compressed data, and looks at filtering and transformations.

Chapter 2, Q Replication Components, discusses three layers—DB2 database layer, the WebSphere MQ layer, and the Q replication layer that make up a Q replication solution and also showed the relationship between *Replication/Publication Queue Map*, *Q subscription*, and *subscription group*.

Chapter 3, The DB2 Database Layer, looks at creating the databases used in Q replication, the Q replication control tables, and their structure.

Chapter 4, WebSphere MQ for the DBA, illustrates the working and setup of WebSphere MQ.

Chapter 5, The ASNCLP Command Interface, illustrates the working and setup of the ASNCLP Command Interface, guides you through some of the Q replication setup tasks, and shows you how to perform them using ASNCLP commands.

Chapter 6, Administration Tasks, focuses on the administrative tasks that we need to perform to set up and administer a Q replication environment.

Chapter 7, Monitoring and Reporting, looks at monitoring and reporting on the Q replication setup. It also describes the Replication Alert Monitor and how to use monitors.

Appendix A, Setup Procedures: Steps to Follow, describes the tools available to set up Q replication, goes through various scenarios, and gives step-by-step instructions. This can be downloaded from `http://www.packtpub.com/sites/default/files/downloads/1544_Appendix.zip`

What you need for this book

In the course of this book, you will need the following software utilities to try out various code examples listed:

- InfoSphere Replication Server 9.7.1
- WebSphere MQ V6.0 or V7.0

Who this book is for

If you are a professional who needs to set up and administer a Q replication or Event Publishing environment, then this is the book you need. The book will give you a clear understanding of how to implement Q replication. The examples are based on a Linux, UNIX, or Windows operating system, but the principles are equally applicable to Q replication on z/OS.

Conventions

In this book, you will find a number of styles of text that distinguish between different kinds of information. Here are some examples of these styles, and an explanation of their meaning.

Code words in text are shown as follows: "A target database is created using the DB2 script file as shown next."

A block of code is set as follows:

```
CONNECT RESET;
DROP DB db2b;
CREATE DB db2b;
UPDATE DB CFG FOR db2b USING logarchmeth1 disk:c:\temp;
BACKUP DATABASE db2b TO c:\temp;
```

When we wish to draw your attention to a particular part of a command-line block, the relevant lines or item(s) are set in bold:

```
SUBNAME     S STATE_TIME
----------  - ------------------------
T10001      A 2006-02-22-18.32.22.112000
T10002      I 2006-02-22-18.22.14.468000
T10003      I 2006-02-22-18.22.14.478002
```

Any command-line input or output is written as follows:

```
$ db2 "select substr(subname,1,10) as subname, state as S, state_time
from asn.ibmqrep_subs"
```

New terms and **important words** are shown in bold. Words that you see on the screen, in menus or dialog boxes for example, appear in the text like this: "There is also a **Sample entries** button, which will give us some default queue names.".

> Warnings or important notes appear in a box like this.

> Tips and tricks appear like this.

Reader feedback

Feedback from our readers is always welcome. Let us know what you think about this book—what you liked or may have disliked. Reader feedback is important for us to develop titles that you really get the most out of.

To send us general feedback, simply send an e-mail to feedback@packtpub.com, and mention the book title via the subject of your message.

If there is a book that you need and would like to see us publish, please send us a note in the **SUGGEST A TITLE** form on www.packtpub.com or e-mail suggest@packtpub.com.

If there is a topic that you have expertise in and you are interested in either writing or contributing to a book, see our author guide on www.packtpub.com/authors.

Customer support

Now that you are the proud owner of a Packt book, we have a number of things to help you to get the most from your purchase.

> **Downloading the example code for this book**
>
> You can download the example code files for all Packt books you have purchased from your account at http://www.PacktPub.com. If you purchased this book elsewhere, you can visit http://www.PacktPub.com/support and register to have the files e-mailed directly to you.

Errata

Although we have taken every care to ensure the accuracy of our content, mistakes do happen. If you find a mistake in one of our books—maybe a mistake in the text or the code—we would be grateful if you would report this to us. By doing so, you can save other readers from frustration and help us improve subsequent versions of this book. If you find any errata, please report them by visiting http://www.packtpub.com/support, selecting your book, clicking on the **errata submission form** link, and entering the details of your errata. Once your errata are verified, your submission will be accepted and the errata will be uploaded on our website, or added to any list of existing errata, under the Errata section of that title. Any existing errata can be viewed by selecting your title from http://www.packtpub.com/support.

Piracy

Piracy of copyright material on the Internet is an ongoing problem across all media. At Packt, we take the protection of our copyright and licenses very seriously. If you come across any illegal copies of our works, in any form, on the Internet, please provide us with the location address or website name immediately so that we can pursue a remedy.

Please contact us at copyright@packtpub.com with a link to the suspected pirated material.

We appreciate your help in protecting our authors, and our ability to bring you valuable content.

Questions

You can contact us at questions@packtpub.com if you are having a problem with any aspect of the book, and we will do our best to address it.

1
Q Replication Overview

Welcome to the start of your journey along the Q replication road. Any journey can be a bumpy ride, but after reading this book and going through the numerous examples, your journey will be a smoother one! In this first chapter, we will take you through the following discussion points:

- Why we want to replicate data.
- What is available today in the IBM world of data replication.
- The toolsets available to set up and administer a replication environment and look at the code that we need to install for a functioning Q replication solution.
- Introduce the architecture of Q replication. We look at the different types of replication available, namely the base replication methods of unidirectional, bidirectional, and peer-to-peer, and the replication architectures built on these base methods.
- Replicating XML data types and compressed tables. We look at some of the design points when considering replicating compressed table.
- Q replication conflict detection.
- Available transformation processing for both regular and XML data.

Why do we want to replicate data

Much has been written about why we need to replicate data, so we will keep this short. What's wrong with just storing our data in one place? Well, in today's 24x7 world where being without data for even a short period of time could be catastrophic to our business, we need a method to be able to take a copy of our data and possibly more than one copy and store it securely in a different location. This copy should be complete and be stored as many miles away as possible. Also the amount of data that has to be stored is ever increasing and being generated at a fast rate, so our method needs to be able to handle large volumes of data very quickly.

Overview of what is available today

In the IBM software world today, there are a number of options available to replicate data:

- InfoSphere (formerly WebSphere) Replication Server
- InfoSphere CDC (formerly the Data Mirror suite of programs)
- The DB2 High Availability Disaster Recovery (HADR) functionality
- Traditional log shipping

In this book, we will cover the first option–InfoSphere Replication Server, which from now on, we will refer to as *DB2 replication*. The other options are outside the scope of this book.

The different replication options

In the world of DB2 replication, we have two main options—SQL replication and Q replication, both of which involve replicating between source and target tables. Event publishing is a subset of Q replication, in that the target is not a table but a WebSphere MQ queue. The choice of replication solution depends on a number of factors, of which the fundamental ones are:

- Type of source
- Type of target
- Operating system support

The DB2 Information Center contains a table, which compares the three types of replication. This table can be used as a quick checklist for determining the best solution to a given business requirement (`http://publib.boulder.ibm.com/infocenter/db2luw/v9r7/topic/com.ibm.swg.im.iis.db.repl.intro.doc/topics/iiyrcintrsbsc.html`).

The following figure shows the basic operations of SQL replication:

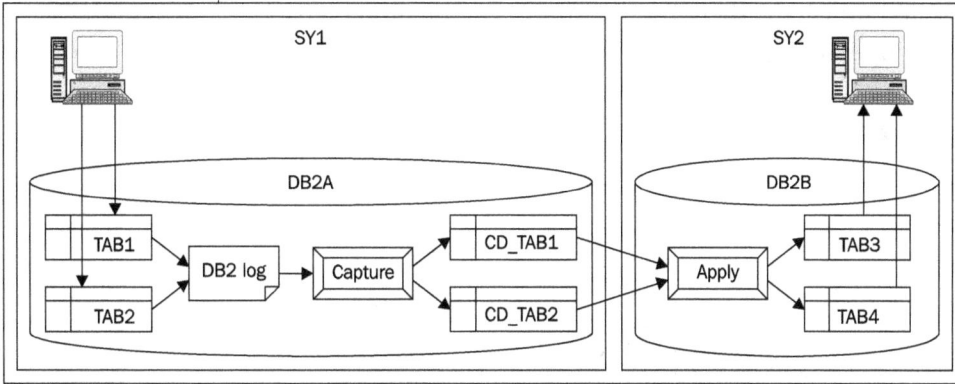

Updates to any tables are logged, and if the table is a registered table (TAB1 and TAB2), then the SQL Capture program (Capture for short) reads the information from the DB2 log and inserts the row into a change data table (CD_<table-name>)—there is one of these for each registered source table. The SQL Apply program (Apply for short) reads from these change data tables and updates the target tables (TAB3 and TAB4).

In Q replication, we do not have the concept of change data tables, as shown in the following figure:

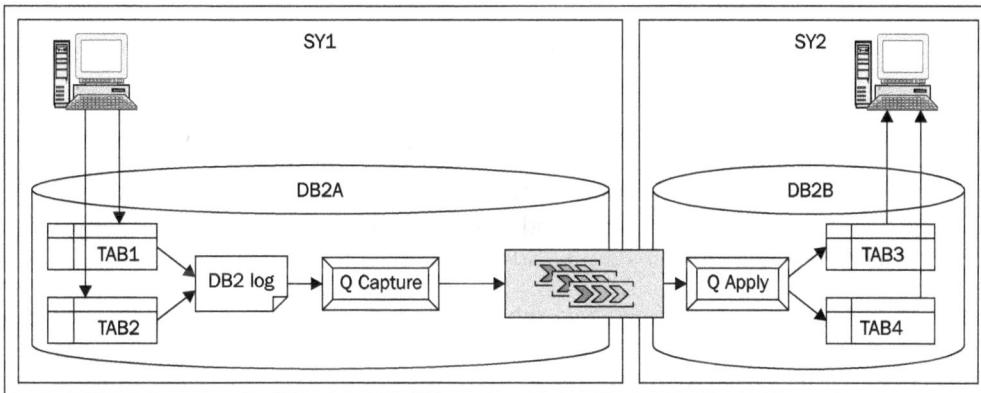

Any updates to registered tables, which the Q Capture program (Q Capture for short) detects are put onto a WebSphere MQ queue. The Q Apply program (Q Apply for short) then reads from these queues and updates the target tables.

In Event Publishing, there is no Q Apply and no target tables as shown in the following diagram:

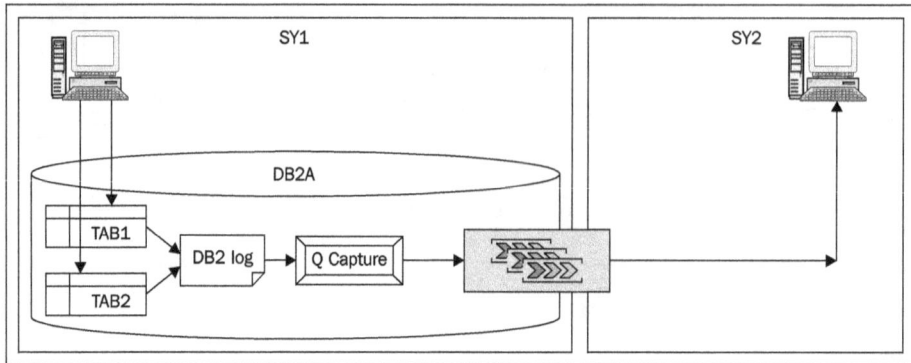

Q Capture puts messages into the WebSphere MQ queues, and it is up to the consuming applications to destructively/non-destructively read from these queues.

Replication toolset

We have three ways of administering a replication environment. We can use:

- The Replication Center GUI
- The ASNCLP command interface
- Standard SQL

We recommend that when you are new to replication, you should use the Replication Center and once you are confident with the process, you can then progress onto the ASNCLP interface. For defining production systems, we recommend using the ASNCLP interface, because the commands can be scripted.

The ASNCLP interface generates SQL, which is run against the appropriate control tables to define and administer the replication environment. Therefore, in theory, it is possible for us to write our own SQL to do this. However, the SQL can be complicated and manual coding could result in errors, and therefore we recommend not using this method.

The Replication Center GUI

The Replication Center GUI can be used to set up and administer a Q replication scenario. See *Chapter 6, Administration Tasks*, for details on accessing and using the Replication Center. The launchpad screen is shown next.

The Replication Center has a series of wizards, which are very useful if we are new to replication. The default wizard screen is the launchpad screen, and it can be accessed from the main replication screen through **Replication Center | Launchpad**. The wizards take us through all the steps necessary to set up a replication environment.

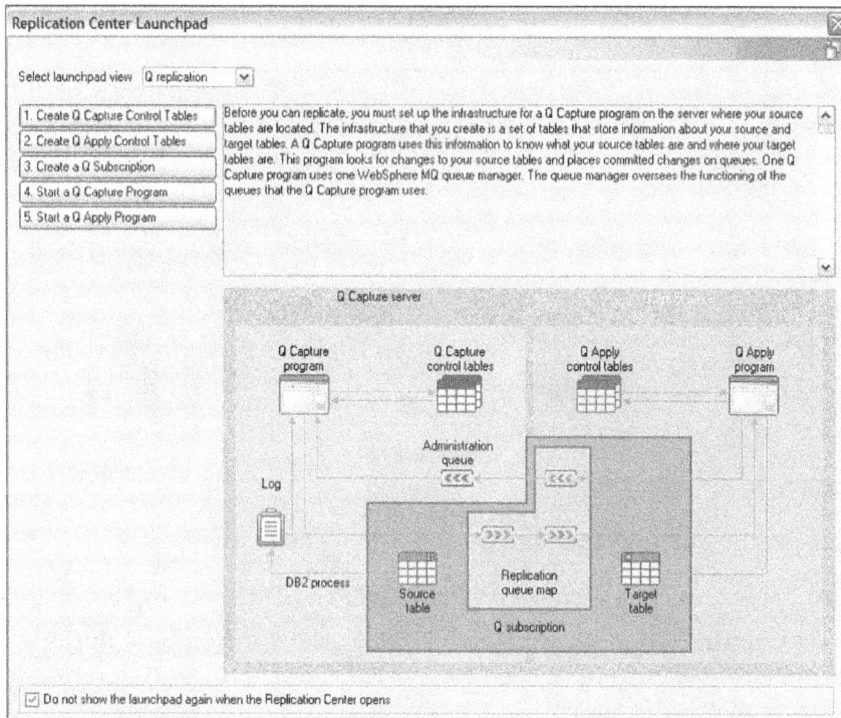

Using the Replication Center, it is possible to generate an SQL script for a particular function. The ability for the Replication Center to generate ASNCLP scripts in addition to SQL scripts is being planned for a future release.

The ASNCLP command interface

The ASNCLP interface (discussed in detail in *Chapter 5, The ASNCLP Command Interface*) allows us to enter commands from the command line, and more importantly, allows us to combine various commands into a script file, which can then be run from the command line. In this book, we will focus on ASNCLP scripts. It is supported on the Linux, UNIX, and Windows platforms. It is also supported on z/OS natively, through USS. We can also administer replication on z/OS from Linux, UNIX, and Windows system if we catalog the z/OS databases on the Linux, UNIX, and Windows system.

In the next section, we will look at the constituent components of Q replication.

Q replication constituent components

We like to think that the Q replication architecture is made up of three interconnected layers: the *DB2 database layer*, the *WebSphere MQ layer*, and finally the *Q replication layer*—each layer needs to be set up and tested before we move on to the next layer. An overview of the Q replication process is shown in the following diagram:

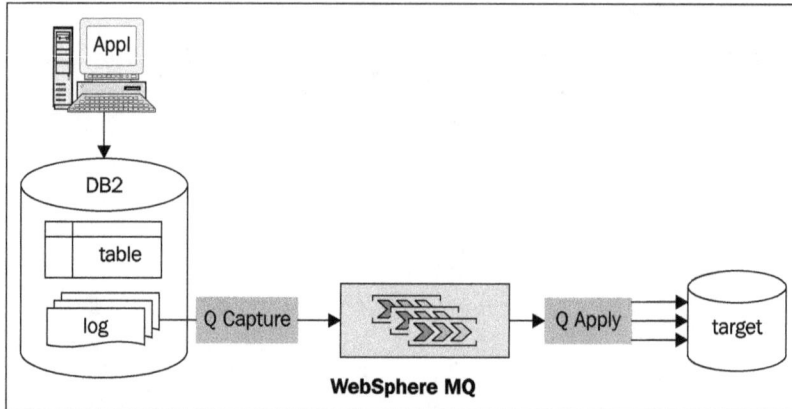

The basic operating architecture of a Q replication system involves:

- An application processing a row in a table and DB2 logging this operation
- A Q Capture program calling the DB2 log reader to "process" the DB2 log and place rows that have been committed and that it wants to replicate onto a WebSphere MQ queue
- A Q Apply program "reading" from this queue and applying the row to the target table

In this setup, we have two components that need to be installed—the Q replication code and the WebSphere MQ code. We will discuss the installation of both of these in some detail.

With the current packaging, the Q replication code for homogeneous replication already comes bundled with the base code for DB2—all we have to install is a replication license key. The license for InfoSphere Replication Server is called isrs.lic and for InfoSphere Data Event Publisher the license is called isep.lic. Use the DB2 db2licm command to install the license key and to confirm that the license key has been successfully applied.

Turning to the WebSphere MQ component, we can use either WebSphere MQ V6 or V7 with DB2 replication.

The WebSphere MQ V6 Information Center can be found at `http://publib.boulder.ibm.com/infocenter/wmqv6/v6r0/index.jsp`.

The WebSphere MQ V7 Information Center can be found at `http://publib.boulder.ibm.com/infocenter/wmqv7/v7r0/index.jsp`.

For the procedure to install WebSphere MQ, consult the WebSphere MQ Information Center and search for *install server*. As an example, we will now take you through installing WebSphere MQ V6 on x86 64-bit Linux (which comes packaged as `C87RUML.tar.gz`). We need to perform the following tasks:

1. As root, use `gunzip` and `tar` to unpack the WebSphere MQ packages:

   ```
   # gunzip C87RUML.tar.gz
   # tar -xvf C87RUML.tar
   ```

2. As root, the first task we need to perform is accept the MQ license, as shown next:

   ```
   # ./mqlicense.sh
   ```

3. Now we can install the base packages. As root, issue the following commands:

   ```
   # rpm -U MQSeriesRuntime-6.0.1-0.x86_64.rpm
   # rpm -U MQSeriesServer-6.0.1-0.x86_64.rpm
   # rpm -U MQSeriesSDK-6.0.1-0.x86_64.rpm
   ```

4. If we want the WebSphere MQ sample programs, which include amqsput, amqsget, amqsgbr, amqsbcg, and so on (which we do!), then we have to install the following package:

   ```
   # rpm -U MQSeriesSamples-6.0.1-0.x86_64.rpm
   ```

For future reference, to uninstall WebSphere MQ, perform the following steps:

1. We can check which packages are installed using the following command:

   ```
   # rpm -q -a | grep MQSeries
   ```

2. We can check what version of WebSphere MQ we are running by using the following command:

   ```
   # dspmqver
   ```

   This should give us an output similar to the following:

   ```
   Name:        WebSphere MQ
   Version:     6.0.0.0
   CMVC level:  p000-L080610
   BuildType:   IKAP - (Production)
   ```

On UNIX systems, if we are running on a 64-bit system, then we need to add the WebSphere MQ library to the LD_LIBRARY_PATH environment variable. If we do not do this, then when we try and start Q Capture (or Q Apply), we will see the following messages in the process log file:

```
2009-09-02-12.47.39.730985 <ASNMQLOD:MQCONN> ASN0584E "Q Capture"
: "ASN" : "AdminThread" : An error occurred while the program was
dynamically loading the WebSphere MQ library "libmqm_r.so". Error
code: "0x90000076", "Cannot load the specified library". Environment
variable ASNUSEMQCLIENT is set to "".
```

The ASN0584E message tells us to set the LD_LIBRARY_PATH environment variable. To check the current setting of this variable, we can either list the current values of all environment variables, using the env command, or we can list the value of this specific variable by using the echo command and prefixing the variable name with a dollar sign:

```
echo $LD_LIBRARY_PATH
```

We can temporarily set the value of this parameter (for the duration of the session in which the command was issued), using the following command:

```
LD_LIBRARY_PATH=/opt/mqm/lib64:$LD_LIBRARY_PATH
```

If we ever need to remove the packages, we would use the commands as shown:

```
#rpm -ev MQSeriesRuntime-6.0.1-0.x86_64.rpm

#rpm -ev MQSeriesServer-6.0.1-0.x86_64.rpm

#rpm -ev MQSeriesSDK-6.0.1-0.x86_64.rpm

#rpm -ev MQSeriesSamples-6.0.1-0.x86_64.rpm
```

The Q Capture and Q Apply programs are discussed in detail in *Chapter 2, The Q Capture and Q Apply programs*. Typically, these programs will be installed on different servers, in which case we have to pay attention to the machine clock time on the servers.

> The machine clock time on all servers involved in replication should be synchronized.

The times on all servers need to be synchronized, because each captured record has a timestamp associated with it, and Q Apply will not apply in the future. Therefore, if the Q Capture server is ahead of the Q Apply server, then Q Apply will wait until it has reached the timestamp in the replicated record before applying it. If the Apply server time is ahead of the Capture server time, then we will not hit the "Apply will not apply in the future" problem, but the latency figures will be out by the time difference.

In the next section, we will look at the different types of Q replication.

The different types of Q replication

There are four basic types of Q replication:

- Unidirectional
- Bidirectional
- Peer-to-peer
- Event Publishing

Replicating to a stored procedure or a Consistent Change Data (CCD) table are a subset of unidirectional replication.

Let's look at each of these in more detail. In the following sections, we talk about source and target tables. You may be wondering, what about views, triggers, and so on? You should check the *Pre-setup evaluation* section of *Appendix A*, for a list of objects to check for, before deciding on whether Q replication is the correct solution.

Unidirectional replication

In unidirectional replication, we can replicate all of the rows and columns of a source table or we can just replicate a subset of the rows and columns. We cannot really perform any transformation on this data. If we want to perform some sort of transformation, then we would need to replicate to a stored procedure, which we will discuss in detail in *Appendix A*.

Replicating to a stored procedure

Stored procedure replication is a subset of unidirectional replication in which the target is not a table as such, but a stored procedure, as shown in the following diagram:

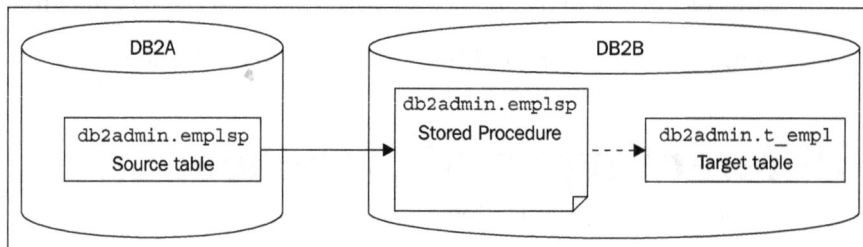

A stored procedure can transform the data and output the results to a target table. This target table is not known to Q Apply. These stored procedures can be written in SQL, C, or Java. An example of replicating to a stored procedure is shown in the *Replication to a stored procedure* section of *Appendix A*.

> Prior to DB2 9.7 the source table and the stored procedure must have the same name, and the target table name can be any name we like.

Bidirectional replication

In bidirectional replication, we replicate copies of tables between two servers, each of which has a copy of the table. Note that we can only set up bidirectional replication between **two** servers. Unlike unidirectional replication, where we can replicate a subset of rows and columns, this is not possible in bidirectional replication. The tables on both servers can have different names, but must have the same number of rows and columns. The columns must have identical column names of compatible data types. It is not possible to do any data transformation using this type of replication.

Because we are updating records on both servers, it is possible that the same record will be updated at the same time on both servers.

> Although Q replication provides a conflict detection mechanism, we strongly advise that the driving application should be written or modified in such a way that such conflicts be avoided. The conflict detection provided by Q replication should be treated as a safety net and not the primary conflict resolution mechanism.

This mechanism allows us to choose which data values are used to detect conflicts (key column values only, changed column values, or all column values) and which server should win if such a conflict is detected. The row in the losing system is rolled back and the record is written to the IBMQSNAP_EXCEPTIONS table for review. Conflict detection is discussed in detail in the *Q replication conflict detection* section.

One of the related subjects to conflict detection is the concept of which server takes precedence in a conflict, or to put it more bluntly, which server is the master and which is the slave! If there is a conflict, then whichever server takes precedence will not apply changes from the other server. This ensures that the servers remain in sync. There is a more egalitarian option, which is that no server takes precedence. In this situation, rows are applied irrespective of whether or not there is a conflict, which ultimately leads to a divergence of the contents of the databases, which is not good!

There are two types of bidirectional replication — the first type is where we have an active/passive setup and the second type is where we have an active/active setup. The type of replication you choose will have implications on which server is defined as the master and which as the slave and what to do if a Q subscription is inadvertently inactivated.

In an active/passive setup, the passive server should be made the master. In an active/active setup, the choice of which system is the master is a decision you have to make. See the *Conflict detection: update/delete conflict* section of *Appendix A* for further discussion.

Peer-to-peer replication

Peer-to-peer replication allows us to replicate data between two or more servers. This is different from bidirectional replication, which is only between two servers. Each server has a copy of the table (which can have a different schema and name), but must have the same number of rows and columns and these columns must have identical column names and compatible data types. It is not possible to do any data transformation using this type of replication.

In peer-to-peer replication, there is no such thing as a master or slave server — each server will have the most recent copy of the table — eventually! What this means is that there will be a slight delay between the first server having a copy of the table and the last server having that copy. This is an asynchronous process, so at any one time the tables might be different, but once applications stop updating them, then the tables will converge to the most recently updated value. This type of processing means that there isn't any "manual" conflict detection as such (it is handled automatically by Q Apply), because the latest update will always win.

If two applications update the same record at exactly the same time, then Q replication uses the server number allocated when the peer-to-peer environment was set up to determine the winner. This type of processing means that two columns are added to each of the tables in the Q replication environment, where the first column is a timestamp of when the row was last updated (GMT) and the second column is the machine number. These updates are performed through triggers on the tables.

Tree replication

Tree replication comes in two flavors: bidirectional, which we call **B-Tree** replication, and unidirectional, which we call **U-Tree** replication.

A variation on the bidirectional replication theme is that it would be nice to be able to replicate from one master to two slaves in a bidirectional manner. This requirement was addressed with B-Tree replication.

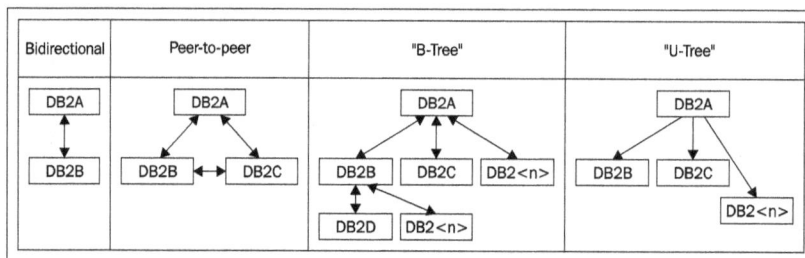

Bidirectional	Peer-to-peer	"B-Tree"	"U-Tree"
DB2A	DB2A	DB2A	DB2A
DB2B	DB2B ↔ DB2C	DB2B DB2C DB2<n>	DB2B DB2C
		DB2D DB2<n>	DB2<n>

A B-Tree replication structure is one, which looks like a tree (as shown in the preceding diagram). DB2A replicates with DB2B, DB2C, and DB2<n> in a bidirectional manner, but DB2B, DB2C, and DB2<n> do not replicate directly with each other — they have to replicate through DB2A, which is what differentiates B-Tree replication from peer-to-peer replication.

For B-Tree replication, we can replicate between one master and many slaves in a bidirectional manner. In SQL replication terms, this was called **Update Anywhere**. Note that it is not possible to set up B-Tree replication using the Replication Center — we need to use ASNCLP commands, which is described in detail in the *Bidirectional replication to two targets (B-Tree)* of *Appendix A*.

We can also replicate from one source to many targets in a unidirectional scenario, which we call a U-Tree scenario. In the preceding figure, DB2A replicates with DB2B, DB2C, and DB2<n> in a unidirectional manner (we can have more than three targets). Note, there is no radio button in the Replication Center to set up unidirectional U-Tree replication. What we have to do is set up unidirectional replication from DB2A to DB2B, and then for DB2A to DB2C, and so on. It is easier to use ASNCLP commands, which are described in detail in the *Unidirectional replication to two targets (U-Tree)* *section* of *Appendix A*.

Replicating to a Consistent Change Data table

Let's first look at the definition of **Consistent Change Data** (CCD) replication. CCD table replication is a subset of unidirectional replication, in which the target is a CCD table, which contains a row for each insert/delete/update that occurs on the source table. These CCD tables can be *complete* and/or *condensed* (this will be explained later).

There are three main uses of CCD table replication:

- To populate an operational data store
- To keep a history of changes made to the source table for audit purposes
- To enable multi-target update

Consider the situation where we want to populate an **Operational Data Store (ODS)** with data from our live system. We want to replicate all operations apart from delete operations. Before the introduction of CCD tables, our only option was to use a stored procedure. One of the parameters that the Q Apply program passes to a stored procedure is the operation (insert, delete, and so on) that occurred on the source system. See the *Replication to a stored procedure* section of *Appendix A*.

We can use CCD tables to keep a history of changes made to a table, or as a feed to InfoSphere DataStage.

The multi-target update scenario uses Q replication to populate the CCD table and then uses SQL Replication to populate the multiple target tables as shown in the following diagram:

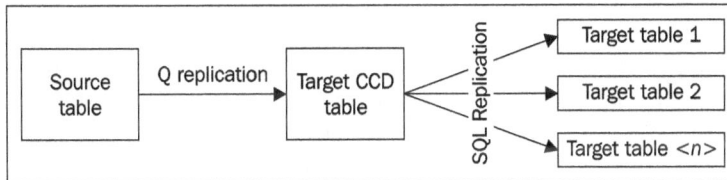

In the *Replicating to a CCD table* section of *Appendix A*, we go through the steps needed to set up replication to a CCD table.

We can only specify that a target table be a CCD table in a unidirectional setup. A CCD target table is made up of the following columns (only four of the metadata columns are compulsory, the other four are optional, and the order of the columns does not matter):

```
<user key columns>

<user nonkey columns>

<user computed columns>

        IBMSNAP_INTENTSEQ              Compulsory auditing columns
        IBMSNAP_OPERATION
        IBMSNAP_COMMITSEQ
        IBMSNAP_LOGMARKER

        IBMSNAP_AUTHID                 Optional auditing columns
        IBMSNAP_AUTHTKN
        IBMSNAP_PLANID
        IBMSNAP_UOWID
```

The IBMSNAP_INTENTSEQ column is a sequence number that uniquely identifies a change and is ascending within a transaction. The IBMSNAP_OPERATION column is a flag that indicates the type of operation for a record. The IBMSNAP_COMMITSEQ column is a sequence number that provides transactional order. The IBMSNAP_LOGMARKER column is the time that the data were committed.

The IBMSNAP_AUTHID column is the authorization ID that is associated with the transaction. This column is for used for Linux, UNIX, Windows, and z/OS. For z/OS, this is the primary authorization ID. The IBMSNAP_AUTHTKN column is the authorization token that is associated with the transaction. This column is for z/OS only and is the correlation ID—it will be NULL for Linux, UNIX, and Windows. The IBMSNAP_PLANID column is the plan name that is associated with the transaction. This column is for z/OS only—it will be NULL for Linux, UNIX, and Windows. And finally, the IBMSNAP_UOWID column is the unit-of-work identifier from the log record for this unit of work. This column is used for Linux, UNIX, Windows, and z/OS.

The <user computed columns> columns will be the before image columns and must be NULLABLE (because there is no before image when we insert a row, the before image is NULL).

Now let's look at what data is stored in a CCD table. With CCD tables we can specify that the target table is: COMPLETE or NONCOMPLETE and CONDENSED or NONCONSENSED. These are interpreted as follows:

- **Complete** (COMPLETE=Y): A complete CCD table contains every row of interest from the source table and is initialized with a full set of source data. All target table loading options are valid for complete CCDs (automatic, manual, or no load).

- **Noncomplete** (COMPLETE=N): A noncomplete CCD table contains only changes to the source table and starts with no data. A noncomplete CCD table records all UPDATE operations at the source. The only valid load option for noncomplete CCD tables is *no load*.

- **Condensed** (CONDENSED=Y): A condensed CCD table contains one row for every key value in the source table and contains only the latest value for the row. For condensed CCD tables, a primary key is required, which is used in case of an update conflict. If such a conflict occurs, all the source columns are forced into the row (CONFLICT_ACTION=F).

- **Noncondensed** (CONDENSED=N): A noncondensed CCD table contains multiple rows with the same key value, one row for every UPDATE, INSERT, or DELETE operation at the source table. When added to the CCD table, all of the rows become INSERT operations. No primary key is required.

The options for handling unexpected conditions at the target are limited for CCD tables:

For condensed and complete, two choices are available:

- Force the source change into the target table (CONFLICT_ACTION=F)
- Ignore the condition and continue (CONFLICT_ACTION=I)

For any combination other than condensed and complete, the only valid option is to force the change into the target table.

For all CCD table types, the only valid conflict rule is to check only key columns (CONFLICT_RULE=K).

Before we move on, let's quickly look at CCD tables in an SQL Replication environment. In SQL Replication, there is the concept of *internal* and *external* CCD tables, which does not exist in Q replication. In SQL Replication terminology, all Q replication CCD tables are *external* CDD tables.

Event Publishing

The Event Publishing functionality captures changes to source tables and converts committed transactional data to messages in an XML format. Each message can contain an entire transaction or only a row-level change. These messages are put on WebSphere MQ message queues and read by a message broker or other applications. We can publish subsets of columns and rows from source tables so that we publish only the data that we need.

DB2 replication sources

In this section, we cover the various DB2 objects that can be used as replication sources, such as XML data types, compressed tables, and large objects.

Replicating XML data types

From DB2 9.5 onwards, we can replicate tables, which contain columns of data type XML, and an example is shown in the *Unidirectional replication for an XML data type* section of *Appendix A*. We can set up unidirectional, bidirectional, and peer-to-peer replication.

From DB2 9.7 onwards, in unidirectional replication, we can use XML expressions to transform XML data between the source and target tables. Examples of supported and unsupported XML expressions are shown next.

Supported XML expressions include XMLATTRIBUTES, XMLCOMMENT, XMLCAST, XMLCONCAT, XMLDOCUMENT, XMLELEMENT, XMLFOREST, XMLNAMESPACES, XMLPARSE, XMLPI, XMLQUERY, XMLROW, XMLSERIALIZE, XMLTEXT, and XMLVALIDATE.

Unsupported XML expressions include XMLAGG, XMLGROUP, XMLTABLE, XMLXSROBJECTID, and XMLTRANSFORM.

For a complete up-to-date list, check out the DB2 Information Center at http://publib.boulder.ibm.com/infocenter/db2luw/v9r7/topic/com.ibm.swg.im.iis.repl.qrepl.doc/topics/iiyrqsubcxmlexpress.html.

Replicating compressed tables

From DB2 9.7 onwards, tables can have both the COMPRESS YES and DATA CAPTURE CHANGES table options set, which means we can now replicate compressed tables.

The issue with replicating a compressed table, is what happens if the compression dictionary is changed while Q Capture is down? Once Q Capture is started again, then it will try and read logs and records that were compressed with the previous compression dictionary, and not succeed. To address this, when a table has both the COMPRESS YES and DATA CAPTURE CHANGES options set, then the table can have two dictionaries: an **active data compression dictionary** and a **historical compression dictionary**.

> We should not create more than one data compression dictionary while Q Capture is down.

If a table is set to DATA CAPTURE NONE, then if a second dictionary exists, it will be removed during the next REORG TABLE operation or during table truncate operations (LOAD REPLACE, IMPORT REPLACE, or TRUNCATE TABLE).

Replicating large objects

If a row change involves columns with **large object** (**LOB**) data, Q Capture copies the LOB data directly from the source table to the send queue.

If we are replicating or publishing data from LOB columns in a source table, then Q Capture will automatically divide the LOB data into multiple messages to ensure that the messages do not exceed the MAX MESSAGE SIZE value of the Replication Queue Map used to transport the data.

If we are going to replicate LOB data, then we need to ensure that the MAXDEPTH value for the Transmission Queue and Administration Queue on the source system, and the Receive Queue on the target system, is large enough to account for divided LOB messages.

If we select columns that contain LOB data types for a Q subscription, we need to make sure that the source table enforces at least one unique database constraint (a unique index, primary key, and so on). Note that we do not need to select the columns that make up this uniqueness property for the Q subscription.

Other DB2 objects

In addition to the previous objects, let's look at some other DB2 objects and see if they can be used as a Q replication source:

- What about **views**? Not at the present time.
- What about **DB2 system tables**? No.
- What about **Materialized Query Tables (MQTs)**? Yes as of DB2 9.7.
- What about **range-partitioned tables**? Yes as of DB2 9.7.
- What about **hash-partitioned tables**? Yes, see the *Q replication in a DPF environment* section.

So now let's move on to looking at Q replication filtering and transformations.

Q replication filtering and transformations

Let's first look at what is possible when it comes to filtering rows and columns, and then move on to look at transformations.

Filtering rows/columns

Let's first look at row filtering. It is only possible to filter rows for replication in a unidirectional scenario, and this is done in the Q subscription. For an example, see the *Creating a Q subscription* section of *Chapter 6*.

What about the number of columns we want to replicate—can we replicate just a subset of the source table columns? For the latest release of code, we can subset the columns to be replicated. Note that we cannot replicate more columns than are defined at the target table or target stored procedure and that the column names must still match, which is shown in the following diagram:

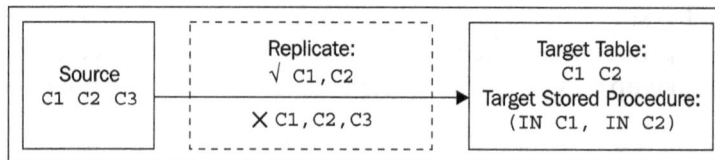

For unidirectional replication only, the target table can have more columns than the source table as shown in the following diagram, but these "non-source" columns cannot be part of the target table key and must be defined as NULLABLE or NOT NULL WITH DEFAULT, as shown next.

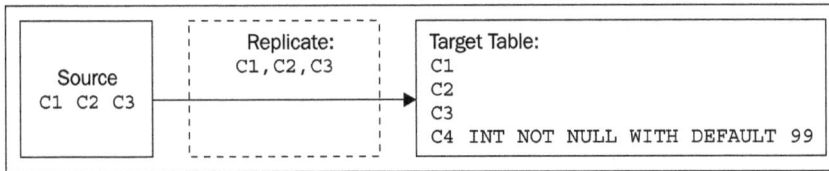

Any filtering of rows or columns in unidirectional replication is specified at Q subscription definition time. At this time, we can specify:

- Which columns to replicate and how they map to columns at the target table (or to parameters in a stored procedure)
- A search condition to determine which rows from the source table are replicated

As stated at the beginning of this chapter, Q replication is built for speed with transformations not being a major factor. However, although Q replication does not have the transformation capabilities of SQL Replication, it does have some transformation capabilities, which are described in the following sections.

Before and After SQL—alternatives

In Q replication, there is no concept of *before and after SQL*, as there is in SQL Replication. In a unidirectional setup, we can use SQL expressions to transform data between the source and target tables. We can map multiple source columns to a single target column, or to create other types of computed columns at the target. An example is shown in the *Q subscription for unidirectional replication* section of *Chapter 5* .

Stored procedure processing

If we want to perform transformations with Q replication, then we need to use stored procedure processing. This allows us to call external routines to perform all the transformations we want. The *Replication to a stored procedure* section of *Appendix A* shows an example of how to set up Q replication to a stored procedure.

We now move on to look at conflict detection in a Q replication environment.

Q replication conflict detection

This section looks at conflict detection, what it is, when it occurs and how we deal with it.

What is conflict detection?

Let's start by defining what we mean by a **conflict**. A conflict occurs in bidirectional replication when the same record is processed at the same time on the two servers. We then have to decide which server is the winner, which we do when we set up the Q subscription for the table.

When do conflicts occur?

In unidirectional replication, the only time we need conflict detection is if we are updating the target table outside of Q replication, which is not recommended! *Q subscription for unidirectional replication* section of *Chapter 5*, covers scenarios where the target table is updated outside of Q replication.

There is no conflict detection with Event Publishing.

We need conflict detection in multi-directional replication. Let's first look at bidirectional replication and then move on to peer-to-peer replication.

Bidirectional replication uses data values (which we can choose) to detect and resolve conflicts. The choice of data values is determined by the CONFLICT RULE parameter we specify when we create a Q subscription. The process is that "before" values at the source server are compared against the "current" values at the target server, and based on the level of conflict detection Q Capture sends a different combination of before and/or after values to Q Apply. The CONFLICT RULE options are:

- **Key column values only**: Q Apply attempts to update or delete the target row by checking the values in the key columns. Q Apply detects the following conflicts:
  - A row is not found in the target table
  - A row is a duplicate of a row that already exists in the target table

  With this conflict rule, Q Capture sends the least amount of data to Q Apply for conflict checking. No before values are sent, only the after values for any changed columns are sent.

- **Key and changed column values**: Q Apply attempts to update or delete the target row by checking the key columns and the columns that changed in the update. Q Apply detects the following conflicts:

  ° A row is not found in the target table

  ° A row is a duplicate of a row that already exists in the target table

  ° A row is updated at both servers simultaneously and the same column values changed

  If a row is updated at both servers simultaneously and the different column values changed, then there is no conflict. With this conflict rule, Q Apply merges updates that affect different columns into the same row. Because Q Apply requires the before values for changed columns for this conflict action, Q Capture sends the before values of changed columns.

- **All column values**: Q Apply attempts to update or delete the target row by checking all columns that are in the target table. With this conflict rule, Q Capture sends the greatest amount of data to Q Apply for conflict checking.

> If we replicate the LOB columns, then conflicts are not detected. This is because Q replication does not replicate "before" values for LOB data types. See the *Replicating large objects* section for more information.

In a peer-to-peer configuration, conflict detection and resolution are managed automatically by Q Apply in a way that assures data convergence. We do not need to set anything up, as was discussed in the *Peer-to-peer replication* section.

The *Conflict detection examples* section of *Appendix A* walks through a couple of conflict detection examples.

Q replication and HADR

We can combine Q replication and the **High Availability Disaster Recovery (HADR)** feature of DB2 in a couple of ways. In the first way, we can use Q replication to replicate data between database DB2A and DB2B and then use HADR to protect the DB2B database, as shown in the following diagram:

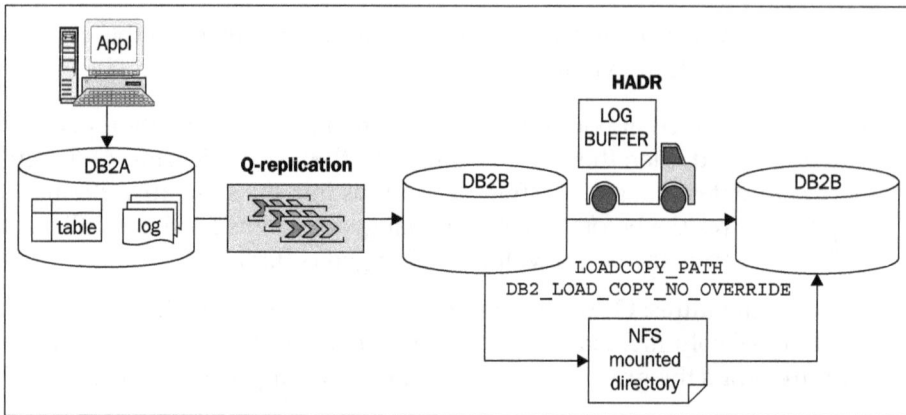

There is a new Q Apply parameter in DB2 9.7 called LOADCOPY_PATH, which can be used instead of the HADR DB2_LOAD_COPY_NO_OVERRIDE registry variable when target tables are loaded by Q Apply using the DB2 LOAD utility.

In the second way, we can use HADR to provide local resilience and Q replication to provide remote resilience, as shown in the following diagram:

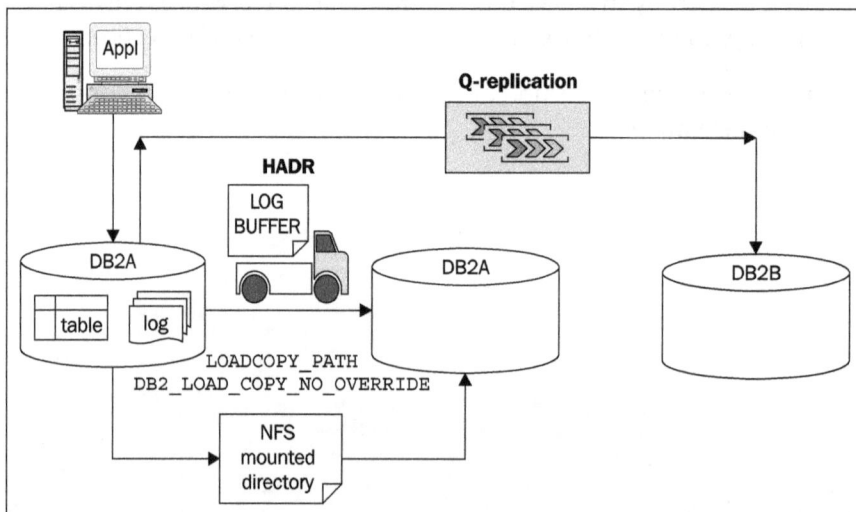

Q replication in a DPF environment

Q replication works well in a **Database Partition Facility (DPF)** environment, but there are a couple of design points to be aware of. Consider the sample configuration shown in the following diagram:

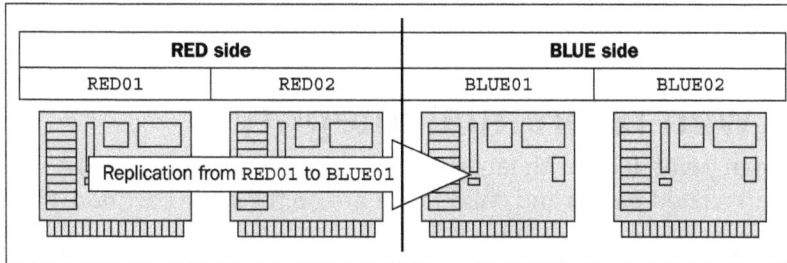

We have four servers called RED01, RED02, BLUE01, and BLUE02. We want to replicate from the RED side to the BLUE side. Each side will have four data partitions and a catalog partition with one DAS instance per box. The instance name is db2i001 and the database name is TP1.

The RED side is shown next. There are five database configuration files (DB CFG) and one database manager configuration file (DBM CFG). It is the "Detailed" table, which is replicated from the RED side to the BLUE side.

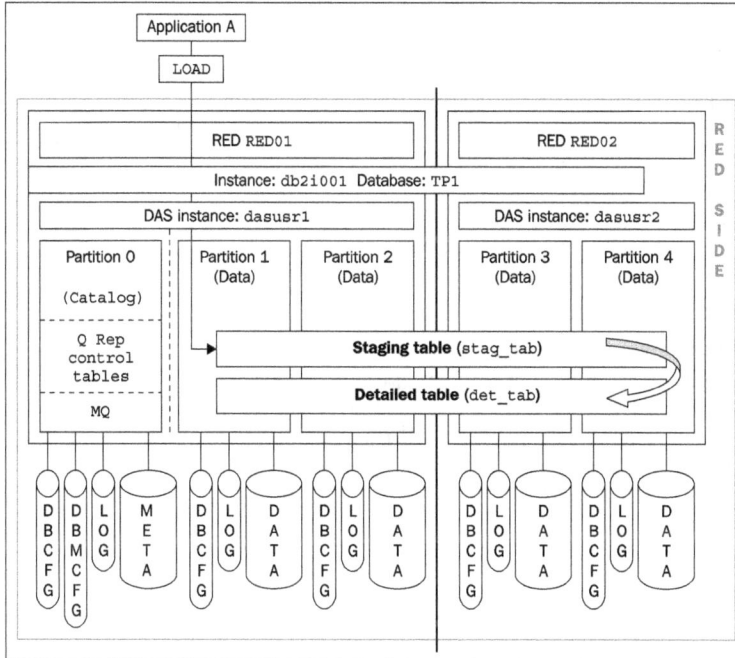

Note the following:

- MQ installed on RED01
- Replication control tables created on partition 0
- Q Capture and Q Apply run on RED01
- EXPLAIN tables defined on RED01

Tables with referential integrity

The first design point deals with tables, which have referential integrity. We need to ensure that all related parent and child tables are on the same partition. If we do not do this and start replication, then we will get ASN7628E errors.

Table load and insert considerations

If we want to load from the application, then the staging table should be partitioned similarly to the detailed table so that we can make use of collocation (therefore, we need the same partition group and same partition key).

If we want to insert from the application, then the staging table should be defined on partition 1 ONLY. If we are using INSERT, then we would use INSERT/SELECT/DELETE to transfer data from the staging table to the detailed table. We also need to perform simple housekeeping tasks on the staging table, for example regular online reorganizations.

An example of an INSERT/SELECT/DELETE statement is shown next:

```
with fred (id,name,trans_date) as
(
  select id,name,trans_date from stag_tab
  (delete from stag_tab where trans_date = current timestamp -10
minutes)
)
select count(*) from fred
(insert into det_tab select id,name,trans_date from fred);
```

Every time we run the above SQL, it will move records that are more than 10 minutes old from stag_tab to det_tab.

Summary

In this chapter, we reviewed the different types of replication available today, and how they are compared. We looked at the different types of Q replication, namely unidirectional/stored procedure/CCD, bidirectional, peer-to-peer, tree replication, and Event Publishing. We discussed various DB2 replication sources including XML data and compressed data and looked at filtering and transformations. Finally, we covered operating Q replication in HADR and DPF environments. Now that we have an overview of what Q replication is, we can look at the Q replication components in more detail, which is what we will do in the next chapter.

2
Q Replication Components

This chapter discusses the three layers, which are needed for Q replication: the **DB2 database layer**, the **WebSphere MQ layer,** and the **Q replication layer**. The individual stages for the different layers are shown in the following diagram:

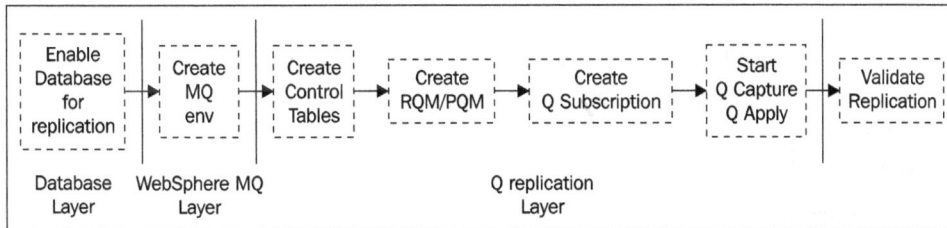

As we go through the following chapters, we will:

- Highlight which layer/stage is being talked about
- Look at how the three layers interact, and review why it is important for each layer/section to be successfully completed for the total solution to function correctly

The DB2 database layer

The first layer is the DB2 database layer, which involves the following tasks:

- For unidirectional replication and all replication scenarios that use unidirectional replication as the base, we need to enable the source database for archive logging (but not the target table). For multi-directional replication, all the source and target databases need to be enabled for archive logging.

- We need to identify which tables we want to replicate. One of the steps is to set the DATA CAPTURE CHANGES flag for each source table, which will be done automatically when the Q subscription is created. This setting of the flag will affect the minimum point in time recovery value for the table space containing the table, which should be carefully noted if table space recoveries are performed.

Before moving on to the WebSphere MQ layer, let's quickly look at the compatibility requirements for the database name, the table name, and the column names. We will also discuss whether or not we need unique indexes on the source and target tables.

Database/table/column name compatibility

In Q replication, the source and target database names and table names do not have to match on all systems. The database name is specified when the control tables are created. The source and target table names are specified in the Q subscription definition.

Now let's move on to looking at whether or not we need unique indexes on the source and target tables. We do not need to be able to identify unique rows on the source table, but we do need to be able to do this on the target table. Therefore, the target table should have one of:

- Primary key
- Unique contraint
- Unique index

If none of these exist, then Q Apply will apply the updates using all columns.

However, the source table must have the same constraints as the target table, so any constraints that exist at the target must also exist at the source, which is shown in the following diagram:

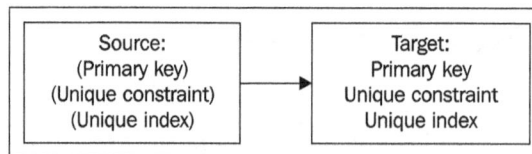

Source: (Primary key) (Unique constraint) (Unique index)	→	Target: Primary key Unique constraint Unique index

The WebSphere MQ layer

This is the second layer we should install and test—if this layer does not work then Q replication will not work!

We can either install the WebSphere MQ Server code or the WebSphere MQ Client code. Throughout this book, we will be working with the WebSphere MQ Server code.

If we are replicating between two servers, then we need to install WebSphere MQ Server on both servers. If we are installing WebSphere MQ Server on UNIX, then during the installation process a user ID and group called mqm are created. If we as a DBA want to issue MQ commands, then we need to get our user ID added to the mqm group.

Assuming that WebSphere MQ Server has been successfully installed, we now need to create the Queue Managers and the queues that are needed for Q replication. The details of what we need to create for each scenario are discussed in *Appendix A*. This section also includes tests that we can perform to check that the MQ installation and setup is correct. The following diagram shows the MQ objects that need to be created for unidirectional replication:

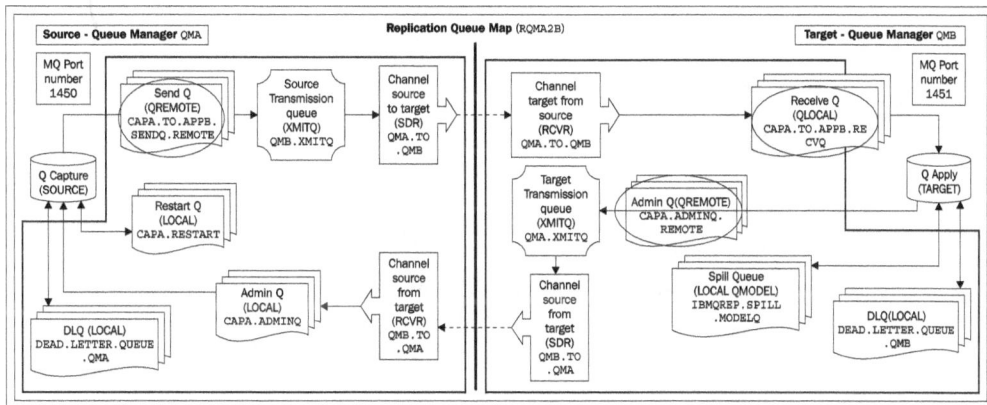

The following figure shows the MQ objects that need to be created for bidirectional replication:

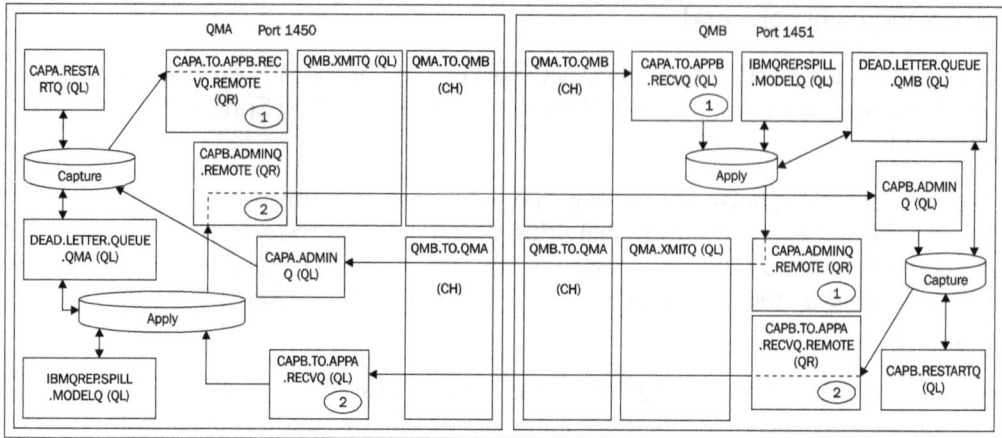

There is a mixture of Local Queue (LOCAL/QL) and Remote Queues (QREMOTE/QR) in addition to Transmission Queues (XMITQ) and channels, which are discussed more in *Chapter 4, WebSphere MQ for the DBA*.

Once we have successfully completed the installation and testing of WebSphere MQ, we can move on to the next layer — the Q replication layer.

The Q replication layer

This is the third and final layer, which comprises the following steps:

- Create the replication control tables on the source and target servers.
- Create the **transport definitions**. What we mean by this is that we somehow need to tell Q replication what the source and target table names are, what rows/columns we want to replicate, and which Queue Managers and queues to use.

The structure of the Q replication control tables are discussed in *Chapter 3, The DB2 Database Layer*, and their creation is discussed in the *To create/drop the Q replication control tables* section of *Chapter 6*.

Some of the terms that are covered in the remainder of this section are:

- Logical table
- Replication Queue Map
- Q subscription
- Subscription group (SUBGROUP)

What is a logical table?

In Q replication, we have the concept of a **logical table**, which is the term used to refer to both the source and target tables in one statement. An example in a peer-to-peer three-way scenario is shown in the following diagram, where the logical table is made up of tables TABA, TABB, and TABC:

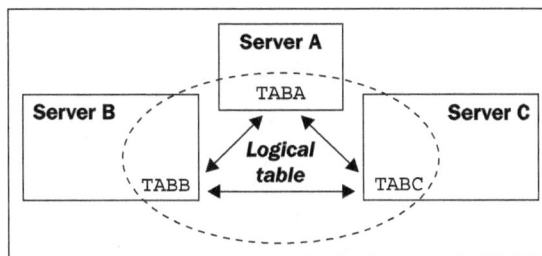

What is a Replication/Publication Queue Map?

The first part of the *transport definitions* mentioned earlier is a definition of **Queue Map**, which identifies the WebSphere MQ queues on both servers that are used to communicate between the servers. In Q replication, the Queue Map is called a Replication Queue Map, and in Event Publishing the Queue Map is called a Publication Queue Map.

Let's first look at **Replication Queue Maps (RQMs)**. RQMs are used by Q Capture and Q Apply to communicate. This communication is Q Capture sending Q Apply rows to apply and Q Apply sending administration messages back to Q Capture. Each RQM is made up of three queues: a queue on the local server called the **Send Queue** (SENDQ), and two queues on the remote server—a **Receive Queue** (RECVQ) and an **Administration Queue** (ADMINQ), as shown in the preceding figures showing the different queues. An RQM can only contain one each of SENDQ, RECVQ, and ADMINQ.

The SENDQ is the queue that Q Capture uses to send source data and informational messages.

The RECVQ is the queue that Q Apply reads for transactions to apply to the target table(s).

The ADMINQ is the queue that Q Apply uses to send control messages back to
Q Capture.

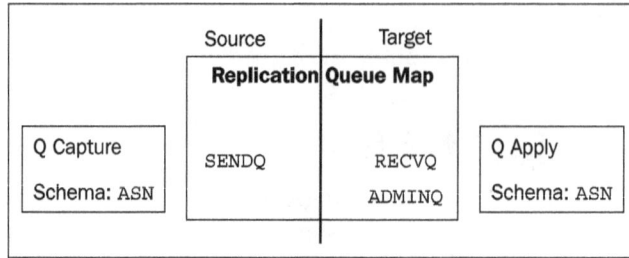

So using the queues in the first "Queues" figure, the Replication Queue Map
definition would be:

- **Send Queue** (SENDQ): CAPA.TO.APPB.SENDQ.REMOTE on Source
- **Receive Queue** (RECVQ): CAPA.TO.APPB.RECVQ on Target
- **Administration Queue** (ADMINQ): CAPA.ADMINQ.REMOTE on Target

Now let's look at **Publication Queue Maps** (**PQMs**). PQMs are used in Event
Publishing and are similar to RQMs, in that they define the WebSphere MQ queues
needed to transmit messages between two servers. The big difference is that because
in Event Publishing, we do not have a Q Apply component, the definition of a PQM
is made up of only a Send Queue.

What is a Q subscription?

The second part of the *transport definitions* is a definition called a **Q subscription**,
which defines a single source/target combination and which Replication Queue Map
to use for this combination. We set up one Q subscription for each source/target
combination.

Each Q subscription needs a Replication Queue Map, so we need to make sure we
have one defined before trying to create a Q subscription. Note that if we are using
the Replication Center, then we can choose to create a Q subscription even though
a RQM does not exist. The wizard will walk you through creating the RQM at the
point at which it is needed.

The structure of a Q subscription is made up of a **source** and **target** section, and we have to specify:

- The Replication Queue Map
- The source and target table
- The type of target table
- The type of conflict detection and action to be used
- The type of initial load, if any, should be performed

The process of creating a Q subscription is discussed in the *Q subscription maintenance* section of *Chapter 6*.

If we define a Q subscription for unidirectional replication, then we can choose the name of the Q subscription—for any other type of replication we cannot.

Q replication does not have the concept of a *subscription set* as there is in SQL Replication, where the subscription set holds all the tables which are related using referential integrity.

> In Q replication, we have to ensure that all the tables that are related through referential integrity use the same Replication Queue Map, which will enable Q Apply to apply the changes to the target tables in the correct sequence.

In the following diagram, Q subscription 1 uses RQM1, Q subscription 2 also uses RQM1, and Q subscription 3 uses RQM3:

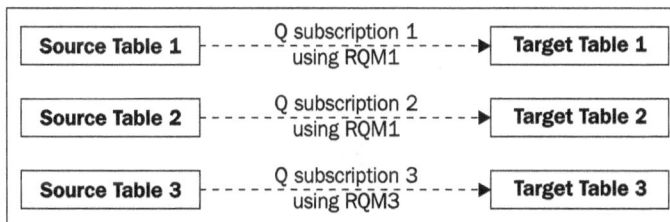

Source Table 1	Q subscription 1 using RQM1	Target Table 1
Source Table 2	Q subscription 2 using RQM1	Target Table 2
Source Table 3	Q subscription 3 using RQM3	Target Table 3

What is a subscription group?

A **subscription group** is the name for a collection of Q subscriptions that are involved in multi-directional replication, and is set using the SET SUBGROUP command. For an example of setting up such a group, see the *Creating a Q subscription* section of *Appendix A*, for peer-to-peer four-way replication.

Q subscription activation

In unidirectional, bidirectional, and peer-to-peer two-way replication, when Q Capture and Q Apply start, then the Q subscription can be automatically activated (if that option was specified). For peer-to-peer three-way replication and higher, when Q Capture and Q Apply are started, only a subset of the Q subscriptions of the subscription group starts automatically, so we need to manually start the remaining Q subscriptions.

The relationship between the components

The following diagram shows the relationship between source/target tables, **Replication Queue Maps (RQMs)**, **Publishing Queue Maps (PQMs)**, and Q subscriptions:

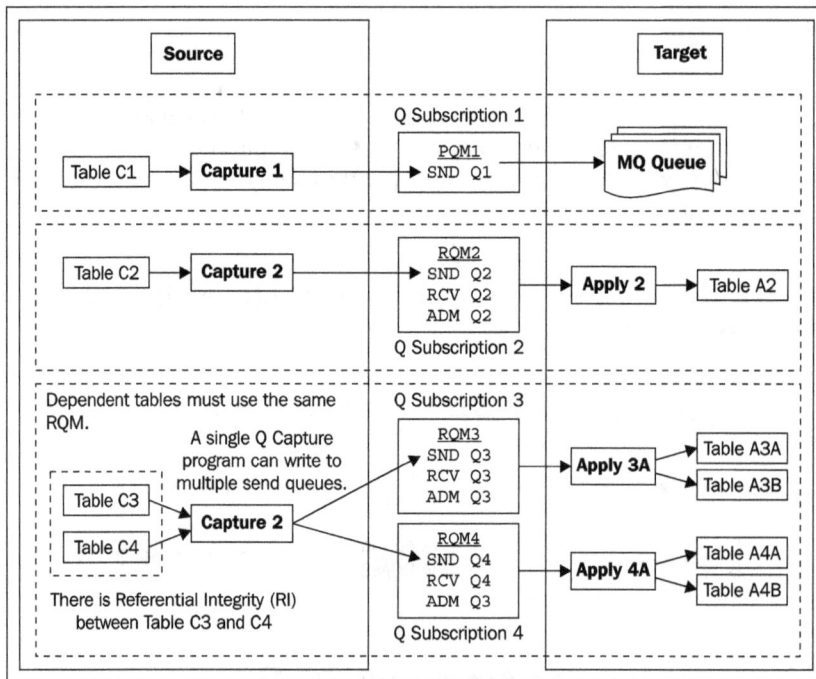

Here are some questions and answers about the Q replication components:

Can two separate Q Captures write to the same Send Queue? No.

Can two Q Subscriptions share a RQM? Yes.

Can we use the same Send Queue for XML publications and replication? No.

Can two RQMs share the same Receive Queue and Send Queue? No.

Can two RQMs share the same Administration Queue? Yes.

The Q Capture and Q Apply programs

It is the Q Capture and Q Apply programs, which form the heart of Q replication as it is these two programs, which read transactions from the source system and apply them to the target table.

The *Q replication constituent components* section from *Chapter 1*, gave a brief introduction to the Q Capture and Q Apply programs. What we will do in this section is examine at a deeper level how these programs work and communicate with each other.

Q Capture internals

Let's review what Q Capture does. Essentially, Q Capture reads transactions for tables that it is interested in from the DB2 log by its transaction thread calling the DB2 log interface API db2ReadLog. It builds complete transactions in memory until it detects a commit or rollback statement in the log. If it detects a rollback statement, then the transaction is flushed from memory. If it detects a commit statement, then Q Capture places the transaction in compressed XML format onto a WebSphere MQ queue called a Send Queue. If the transaction is large, then Q Capture will break the transaction up into smaller chunks before putting them onto the Send Queue.

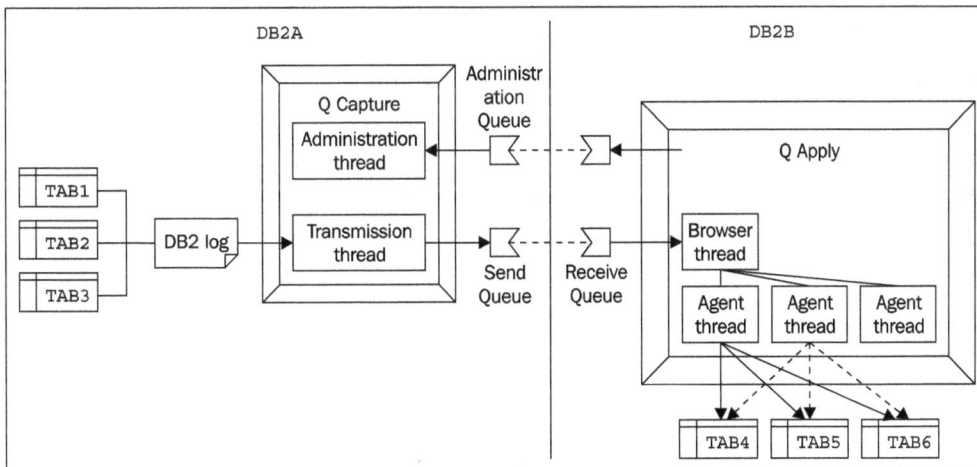

Once Q Capture puts a transaction onto the Send Queue, it records the fact in its Restart Queue, so that if Q Capture is stopped (meaning that any in flight transactions in memory will be lost), and then restarted, Q Capture knows the **log sequence number** (**LSN**) of the last record it had put onto the Send Queue, and will request the log information from that point onwards.

The work that we have just described that Q Capture does is performed by Q Capture **threads**. Q Capture consists of the following threads:

- `Administration`: This thread handles control messages that are put by Q Apply or a user application on the Administration Queue, and is also used for error logging and monitoring.
- `Hold1`: This thread prevents two Q Captures with the same schema from running on a server, and handles signals sent to Q Capture.
- `Prune`: This thread deletes old data from some of the Q Capture control tables.
- `Transaction`: This thread reads the DB2 recovery log, captures changes for subscribed tables, and rebuilds log records into transactions in memory before passing them to the worker thread. For Oracle sources, the transaction thread starts the Oracle LogMiner utility, reads from the `V$LOGMNR_CONTENTS` view to find changes for subscribed tables, and stops LogMiner.
- `Worker`: This thread receives completed transactions from the `Transaction` thread, turns transactions into WebSphere MQ messages, and puts the messages onto Send Queues.

`Administration`, `Prune`, and `Worker` threads are typically in `running` or `resting` states. `Hold1` threads are typically in a `waiting` state. If the `worker` thread is in a `running` state but data is not being captured, check the `IBMQREP_CAPTRACE` table for messages and possible reasons.

The state of these threads can be any of the following:

Status	Description
`Exists`	The thread exists but cannot start.
`Initializing`	The thread is initialized but cannot work.
`Resting`	The thread is sleeping and will wake up when there is work to do.
`Running`	The thread is actively processing.
`Started`	The thread started but cannot initialize. Investigate potential system resource problems, such as too many threads or not enough processing power.
`Stopped`	The thread is not running. Check for messages in the `IBMQREP_CAPTRACE`, `IBMQREP_APPLYTRACE`, or `IBMSNAP_MONTRACE` control tables.

The reading of the DB2 log and the gathering of committed transactions is asynchronous to the rest of Q Capture processing and is performed by the `transaction` thread.

Let's quickly look at Q Capture **memory usage**. There are three main areas of Q Capture memory usage:

- To store information about what source data we want to replicate or publish.
- To store information about Q subscriptions or Q publications. Each of these consumes a maximum of 1000 bytes of memory.
- To build the transactions from the DB2 logs until a commit or rollback is encountered. Clearly, if we have large transactions with few commit/rollback points, then Q Capture will require a large amount of memory to handle this. If Q Capture runs out of assigned memory, it will spill part of the transaction data to a file.

Once Q Capture puts a transaction onto the Send Queue, its processing is complete. We now turn our attention to Q Apply processing.

Q Apply internals

For each Send Queue that Q Capture puts messages onto, there is a corresponding and connected **Receive Queue** that Q Apply reads from, and it starts a `browser` thread for each Receive Queue. This browser thread launches one or more agents to process the transactions on the Receive Queue. These agents try and work in parallel, to maximize throughput. Note that if transactions affect the same rows in the same table, then they will always be handled in order by a single agent. In addition to that, transactions affecting referential integrity between tables are also processed by a single agent.

The number of agents available to Q Apply is not determined by a Q Apply parameter, but is set for each Replication Queue Map using the `num_apply_agents` parameter. A value of higher than 1 for `num_apply_agents` allows Q Apply to process transactions in parallel.

The various Q Apply threads are as follows:

- `Agent`: This thread rebuilds transactions in memory and applies them to targets. We set the number of agent threads that will be used for parallel processing of transactions when we create a Replication Queue Map.

- `Browser`: This thread reads transaction messages from a Receive Queue, maintains dependencies between transactions, and launches one or more agent threads. Q Apply launches one browser thread for each Receive Queue.

- `Housekeeping`: This thread maintains the Q Apply control tables by saving and deleting data.

- `Monitor`: This thread logs information about Q Apply's performance into the `IBMQREP_APPLYMON` control table.

- `Spill agent`: This thread rebuilds transactions that were held in a Spill Queue and applies them to targets. Spill agents terminate after the Spill Queue is emptied and the Q subscription becomes active.

`Agent`, `Browser`, and `Housekeeping` threads are typically in a `running` state. Check the `IBMQREP_APPLYTRACE` table if agent threads are in a `running` state but data is not being applied.

The state of these threads is similar to the description for Q Capture in the previous section.

And let's look at memory requirements for Q Apply. As with Q Capture, Q Apply consumes a maximum of 1000 bytes worth of memory for each active Q subscription. The other major area of memory usage is when Q Apply rebuilds the transactions from the Receive Queues before applying them to the target tables.

How do Q Capture and Q Apply communicate?

In the previous sections, we talked about how Q Capture and Q Apply put messages onto and read from various WebSphere MQ queues. Q Capture and Q Apply need to be able to communicate with each other, for example to exchange information on which records have been processed. This process is shown in the following diagram:

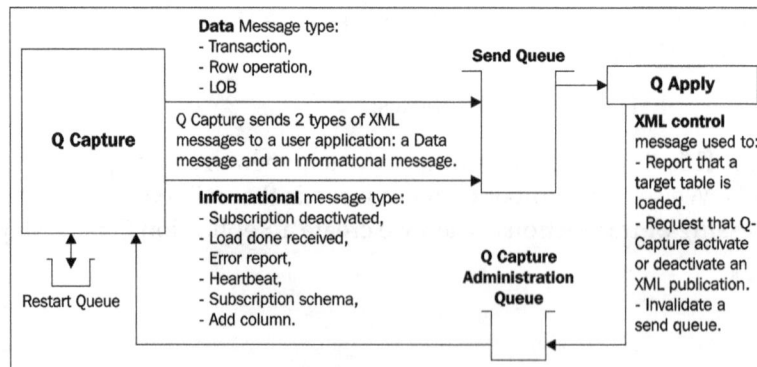

Q Capture communicates with Q Apply by putting messages onto its Send Queue (which Q Apply sees as a Receive Queue). Q Apply communicates back to Q Capture using its Administration Queue.

There are two types of message sent: **Data messages** and **Informational messages.** Let's discuss these in more detail.

- **Data messages**: There are three types of data messages, and these messages contain the data/operation:
    - ◦ **Large object (LOB)**: This contains some or all of the data from a LOB value in the source table. LOB messages are sent separately from the transaction messages and row operation messages that the LOB values belong to if they are not inlined.
    - ◦ **Row operation**: This contains a single insert, delete, or update operation to a source table. It also contains commit information about the database transaction that this row is part of.
    - ◦ **Transaction**: This contains one or more insert, delete, or update operations to a source table. These operations belong to the same database transaction. It also contains commit information for the transaction.

- **Informational messages**: There are six informational messages and they describe the action being transmitted:
    - ◦ **Add column**: This contains information about a column that was added to an existing subscription.
    - ◦ **Error report**: This tells the user application that Q Capture encountered a publication error.
    - ◦ **Heartbeat**: This tells the user application that Q Capture is still running when it has no data messages to send.
    - ◦ **Load done received**: This acknowledges that Q Capture received the message that the target table is loaded.
    - ◦ **Subscription deactivated**: This tells the user application that Q Capture deactivated a subscription.
    - ◦ **Subscription schema**: This contains information about the source table and its columns. It also contains data-sending options, Send Queue name, and information about Q Capture and the source database.

- **XML control messages**: There are four control messages which provide information to Q Capture:

    ° **Activate subscription**: This requests that Q Capture activates a subscription.

    ° **Deactivate subscription**: This requests that Q Capture deactivates a subscription.

    ° **Invalidate Send Queue**: This requests that Q Capture invalidates a Send Queue by performing the queue error action that was specified.

    ° **Load done**: This tells Q Capture that the target table for a subscription is loaded.

Summary

In this chapter, we looked at the DB2 database layer, the WebSphere MQ layer, and the Q replication layer that make up a Q replication solution. We introduced the terms *Replication/Publication Queue Map*, *Q subscription*, and *subscription group* and showed their relationship with each other. We then moved on to look at the internals of the Q Capture and Q Apply programs and finished with how they communicate.

Now that we have introduced the three layers which make up a Q replication environment, let's move on to look at them in more detail in the following chapters. We will start with the DB2 database layer.

3
The DB2 Database Layer

This chapter covers the DB2 database layer, which is the first layer we will look at. The following diagram shows this, and all the sections or layers we will look at in subsequent chapters and sections.

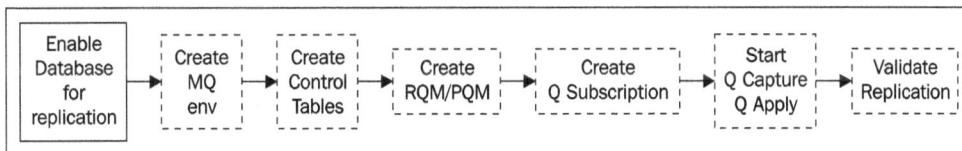

Enable Database for replication	Create MQ env	Create Control Tables	Create RQM/PQM	Create Q Subscription	Start Q Capture Q Apply	Validate Replication

In this chapter, we will take a look at:

- Creating the databases used in Q replication
- The Q replication control tables, their structure, and how they are pruned

We will not look at the commands to create the control tables in this chapter; this topic is covered in the *To create/drop the Q replication control tables* section of *Appendix A*. We will look at the IBMQREP_SIGNAL table, which is used to communicate with Q Capture.

Database creation

When we set up Q replication, we can either use an existing database or create a new database. For Q Capture to operate, the source database must be using **archive logging**, see the *Database creation* section of *Appendix A* for more details.

> The source and target databases can be created with different code page settings if that is required, but it is recommended that the source and target databases (and servers) all use the same code page setting.

There are also considerations regarding table referential integrity, triggers, and so on. All these points are discussed in the *Pre-setup evaluation* section of *Appendix A*.

The control tables

For Q replication to function, it needs to store information about its Replication Queue Maps and Q subscriptions in control tables, located on the source and target servers.

The control tables are called `<schema>.<table-name>`, where `<schema>` defaults to ASN. Some of the control tables are user updateable, and others are internal tables that should only be updated by Q Capture and Q Apply.

In the following table descriptions:

Column descriptions marked with (97) at the end are columns new in DB2 9.7 compared with previous releases of DB2.

We use the following nomenclature:

CHAR means CHARACTER, NNWD means NOT NULL WITH DEFAULT, VCHAR means VARCHAR, INT means INTEGER, NN means NOT NULL, and FBD means FOR BIT DATA.

> Not all the control tables are initially created for each scenario, for example, the IBMQREP_EOLFLUSH control table is only created for replication from an Oracle source (new in DB2 9.7.1).

The Q Capture control tables

In this section, we look at the structure of the Q Capture control tables.

The default table space generated by Q replication is of the form:

```
QC<schema>4 MANAGED BY SYSTEM USING ('QC<schema>4_TSC')
```

In DB2 9.7, there are 15 possible Q Capture control tables as follows:

IBMQREP_ADMINMSG	IBMQREP_CAPQMON	IBMQREP_SENDQUEUES
IBMQREP_CAPENQ	IBMQREP_CAPTRACE	IBMQREP_SIGNAL
IBMQREP_CAPENVINFO	IBMQREP_EOLFLUSH	IBMQREP_SRCH_COLS
IBMQREP_CAPMON	IBMQREP_IGNTRAN	IBMQREP_SRC_COND
IBMQREP_CAPPARMS	IBMQREP_IGNTRANTRC	IBMQREP_SUBS

Let's look at each of these tables in detail:

- IBMQREP_ADMINMSG: This is an internal table, which contains administrative messages received by Q Capture.

  ```
  MQMSGID                        CHAR(24) FOR BIT DATA NOT NULL
  MSG_TIME                       TS NNWD CURRENT TS

  PRIMARY KEY(MQMSGID);
  ALTER TABLE ASN.IBMQREP_ADMINMSG VOLATILE CARDINALITY;
  ```

- IBMQREP_CAPENQ: This table ensures that only one Q Capture with a given schema is running per Q Capture server.

  ```
  LOCKNAME                       INT
  ```

- IBMQREP_CAPENVINFO: This table contains eight rows that are used to store the value of runtime environment variables and other information that the replication administration tools use to access remote programs.

  ```
  NAME                           VARCHAR(30) NOT NULL        (97)
  VALUE                          VARCHAR(3800)               (97)
  ```

- IBMQREP_CAPMON: This table contains statistics about the performance of Q Capture.

  ```
  MONITOR_TIME                   TS NOT NULL
  CURRENT_LOG_TIME               TS NOT NULL

  CAPTURE_IDLE                   INT NOT NULL
  CURRENT_MEMORY                 INT NOT NULL
  ROWS_PROCESSED                 INT NOT NULL
  TRANS_SKIPPED                  INT NOT NULL
  TRANS_PROCESSED                INT NOT NULL
  TRANS_SPILLED                  INT NOT NULL
  MAX_TRANS_SIZE                 INT NOT NULL
  QUEUES_IN_ERROR                INT NOT NULL
  RESTART_SEQ                    CHAR(10) FOR BIT DATA NOT NULL
  CURRENT_SEQ                    CHAR(10) FOR BIT DATA NOT NULL
  LAST_EOL_TIME                  TS
  ```

```
LOGREAD_API_TIME              INT   (97)
NUM_LOGREAD_CALLS             INT   (97)
NUM_END_OF_LOGS               INT   (97)
LOGRDR_SLEEPTIME              INT   (97)

PRIMARY KEY(MONITOR_TIME);
ALTER TABLE ASN.IBMQREP_CAPMON VOLATILE CARDINALITY;
UNIQUE INDEX ASN.IX1CAPMON ON ASN.IBMQREP_CAPMON(MONITOR_TIME
DESC);
```

> In multi-directional replication, Q Capture can produce the following error:
>
> ```
> ASN0565E "Q Capture" : "ASN" : "AdminThread" : The
> program cannot insert statistics into the table
> "IBMQREP_CAPMON".  The SQL return code is "-803".  The
> data for this interval will be skipped and included in
> the next interval.
> ```
>
> To rectify this problem, drop the unique index on the table (see the index for IBMQREP_CAPQMON):
>
> ```
> $ db2 DROP INDEX asn.ix1capmon
> ```

- IBMQREP_CAPPARMS: This table contains parameters that control the operations of Q Capture.

```
QMGR                      VCHAR(48)  NOT NULL
REMOTE_SRC_SERVER         VCHAR(18)
RESTARTQ                  VCHAR(48)  NOT NULL
ADMINQ                    VCHAR(48)  NOT NULL
STARTMODE                 VCHAR(6)  NNWD 'WARMSI'
MEMORY_LIMIT              INT NNWD 500
COMMIT_INTERVAL           INT NNWD 500
AUTOSTOP                  CHAR(1)  NNWD 'N'
MONITOR_INTERVAL          INT NNWD 300000
MONITOR_LIMIT             INT NNWD 10080
TRACE_LIMIT               INT NNWD 10080
SIGNAL_LIMIT              INT NNWD 10080
PRUNE_INTERVAL            INT NNWD 300
SLEEP_INTERVAL            INT NNWD 5000
LOGREUSE                  CHAR(1)  NNWD 'N'
LOGSTDOUT                 CHAR(1)  NNWD 'N'
TERM                      CHAR(1)  NNWD 'Y'
CAPTURE_PATH              VCHAR(1040)  WITH DEFAULT NULL
ARCH_LEVEL                CHAR(4)  NNWD '0907'
COMPATIBILITY             CHAR(4)  NNWD '0907'
```

```
LOB_SEND_OPTION                     CHAR(1) NNWD 'I'  (97)
QFULL_NUM_RETRIES                   INTEGER NNWD 30   (97)
QFULL_RETRY_DELAY                   INTEGER NNWD 250  (97)
MSG_PERSISTENCE                     CHAR(1) NNWD 'Y'  (97)
LOGRDBUFSZ                          INTEGER NNWD 256  (97)

ALTER TABLE ASN.IBMQREP_CAPPARMS  VOLATILE CARDINALITY;
UNIQUE INDEX ASN.IX1CQMGRCOL ON ASN.IBMQREP_CAPPARMS( QMGR ASC);
```

The following query shows the default values when the Q Capture control tables are created:

```
INSERT INTO ASN.IBMQREP_CAPPARMS
(qmgr, restartq, adminq, startmode, memory_limit,
commit_interval, autostop, monitor_interval, monitor_limit,
trace_limit, signal_limit, prune_interval, sleep_interval,
logreuse, logstdout, term, arch_level,compatibility,
lob_send_option, qfull_num_retries, qfull_retry_delay
,msg_persistence, logrdbufsz)
VALUES(
'QMA', 'CAPA.RESTARTQ', 'CAPA.ADMINQ', 'WARMSI', 500,
500, 'N', 300000, 10080,
10080, 10080, 300, 5000,
'N', 'N', 'Y', '0907', '0907',
'I', 30, 250,
'Y', 256);
```

The following shows the three queries to list out the startup parameters:

```
db2 "SELECT SUBSTR(qmgr,1,5) AS qmgr, SUBSTR(remote_src_
server,1,10) AS remsrv, SUBSTR(restartq,1,20) AS restartq,
SUBSTR(adminq,1,20) AS adminq, startmode FROM asn.ibmqrep_
capparms"

QMGR  REMSRV      RESTARTQ               ADMINQ
STARTMODE
----- ---------- -------------------- -------------------- -------
--

QMA   -           CAPA.RESTARTQ          CAPA.ADMINQ          WARMSI
```

```
db2 "SELECT SUBSTR(qmgr,1,5) AS qmgr, CAST(memory_limit AS
char(8)) AS meml, CAST(commit_interval AS char(8)) AS comi,
autostop AS a, CAST(monitor_interval AS CHAR(8)) AS moni,
CAST(monitor_limit as CHAR(8)) AS monl, CAST(trace_limit AS
CHAR(8)) AS trcl, CAST(signal_limit AS CHAR(8)) AS sigl FROM asn.
ibmqrep_capparms"
```

```
QMGR    MEML      COMI      A MONI      MONL      TRCL      SIGL
-----  --------  --------  - --------  --------  --------  --------
QMA     500       500      N 300000    10080     10080     10080
```

db2 "SELECT SUBSTR(qmgr,1,5) AS qmgr, CAST(prune_interval AS CHAR(8)) AS prui, CAST(sleep_interval AS CHAR(8)) AS slpi, logreuse AS l, logstdout AS o, term AS t, substr(capture_path,1,20) AS cappath FROM asn.ibmqrep_capparms"

```
QMGR    PRUI      SLPI      L O T CAPPATH
-----  --------  --------  - - - --------------------
QMA     300       5000      N N Y -
```

- IBMQREP_CAPQMON: This table contains statistics about the performance of Q Capture for each **Send Queue**.

```
MONITOR_TIME                TS NOT NULL
SENDQ                       VCHAR(48) NOT NULL
ROWS_PUBLISHED              INT NOT NULL
TRANS_PUBLISHED             INT NOT NULL
CHG_ROWS_SKIPPED            INT NOT NULL
DELROWS_SUPPRESSED          INT NOT NULL
ROWS_SKIPPED               INT NOT NULL
QFULL_ERROR_COUNT          INTEGER NOT NULL,  (97)
LOBS_TOO_BIG               INTEGER NNWD 0,    (97)
XMLDOCS_TOO_BIG            INTEGER NNWD 0,    (97)
MQ_BYTES                   INTEGER,           (97)
MQ_MESSAGES                INTEGER,           (97)
CURRENT_SEQ                CHARACTER(10) FBD (97)
RESTART_SEQ                CHARACTER(10) FBD (97)


UNIQUE INDEX ASN.IX1CAPQMON ON ASN.IBMQREP_CAPQMON (MONITOR_TIME
DESC,SENDQ ASC) ;
ALTER TABLE ASN.IBMQREP_CAPQMON VOLATILE CARDINALITY;
ALTER TABLE IBMQREP_CAPQMON
ADD CONSTRAINT IBMQREP_CAPQMON_IBMQREP_SENDQUEUES_FK
FOREIGN KEY (SENDQ) REFERENCES IBMQREP_SENDQUEUES (SENDQ) NOT
ENFORCED;
```

> In multi-directional replication, Q Capture can produce the ASN0565E error, as for the IBMQREP_CAPMON table. The remedy, as seen earlier, is to drop the unique index on the table as:
> **$ db2 DROP INDEX asn.ix1capqmon**

- IBMQREP_CAPTRACE: This table contains informational, warning, and error messages from Q Capture.

```
OPERATION                 CHAR(8) NOT NULL
TRACE_TIME                TS NOT NULL
DESCRIPTION               VCHAR(1024) NOT NULL
REASON_CODE               INTEGER                    (97)
MQ_CODE                   INTEGER                    (97)

INDEX ASN.IX1CTRCTMCOL ON ASN.IBMQREP_CAPTRACE (TRACE_TIME DESC);
```

- IBMQREP_EOLFLUSH: This table is an internal table that Q Capture writes to, when Oracle LogMiner has not responded within the time that is specified by the commit_interval parameter. Writing to this table helps determine if any buffered but unreturned log records are available for Q Capture to process (new in DB2 9.7.1).

```
EOL_TIMEOUT               TS NOT NULL
```

- IBMQREP_IGNTRAN: This table can be used to inform Q Capture about transactions that we do not want to be captured from the DB2 recovery log. We use SQL to insert rows in the table that inform the programs to ignore transactions based on authorization ID, authorization token (z/OS only), or plan name (z/OS only).

```
AUTHID                    CHAR(128)
AUTHTOKEN                 CHAR(30)
PLANNAME                  CHAR(8)
IGNTRANTRC                CHAR(1) NNWD 'N' (97)

UNIQUE INDEX ASN.IGNTRANX ON ASN.IBMQREP_IGNTRAN (AUTHID
ASC,AUTHTOKEN ASC,PLANNAME ASC);
```

- IBMQREP_IGNTRANTRC: This table records information about transactions that were specified to be ignored.

```
IGNTRAN_TIME    TIMESTAMP NOT NULL WITH DEFAULT CURRENT TIMESTAMP
(97)
AUTHID          CHARACTER(128)
AUTHTOKEN       CHARACTER(30)
PLANNAME        CHARACTER(8)
TRANSID         CHARACTER(10) FOR BIT DATA NOT NULL
COMMITLSN       CHARACTER(10) FOR BIT DATA NOT NULL

INDEX ASN.IGNTRCX ON ASN.IBMQREP_IGNTRANTRC(IGNTRAN_TIME ASC);
```

In DB2 9.5, the first column is called PUBQMAPNAME VARCHAR(128).

- **IBMQREP_SENDQUEUES**: This table contains information about the **WebSphere MQ** queues that a Q Capture uses to send transaction, row operation, large object, or informational messages.

PUBQMAPNAME	VCHAR(128) NOT NULL
SENDQ	VCHAR(48) NOT NULL
RECVQ	VCHAR(48)
MESSAGE_FORMAT	CHAR(1) NNWD 'C'
MSG_CONTENT_TYPE	CHAR(1) NNWD 'T'
STATE	CHAR(1) NNWD 'A'
STATE_TIME TS	NNWD CURRENT TS
STATE_INFO	CHAR(8)
ERROR_ACTION	CHAR(1) NNWD 'S'
HEARTBEAT_INTERVAL	INT NNWD 60
MAX_MESSAGE_SIZE	INT NNWD 64
APPLY_SERVER	VCHAR(18)
APPLY_ALIAS	VCHAR(8)
APPLY_SCHEMA	VCHAR(128)
DESCRIPTION	VCHAR(254)
MESSAGE_CODEPAGE	INT
COLUMN_DELIMITER	CHAR(1) (97)
STRING_DELIMITER	CHAR(1) (97)
RECORD_DELIMITER	CHAR(1) (97)
DECIMAL_POINT	CHAR(1) (97)
SENDRAW_IFERROR	CHAR(1) NNWD 'N' (97)
LOB_TOO_BIG_ACTION	CHAR(1) NNWD 'Q' (97)
XML_TOO_BIG_ACTION	CHAR(1) NNWD 'Q' (97)

```
PRIMARY KEY(SENDQ)
ALTER TABLE ASN.IBMQREP_SENDQUEUES VOLATILE CARDINALITY;
CREATE UNIQUE INDEX ASN.IX1PUBMAPCOL ON ASN.IBMQREP_
SENDQUEUES(PUBQMAPNAME ASC);
```

We can use the following queries to interrogate the table:

```
db2 "select substr(pubqmapname,1,10) as RQM, substr(sendq,1,30) as
SENDQ, substr(recvq,1,20) as RECVQ FROM asn.ibmqrep_sendqueues"
```

RQM	SENDQ	RECVQ
----------	------------------------------	--------------------
RQMA2B	CAPA.TO.APPB.SENDQ.REMOTE	CAPA.TO.APPB.RECVQ

```
db2 "select substr(pubqmapname,1,10) as RQM, apply_alias as APPAL,
substr(apply_schema,1,10) AS appschema, substr(apply_server,1,5)
as APPS FROM asn.ibmqrep_sendqueues"
RQM          APPAL    APPSCHEMA  APPS
----------   -------- ---------- -----
RQMA2B       DB2B     ASN        DB2B

db2 "select substr(pubqmapname,1,10) as RQM, state, state_time,
state_info, error_action as EA FROM asn.ibmqrep_sendqueues"
RQM          STATE STATE_TIME                 STATE_INFO EA
----------   ----- -------------------------- ---------- --
RQMA2B       A     2010-01-24-16.21.23.656000 -          S
```

- IBMQREP_SIGNAL: This table contains signals that are used to prompt Q Capture. These signals are inserted by a user or subscribing application, or by Q Capture after it receives a control message from Q Apply.

```
SIGNAL_TIME                     TS NNWD CURRENT TS
SIGNAL_TYPE                     VCHAR(30) NOT NULL
SIGNAL_SUBTYPE                  VCHAR(30)
SIGNAL_INPUT_IN                 VCHAR(500)
SIGNAL_STATE                    CHAR(1) NNWD 'P'
SIGNAL_LSN                      CHAR(10) FOR BIT DATA

DATA CAPTURE CHANGES;
ALTER TABLE ASN.IBMQREP_SIGNAL VOLATILE CARDINALITY;
```

The columns for this table are discussed in the *The IBMQREP_SIGNAL control table* section later in this chapter.

In bidirectional replication, Q Apply inserts a signal into the IBMQREP_SIGNAL table for every transaction that it receives and applies to make sure that Q Capture does not recapture the transaction.

- IBMQREP_SRC_COLS: This table identifies columns in the source table, which are replicated or published for a Q subscription or XML publication.

```
SUBNAME                         VCHAR(132) NOT NULL
SRC_COLNAME                     VCHAR(128) NOT NULL
IS_KEY SMALLINT                 NNWD 0
COL_OPTIONS_FLAG                CHAR(10) NNWD 'NNNNNNNNNN'

PRIMARY KEY(SUBNAME, SRC_COLNAME),CONSTRAINT FKSUBS FOREIGN
KEY(SUBNAME) REFERENCES ASN.IBMQREP_SUBS(SUBNAME))

ALTER TABLE ASN.IBMQREP_SRC_COLS VOLATILE CARDINALITY;
```

```
ALTER TABLE IBMQREP_SRC_COLS
ADD CONSTRAINT FKSUBS
FOREIGN KEY (SUBNAME) REFERENCES IBMQREP_SUBS (SUBNAME);
```

- IBMQREP_SRCH_COND: This table is an internal table that Q Capture uses to evaluate the search conditions that were specified for a Q subscription or publication.

ASNQREQD	INT

- IBMQREP_SUBS: This table contains information about Q subscriptions and publications, including subscription type, source tables, search conditions, data sending options, target loading options, and states.

SUBNAME	VCHAR(132) NOT NULL
SOURCE_OWNER	VCHAR(128) NOT NULL
SOURCE_NAME	VCHAR(128) NOT NULL
TARGET_SERVER	VCHAR(18)
TARGET_ALIAS	VCHAR(8)
TARGET_OWNER	VCHAR(128)
TARGET_NAME	VCHAR(128)
TARGET_TYPE	INT
APPLY_SCHEMA	VCHAR(128)
SENDQ	VCHAR(48) NOT NULL
SEARCH_CONDITION	VCHAR(2048) WITH DEFAULT NULL
SUB_ID	INT WITH DEFAULT NULL
SUBTYPE	CHAR(1) NNWD 'U'
ALL_CHANGED_ROWS	CHAR(1) NNWD 'N'
BEFORE_VALUES	CHAR(1) NNWD 'N'
CHANGED_COLS_ONLY	CHAR(1) NNWD 'Y'
HAS_LOADPHASE	CHAR(1) NNWD 'I'
STATE	CHAR(1) NNWD 'N'
STATE_TIME	TS NNWD CURRENT TS
STATE_INFO	CHAR(8)
STATE_TRANSITION	VCHAR(256) FOR BIT DATA
SUBGROUP	VCHAR(30) WITH DEFAULT NULL
SOURCE_NODE	SMALLINT NNWD 0
TARGET_NODE	SMALLINT NNWD 0
GROUP_MEMBERS	CHAR(254) FBD WITH DEFAULT NULL
OPTIONS_FLAG	CHAR(4) NNWD 'NNNN'
SUPPRESS_DELETES	CHAR(1) NNWD 'N'
DESCRIPTION	VCHAR(200)
TOPIC	VCHAR(256)

```
CAPTURE_LOAD                    CHAR(1) NNWD 'W' (97)
```

```
PRIMARY KEY(SUBNAME)
CONSTRAINT FKSENDQ FOREIGN KEY(SENDQ) REFERENCES ASN.IBMQREP_
SENDQUEUES(SENDQ)
```

```
ALTER TABLE ASN.IBMQREP_SUBS VOLATILE CARDINALITY;
ALTER TABLE ASN.IBMQREP_SUBS
ADD CONSTRAINT FKSENDQ
FOREIGN KEY (SENDQ) REFERENCES IBMQREP_SENDQUEUES (SENDQ);
```

The STATE column is updated by Q Capture to indicate the current state of the Q subscription or publication. The initial state is N, and the STATE_INFO field is initially set to ASN7024I (new Q subscription or publication):

- ° N: This is the default state and it indicates that the Q subscription or publication is new. Q Capture automatically activates this Q subscription or publication when the program is started or reinitialized.

- ° A: This indicates that the Q subscription or publication is active. If there is a load phase, Q Capture will process the LOADDONE signal and send a load done received message to Q Apply or the user application. Q Capture is sending data messages based on the options defined for the Q subscription or publication.

- ° G: This is an internal state that indicates that Q Capture read a CAPSTOP signal in the log for this peer-to-peer Q subscription, and the subscription is being deactivated within the peer-to-peer group.

- ° I: This indicates that the Q subscription or publication is inactive. Q Capture saw a CAPSTOP signal in the log, or an error occurred and the Q subscription or publication was deactivated. Q Capture stopped sending messages for this Q subscription or publication but continued with others.

- ° L: This indicates that the Q subscription is loading. Q Capture processed the CAPSTART signal, and sent the subscription schema message to Q Apply or user application. Q Capture is sending transaction messages that include before values for all columns, and it is waiting for the LOADDONE signal.

- ° T: This is an internal state that indicates that Q Capture read a CAPSTART signal in the log for this peer-to-peer Q subscription, and the Q subscription is being initialized within the peer-to-peer group.

The STATE_TIME column is the timestamp of the last change in Q subscription or publication state, and has a default value of the current timestamp.

The STATE_INFO column contains the number for the ASN message about the Q subscription state.

We can list the values for a Q subscription by using the following queries:

```
db2 "SELECT SUBSTR(subname,1,10) AS subname, SUBSTR(source_owner,1,10) AS
srcowner, SUBSTR(source_name,1,10) AS srcname, SUBSTR(target_server,1,10)
AS trgsrv, SUBSTR(target_alias,1,8) AS trgalias, SUBSTR(target_
owner,1,10) AS trgowner, SUBSTR(target_name,1,10) as trgname,
CAST(target_type AS char) AS tt FROM asn.ibmqrep_subs "
```

SUBNAME	SRCOWNER	SRCNAME	TRGSRV	TRGALIAS	TRGOWNER	TRGNAME	TT
TAB1	ERIC	T1	DB2B	DB2B	FRED	T1	1

```
db2 "SELECT SUBSTR(subname,1,10) AS subname, SUBSTR(apply_schema,1,10) AS
appschema, SUBSTR(sendq,1,30) AS sendq, sub_id FROM asn.ibmqrep_subs"
```

SUBNAME	APPSCHEMA	SENDQ	SUB_ID
TAB1	ASN	CAPA.TO.APPB.SENDQ.REMOTE	1

```
db2 "SELECT SUBSTR(subname,1,10) AS subname, all_changed_rows AS c,
before_values AS b, changed_cols_only AS h, has_loadphase AS l, state AS
s, state_time,SUBSTR(subgroup,1,10) AS subgp, CAST(source_node AS CHAR)
AS sn, CAST(target_node AS CHAR) AS tn FROM asn.ibmqrep_subs "
```

SUBNAME	C	B	H	L	S	STATE_TIME	SUBGP	SN	TN
TAB1	N	N	N	I	A	2010-01-23-13.42.35.756000	-	0	0

The Q Apply control tables

In this section, we look at the structure of the Q Apply control tables.

The default table space generated is of the form:

```
QC<schema>N4 MANAGED BY SYSTEM USING ('QC<schema>4_TSC')
```

In DB2 9.7, there are 14 possible Q Apply control tables:

IBMQREP_APPENQ	IBMQREP_DELTOMB	IBMQREP_SPILLEDROW
IBMQREP_APPENVINFO	IBMQREP_DONEMSG	IBMQREP_SPILLQS
IBMQREP_APPLYMON	IBMQREP_EXCEPTIONS	IBMQREP_TARGETS
IBMQREP_APPLYPARMS	IBMQREP_RECVQUEUES	IBMQREP_TRG_COLS
IBMQREP_APPLYTRACE	IBMQREP_SAVERI	

Let's look at each of these tables in detail:

- IBMQREP_APPENQ: This table ensures that only one Q Apply with a given schema is running per Q Apply server.

LOCKNAME	INT

- IBMQREP_APPENVINFO: This table contains eight rows that are used to store the value of runtime environment variables and other information that the replication administration tools use to access remote programs.

NAME	VARCHAR(30) NOT NULL
VALUE	VARCHAR(3800)

- IBMQREP_APPLYMON: This table contains statistics about the performance of Q Apply for each **Receive Queue**.

MONITOR_TIME	TS NOT NULL
RECVQ	VCHAR(48) NOT NULL
QSTART_TIME	TS NOT NULL
CURRENT_MEMORY	INT NOT NULL
QDEPTH	INT NOT NULL
END2END_LATENCY	INT NOT NULL
QLATENCY	INT NOT NULL
APPLY_LATENCY	INT NOT NULL
TRANS_APPLIED	INT NOT NULL
ROWS_APPLIED	INT NOT NULL
TRANS_SERIALIZED	INT NOT NULL
RI_DEPENDENCIES	INT NOT NULL
RI_RETRIES	INT NOT NULL
DEADLOCK_RETRIES	INT NOT NULL
ROWS_NOT_APPLIED	INT NOT NULL
MONSTER_TRANS	INT NOT NULL
MEM_FULL_TIME	INT NOT NULL
APPLY_SLEEP_TIME	INT NOT NULL
SPILLED_ROWS	INT NOT NULL
SPILLEDROWSAPPLIED	INT NOT NULL
OLDEST_TRANS	TS NOT NULL
OKSQLSTATE_ERRORS	INT NOT NULL

```
HEARTBEAT_LATENCY              INT NOT NULL
KEY_DEPENDENCIES               INT NOT NULL
UNIQ_DEPENDENCIES              INT NOT NULL
UNIQ_RETRIES                   INT NOT NULL
OLDEST_INFLT_TRANS             TS
JOB_DEPENDENCIES               INTEGER                              (97)
CAPTURE_LATENCY                INTEGER                              (97)
OLDEST_COMMIT_LSN              CHARACTER(10) FOR BIT DATA           (97)
ROWS_PROCESSED                 INTEGER                              (97)
Q_PERCENT_FULL                 SMALLINT WITH DEFAULT NULL           (97)
OLDEST_COMMIT_SEQ              CHARACTER(10) FOR BIT DATA           (97)

PRIMARY KEY(MONITOR_TIME, RECVQ)

ALTER TABLE ASN.IBMQREP_APPLYMON VOLATILE CARDINALITY;
ALTER TABLE IBMQREP_APPLYMON
ADD CONSTRAINT IBMQREP_APPLYMON_IBMQREP_RECVQUEUES_FK
FOREIGN KEY (RECVQ) REFERENCES IBMQREP_RECVQUEUES (RECVQ) NOT
ENFORCED;
```

- `IBMQREP_APPLYPARMS`: This table contains parameters that we can specify to control the operation of Q Apply.

```
QMGR                  VCHAR(48) NOT NULL
MONITOR_LIMIT         INT NNWD 10080
TRACE_LIMIT           INT NNWD 10080
MONITOR_INTERVAL      INT NNWD 300000
PRUNE_INTERVAL        INT NNWD 300
AUTOSTOP              CHAR(1) NNWD 'N'
LOGREUSE              CHAR(1) NNWD 'N'
LOGSTDOUT             CHAR(1) NNWD 'N'
APPLY_PATH            VCHAR(1040) WITH DEFAULT NULL
ARCH_LEVEL            CHAR(4) NNWD '0901'
TERM                  CHAR(1) NNWD 'Y'
PWDFILE               VCHAR(48) WITH DEFAULT NULL
DEADLOCK_RETRIES      INT NNWD 3
SQL_CAP_SCHEMA        VCHAR(128) WITH DEFAULT NULL
LOADCOPY_PATH         VARCHAR(1040) WITH DEFAULT NULL     (97)
NICKNAME_COMMIT_CT    INTEGER WITH DEFAULT 10             (97)
SPILL_COMMIT_COUNT    INTEGER WITH DEFAULT 10             (97)
LOAD_DATA_BUFF_SZ     INTEGER WITH DEFAULT 8              (97)
CLASSIC_LOAD_FL_SZ    INTEGER WITH DEFAULT 500000         (97)
MAX_PARALLEL_LOADS    INTEGER WITH DEFAULT 15             (97)
```

```
COMMIT_COUNT              INTEGER WITH DEFAULT 1          (97)
INSERT_BIDI_SIGNAL        CHAR(1) NOT NULL WITH DEFAULT 'Y'  (97)

ALTER TABLE ASN.IBMQREP_APPLYPARMS VOLATILE CARDINALITY;
UNIQUE INDEX ASN.IX1AQMGRCOL ON ASN.IBMQREP_APPLYPARMS(QMGR ASC);
```

The following are the default values when the Q Apply control tables are created:

```
INSERT INTO ASN.IBMQREP_APPLYPARMS
(qmgr, monitor_limit, trace_limit, monitor_interval,
prune_interval, autostop, logreuse, logstdout, arch_level,
term, deadlock_retries, nickname_commit_ct, spill_commit_count,
load_data_buff_sz, classic_load_fl_sz, max_parallel_loads,
commit_count, insert_bidi_signal)
VALUES(
'QMB', 10080, 10080, 300000,
300, 'N', 'N', 'N', '0907',
'Y', 3, 10, 10,
8, 500000, 15,
1, 'Y');
```

The following is a query to list the Q Apply startup parameters:

```
db2 "SELECT SUBSTR(qmgr,1,5) AS qmgr, CAST(monitor_limit
AS CHAR(8)) AS monl, CAST(trace_limit AS CHAR(8)) AS trcl,
CAST(monitor_interval AS CHAR(8)) AS moni, CAST(prune_
interval AS char(8)) AS prui, autostop AS a, logreuse AS l,
logstdout AS o, substr(apply_path,1,5) AS APPLPATH, term AS t,
SUBSTR(pwdfile,1,10) AS pwdfile, CAST(deadlock_retries AS CHAR) AS
dear FROM asn.ibmqrep_applyparms"
```

The default start up values are:

```
QMGR  MONL      TRCL      MONI      PRUI A L O APPLPATH T PWDFILE
DEAR
----- --------- --------- --------- ---- - - - -------- - --------
QMB   10080     10080     300000    300  N N N -        Y -        3
```

- IBMQREP_APPLYTRACE: This table contains informational, warning, and error messages from Q Apply.

```
OPERATION                 CHAR(8) NOT NULL
TRACE_TIME                TS NOT NULL
DESCRIPTION               VCHAR(1024) NOT NULL
REASON_CODE               INTEGER                (97)
MQ_CODE                   INTEGER                (97)
```

```
ALTER TABLE ASN.IBMQREP_APPLYTRACE VOLATILE CARDINALITY
INDEX ASN.IX1TRCTMCOL ON ASN.IBMQREP_APPLYTRACE( TRACE_TIME ASC)
```

- IBMQREP_DELTOMB: This table is an internal table used by Q Apply to record conflicting deletes in peer-to-peer replication (this table is only created when peer-to-peer replication is being used).

TARGET_OWNER	VARCHAR(30)
TARGET_NAME	VARCHAR(128)
VERSION_TIME	TS
VERSION_NODE	SI(2)
KEY_HASH	INT
PACKED_KEY	VARCHAR(4096)

- IBMQREP_DONEMSG: This table is an internal table used by Q Apply to record which messages were processed.

RECVQ	VCHAR(48) NOT NULL
MQMSGID	CHAR(24) FOR BIT DATA NOT NULL

```
PRIMARY KEY(RECVQ, MQMSGID)
ALTER TABLE ASN.IBMQREP_DONEMSG VOLATILE CARDINALITY APPEND ON
ALTER TABLE IBMQREP_DONEMSG
ADD CONSTRAINT IBMQREP_DONEMSG_IBMQREP_RECVQUEUES_FK
FOREIGN KEY (RECVQ) REFERENCES IBMQREP_RECVQUEUES (RECVQ)
NOT ENFORCED
```

- IBMQREP_EXCEPTIONS: This table contains row changes that could not be applied because of conflicts, errors, or rollbacks.

EXCEPTION_TIME	TS NNWD CURRENT TIMESTAMP,
RECVQ	VCHAR(48) NOT NULL
SRC_COMMIT_LSN	VCHAR(48) FOR BIT DATA NOT NULL
SRC_TRANS_TIME	TS NOT NULL
SUBNAME	VCHAR(132) NOT NULL
REASON	CHAR(12) NOT NULL
SQLCODE	INT
SQLSTATE	CHAR(5)
SQLERRMC	VCHAR(70) FOR BIT DATA
OPERATION	VCHAR(18) NOT NULL
TEXT	CLOB(32768) NOT LOGGED NOT COMPACT
NOT NULL	
IS_APPLIED	CHAR(1) NOT NULL
CONFLICT_RULE	CHAR(1)
SRC_TRANS_ID	VARCHAR(48) FOR BIT DATA (97)

```
ALTER TABLE IBMQREP_EXCEPTIONS
ADD CONSTRAINT IBMQREP_EXCEPTIONS_IBMQREP_RECVQUEUES_FK
FOREIGN KEY (RECVQ)
REFERENCES IBMQREP_RECVQUEUES (RECVQ) NOT ENFORCED
```

The REASON column can contain:

- CHECKFAILED: This indicates that the conflict detection rule was to check all values or check changed values, and whether a non-key value was not as expected.

- DUPLICATE: This indicates an attempt to insert a row that was already present.

- LOBXMLTOOBIG: This indicates that a large object (LOB) value or XML document was too large to fit into a transaction message. The TEXT column specifies which data type was too large.

- NOTFOUND: This indicates that an attempt to delete or update a row that did not exist.

- OKSQLSTATE: This indicates that an SQL error occurred, and it was on the list of acceptable errors in the OKSQLSTATES column of the IBMQREP_TARGETS table.

- P2PDUPKEY: This indicates that in peer-to-peer replication, a key update failed because a target row with the same key already exists, but is newer than the previous one..

- P2PINSERTED: This indicates that in peer-to-peer replication, a key update was successfully applied as an insert, because the old key row and the new key row were not found. The new key row was inserted into the target table.

- P2PNOTFOUND: This indicates that in peer-to-peer replication, a delete or update failed, because the target row did not exist.

- P2PVERLOSER: This indicates that in peer-to-peer replication, a delete or update failed, because the target row was newer than the row in the change message.

- SQLERROR: This indicates that an SQL error occurred, and it was not on the list of acceptable errors in the OKSQLSTATES column of the IBMQREP_TARGETS table.

The IS_APPLIED column contains a flag that indicates whether the row was applied to the target table even though it was entered into the IBMQREP_EXCEPTIONS table:

- ° N: It indicates that the transaction was not applied.

- ° Y: It indicates that the row was applied because the CONFLICT_ACTION specified for the Q subscription was F (force).

- IBMQREP_RECVQUEUES: This table identifies queues that Q Apply uses to receive transaction messages and send control message, and contains some operation parameters for Q Apply.

REPQMAPNAME	VCHAR(128) NOT NULL
RECVQ	VCHAR(48) NOT NULL
SENDQ	VCHAR(48) WITH DEFAULT NULL
ADMINQ	VCHAR(48) NOT NULL
NUM_APPLY_AGENTS	INT NNWD 16
MEMORY_LIMIT	INT NNWD 64
CAPTURE_SERVER	VCHAR(18) NOT NULL
CAPTURE_ALIAS	VCHAR(8) NOT NULL
CAPTURE_SCHEMA	VCHAR(128) NNWD 'ASN'
STATE	CHAR(1) NNWD 'A'
STATE_TIME	TS NNWD CURRENT TIMESTAMP
STATE_INFO	CHAR(8)
DESCRIPTION	VCHAR(254)
SOURCE_TYPE	CHAR(1) WITH DEFAULT ' '
MAXAGENTS_CORRELID	INTEGER WITH DEFAULT NULL (97)

```
PRIMARY KEY(RECVQ)
ALTER TABLE ASN.IBMQREP_RECVQUEUES VOLATILE CARDINALITY
UNIQUE INDEX ASN.IX1REPMAPCOL ON ASN.IBMQREP_RECVQUEUES(
REPQMAPNAME ASC)
```

The STATE column contains a flag that shows the current status of the Receive Queue:

- ° A: This is a default flag and it indicates that the receive queue is active, which means that Q Apply is processing and applying the transactions from this queue.

- ° I: This indicates that the Receive Queue is inactive, which means that there is a problem with the queue.

We can use the following query to interrogate the table:

```
db2 "select substr(repqmapname,1,10) as RQMNAME,
```

```
ubstr(sendq,1,25) as SENDQ, substr(recvq,1,25) as RECVQ,
substr(adminq,1,25) as ADMINQ, substr(capture_server,1,5) as CAPS
from ASN.IBMQREP_RECVQUEUES"
```

- IBMQREP_SAVERI: This is an internal table that Q Apply uses to store referential integrity constraints that are dropped while targets are being loaded.

SUBNAME	VCHAR(132) NOT NULL
RECVQ	VCHAR(48) NOT NULL
CONSTNAME	VCHAR(128) NOT NULL
TABSCHEMA	VCHAR(128) NOT NULL
TABNAME	VCHAR(128) NOT NULL
REFTABSCHEMA	VCHAR(128) NOT NULL
REFTABNAME	VCHAR(128) NOT NULL
ALTER_RI_DDL	VCHAR(1680) NOT NULL
TYPE_OF_LOAD	CHAR(1) NOT NULL
DELETERULE	CHAR(1)
UPDATERULE	CHAR(1)

```
ALTER TABLE ASN.IBMQREP_SAVERI VOLATILE CARDINALITY
ALTER TABLE IBMQREP_SAVERI
ADD CONSTRAINT IBMQREP_SAVERI_IBMQREP_RECVQUEUES_FK
FOREIGN KEY (RECVQ) REFERENCES IBMQREP_RECVQUEUES (RECVQ) NOT
ENFORCED
```

- IBMQREP_SPILLEDROW: This is an internal table that Q Apply uses to keep track of rows sent to a temporary Spill Queue.

SPILLQ	VCHAR(48) NOT NULL
MQMSGID	CHAR(24) FOR BIT DATA NOT NULL

```
PRIMARY KEY(SPILLQ, MQMSGID)
ALTER TABLE ASN.IBMQREP_SPILLEDROW VOLATILE CARDINALITY
ALTER TABLE IBMQREP_SPILLEDROW
ADD CONSTRAINT IBMQREP_SPILLEDROW_IBMQREP_SPILLQS_FK
FOREIGN KEY (SPILLQ)
REFERENCES IBMQREP_SPILLQS (SPILLQ) NOT ENFORCED
```

- IBMQREP_SPILLQS: This table identifies temporary Spill Queues that will hold changes to source tables before they are applied to targets.

SPILLQ	VCHAR(48) NOT NULL
SUBNAME	VCHAR(132) NOT NULL
RECVQ	VCHAR(48) NOT NULL

```
PRIMARY KEY(SPILLQ)
```

```
ALTER TABLE ASN.IBMQREP_SPILLQS VOLATILE CARDINALITY
ALTER TABLE IBMQREP_SPILLQS
ADD CONSTRAINT IBMQREP_SPILLQS_IBMQREP_RECVQUEUES_FK
FOREIGN KEY (RECVQ) REFERENCES IBMQREP_RECVQUEUES (RECVQ) NOT
ENFORCED
```

- IBMQREP_TARGETS: This table contains information about target tables or stored procedures, and options for Q subscriptions.

SUBNAME	VCHAR(132) NOT NULL
RECVQ	VCHAR(48) NOT NULL
SUB_ID	INT WITH DEFAULT NULL
SOURCE_SERVER	VCHAR(18) NOT NULL
SOURCE_ALIAS	VCHAR(8) NOT NULL
SOURCE_OWNER	VCHAR(128) NOT NULL
SOURCE_NAME	VCHAR(128) NOT NULL
SRC_NICKNAME_OWNER	VCHAR(128)
SRC_NICKNAME	VCHAR(128)
TARGET_OWNER	VCHAR(128) NOT NULL
TARGET_NAME	VCHAR(128) NOT NULL
TARGET_TYPE	INT NNWD 1,
FEDERATED_TGT_SRVR	VCHAR(18) WITH DEFAULT NULL
STATE	CHAR(1) NNWD 'I'
STATE_TIME	TS NNWD CURRENT TIMESTAMP
STATE_INFO	CHAR(8)
SUBTYPE	CHAR(1) NNWD 'U'
CONFLICT_RULE	CHAR(1) NNWD 'K'
CONFLICT_ACTION	CHAR(1) NNWD 'I'
ERROR_ACTION	CHAR(1) NNWD 'Q'
SPILLQ	VCHAR(48) WITH DEFAULT NULL
OKSQLSTATES	VCHAR(128) WITH DEFAULT NULL
SUBGROUP	VCHAR(30) WITH DEFAULT NULL
SOURCE_NODE	SI NNWD 0
TARGET_NODE	SI NNWD 0
GROUP_INIT_ROLE	CHAR(1) WITH DEFAULT NULL
HAS_LOADPHASE	CHAR(1) NNWD 'N'
LOAD_TYPE	SI NNWD 0
DESCRIPTION	VCHAR(254)
SEARCH_CONDITION	VCHAR(2048) WITH DEFAULT NULL
MODELQ	VCHAR(36) NNWD 'IBMQREP.SPILL.MODELQ'
CCD_CONDENSED	CHAR(1) WITH DEFAULT 'Y'
CCD_COMPLETE	CHAR(1) WITH DEFAULT 'Y'

```
SOURCE_TYPE                     CHAR(1) WITH DEFAULT ' '
```

ALTER TABLE ASN.IBMQREP_TARGETS VOLATILE CARDINALITY

UNIQUE INDEX ASN.IX1TARGETS ON ASN.IBMQREP_TARGETS(SUBNAME ASC, RECVQ ASC)

UNIQUE INDEX ASN.IX2TARGETS ON ASN.IBMQREP_TARGETS(TARGET_OWNER ASC, TARGET_NAME ASC, RECVQ ASC, SOURCE_OWNER ASC, SOURCE_NAME ASC)

INDEX ASN.IX3TARGETS ON ASN.IBMQREP_TARGETS(RECVQ ASC, SUB_ID ASC)

ALTER TABLE IBMQREP_TARGETS

ADD CONSTRAINT IBMQREP_TARGETS_IBMQREP_RECVQUEUES_FK

FOREIGN KEY (RECVQ) REFERENCES IBMQREP_RECVQUEUES (RECVQ) NOT ENFORCED

ALTER TABLE IBMQREP_TARGETS

ADD CONSTRAINT IBMQREP_TARGETS_IBMQREP_SPILLQS_FK

FOREIGN KEY (SPILLQ) REFERENCES IBMQREP_SPILLQS (SPILLQ) NOT ENFORCED

The following is a query to interrogate the table:

db2 "SELECT SUBSTR(subname,1,20) AS subname, SUBSTR(recvq,1,30) AS recvq, conflict_rule AS r, conflict_action AS a, error_action AS e, has_loadphase as L, cast(load_type as char) AS t FROM asn. ibmqrep_targets "

```
SUBNAME                 RECVQ                           R A E L T
------------------- ----------------------------- - - - - -

T10002                  CAPB.TO.APPA.RECVQ              K I Q I 0
```

The columns map as follows:

```
subname,
substr(recvq,1,30) as RECVQ,
conflict_rule as R,
conflict_action as A,
error_action as E,
has_loadphase as L,
cast(load_type as char) as T
```

Note that the T column value is zero.

- IBMQREP_TRG_COLS: This table contains information about the mapping between source and target columns.

```
RECVQ                     VCHAR(48) NOT NULL
SUBNAME                   VCHAR(132) NOT NULL
SOURCE_COLNAME            VCHAR(254) NOT NULL
```

```
TARGET_COLNAME              VCHAR(128) NOT NULL
TARGET_COLNO               INT WITH DEFAULT NULL
MSG_COL_CODEPAGE           INT WITH DEFAULT NULL
MSG_COL_NUMBER             SI WITH DEFAULT NULL
MSG_COL_TYPE               SI WITH DEFAULT NULL
MSG_COL_LENGTH             INT WITH DEFAULT NULL
IS_KEY                     CHAR(1) NOT NULL
MAPPING_TYPE               CHAR(1) WITH DEFAULT NULL
SRC_COL_MAP                VCHAR(2000) WITH DEFAULT NULL
BEF_TARG_COLNAME           VCHAR(128) WITH DEFAULT NULL

ALTER TABLE ASN.IBMQREP_TRG_COLS VOLATILE CARDINALITY
UNIQUE INDEX ASN.IX1TRGCOL ON ASN.IBMQREP_TRG_COLS( RECVQ ASC,
SUBNAME ASC, TARGET_COLNAME ASC)
ALTER TABLE IBMQREP_TRG_COLS
ADD CONSTRAINT IBMQREP_TRG_COLS_IBMQREP_RECVQUEUES_FK
FOREIGN KEY (RECVQ) REFERENCES IBMQREP_RECVQUEUES (RECVQ) NOT
ENFORCED
```

The Replication Alert Monitor control tables

In this section, we will look at the structure of the **Replication Alert Monitor (RAM)** control tables.

There are three default table spaces that are created:

```
CREATE TABLESPACE REPLMONTS1 IN NODEGROUP IBMCATGROUP MANAGED BY
DATABASE USING ( FILE 'REPLMONTS1' 5M)

CREATE TABLESPACE REPLMONTS2 IN NODEGROUP IBMCATGROUP MANAGED BY
DATABASE USING ( FILE 'REPLMONTS2' 5M)

CREATE TABLESPACE REPLMONTS3 IN NODEGROUP IBMCATGROUP MANAGED BY
DATABASE USING ( FILE 'REPLMONTS3' 5M)
```

In DB2 9.7, there are 12 Replication Alert Monitor control tables:

```
IBMSNAP_ALERTS        IBMSNAP_GROUPS       IBMSNAP_MONTRACE
IBMSNAP_CONDITIONS    IBMSNAP_MONENQ       IBMSNAP_MONTRAIL
IBMSNAP_CONTACTGRP    IBMSNAP_MONPARMS     IBMSNAP_SUSPENDS
IBMSNAP_CONTACTS      IBMSNAP_MONSERVERS   IBMSNAP_TEMPLATES
```

Let's look at each of these tables in detail:

- `IBMSNAP_ALERTS`: This table contains a record of all the alerts issued by the Replication Alert Monitor (table space: `REPLMONTS2`).

```
MONITOR_QUAL                    CHAR(18) NOT NULL
ALERT_TIME                      TS NOT NULL
COMPONENT                       CHAR( 1) NOT NULL
SERVER_NAME                     CHAR(18) NOT NULL
SERVER_ALIAS                    CHAR( 8)
SCHEMA_OR_QUAL                  VARCHAR(128) NOT NULL
SET_NAME                        CHAR(18) NNWD ' '
CONDITION_NAME                  CHAR(18) NOT NULL
OCCURRED_TIME                   TS NOT NULL
ALERT_COUNTER                   SI NOT NULL
ALERT_CODE                      CHAR( 10) NOT NULL
RETURN_CODE                     INT NOT NULL
NOTIFICATION_SENT               CHAR(1) NOT NULL
ALERT_MESSAGE                   VCHAR(1024) NOT NULL)
```

```
INDEX ASN.IBMSNAP_ALERTXON ASN.IBMSNAP_ALERTS(MONITOR_QUAL
ASC,COMPONENT ASC,SERVER_NAME ASC,SCHEMA_OR_QUAL ASC,SET_NAME
ASC,CONDITION_NAME ASC,ALERT_CODE ASC)
ALTER TABLE ASN.IBMSNAP_ALERTS VOLATILE CARDINALITY
```

- `IBMSNAP_CONDITIONS`: This table contains the alert conditions for which the Replication Alert Monitor will contact someone, and contains the group or individual's name to contact if a particular condition occurs (table space: `REPLMONTS1`).

```
MONITOR_QUAL                    CHAR(18) NOT NULL
SERVER_NAME                     CHAR(18) NOT NULL
COMPONENT                       CHAR( 1) NOT NULL
SCHEMA_OR_QUAL                  VCHAR(128) NOT NULL
SET_NAME                        CHAR(18) NNWD ' '
SERVER_ALIAS                    CHAR( 8)
ENABLED                         CHAR( 1) NOT NULL
CONDITION_NAME                  CHAR(18) NOT NULL
PARM_INT                        INT
PARM_CHAR                       VCHAR(128)
CONTACT_TYPE                    CHAR( 1) NOT NULL
CONTACT                         VCHAR(127) NOT NULL
```

```
UNIQUE INDEX ASN.IBMSNAP_MONCONDX ON ASN.IBMSNAP_
CONDITIONS(MONITOR_QUAL ASC, SERVER_NAME ASC, COMPONENT ASC,
SCHEMA_OR_QUAL ASC, SET_NAME ASC, CONDITION_NAME ASC)
ALTER TABLE ASN.IBMSNAP_CONDITIONS VOLATILE CARDINALITY
```

- IBMSNAP_CONTACTGRP: This table contains the individual contacts that make up the contact groups (table space: REPLMONTS1).

GROUP_NAME	VCHAR(127) NOT NULL
CONTACT_NAME	VCHAR(127) NOT NULL)

  ```
  UNIQUE INDEX ASN.IBMSNAP_CONTACTGPX ON ASN.IBMSNAP_
  CONTACTGRP(GROUP_NAME ASC, CONTACT_NAME ASC)
  ALTER TABLE ASN.IBMSNAP_CONTACTGRP VOLATILE CARDINALITY
  ```

- IBMSNAP_CONTACTS: This table contains information on how the Replication Alert Monitor notifies each person or group, when an alert condition that is associated with that contact name occurs (table space: REPLMONTS1).

CONTACT_NAME	VARCHAR(127) NOT NULL
EMAIL_ADDRESS	VARCHAR(128) NOT NULL
ADDRESS_TYPE	CHAR(1) NOT NULL
DELEGATE	VARCHAR(127)
DELEGATE_START	DATE
DELEGATE_END	DATE
DESCRIPTION	VARCHAR(1024))

  ```
  UNIQUE INDEX ASN.IBMSNAP_CONTACTSXON ASN.IBMSNAP_CONTACTS(CONTACT_
  NAME ASC)
  ALTER TABLE ASN.IBMSNAP_CONTACTS VOLATILE CARDINALITY
  ```

- IBMSNAP_GROUPS: This table contains the name and description of each contact group (table space: REPLMONTS1).

GROUP_NAME	VCHAR(127) NOT NULL
DESCRIPTION	VCHAR(1024)

  ```
  UNIQUE INDEX ASN.IBMSNAP_GROUPSX ON ASN.IBMSNAP_GROUPS(GROUP_NAME
  ASC);
  ALTER TABLE ASN.IBMSNAP_GROUPS VOLATILE CARDINALITY
  ```

- IBMSNAP_MONENQ: This table is used to ensure that only one Replication Alert Monitor program is running per monitor qualifier (table space: REPLMONTS1).

MONITOR_QUAL	CHAR(18) NOT NULL)

- IBMSNAP_MONPARMS: This table contains parameters that can be modified to control the operations of the monitor program (table space: REPLMONTS3).

MONITOR_QUAL	CHAR(18) NOT NULL
ALERT_PRUNE_LIMIT	INT WITH DEFAULT 10080
AUTOPRUNE	CHAR(1) WITH DEFAULT 'Y'
EMAIL_SERVER	VCHAR(128)
LOGREUSE	CHAR(1) WITH DEFAULT 'N'

```
LOGSTDOUT                    CHAR(1) WITH DEFAULT 'N'
NOTIF_PER_ALERT              INT WITH DEFAULT 3
NOTIF_MINUTES                INT WITH DEFAULT 60
MONITOR_ERRORS               VCHAR(128)
MONITOR_INTERVAL             INT WITH DEFAULT 300000
MONITOR_PATH                 VCHAR(1040)
RUNONCE                      CHAR(1) WITH DEFAULT 'N'
TERM                         CHAR(1) WITH DEFAULT 'N'
TRACE_LIMIT                  INT WITH DEFAULT 10080
ARCH_LEVEL                   CHAR(4) WITH DEFAULT '0901')
```

```
UNIQUE INDEX ASN.IBMSNAP_MONPARMSXON ASN.IBMSNAP_MONPARMS(MONITOR_
QUAL ASC)
```

```
ALTER TABLE ASN.IBMSNAP_MONPARMS VOLATILE CARDINALITY
```

- IBMSNAP_MONSERVERS: This table contains the latest time that a server was monitored by a Replication Alert Monitor program, identified by a monitor qualifier (table space: REPLMONTS1).

```
MONITOR_QUAL                 CHAR(18) NOT NULL
SERVER_NAME                  CHAR(18) NOT NULL
SERVER_ALIAS                 CHAR(8)
LAST_MONITOR_TIME            TS NOT NULL
START_MONITOR_TIME           TS
END_MONITOR_TIME             TS
LASTRUN                      TS NOT NULL
LASTSUCCESS                  TS
STATUS                       SI NOT NULL
```

```
UNIQUE INDEX ASN.IBMSNAP_MONSERVERX ON ASN.IBMSNAP_
MONSERVERS(MONITOR_QUAL ASC, SERVER_NAME ASC)
```

```
ALTER TABLE ASN.IBMSNAP_MONSERVERS VOLATILE CARDINALITY
```

- IBMSNAP_MONTRACE: This table contains important messages from the monitor program (table space: REPLMONTS3).

```
MONITOR_QUAL                 CHAR(18) NOT NULL
TRACE_TIME                   TS NOT NULL
OPERATION                    CHAR( 8) NOT NULL
DESCRIPTION                  VCHAR(1024) NOT NULL
```

```
INDEX ASN.IBMSNAP_MONTRACEXON ASN.IBMSNAP_MONTRACE(MONITOR_QUAL
ASC, TRACE_TIME ASC)
```

```
ALTER TABLE ASN.IBMSNAP_MONTRACE VOLATILE CARDINALITY
```

- `IBMSNAP_MONTRAIL`: This table contains important information about each monitor cycle (table space: `REPLMONTS3`).

MONITOR_QUAL	CHAR(18) NOT NULL
SERVER_NAME	CHAR(18) NOT NULL
SERVER_ALIAS	CHAR(8)
STATUS	SI NOT NULL
LASTRUN	TS NOT NULL
LASTSUCCESS	TS
ENDTIME	TS NNWD
LAST_MONITOR_TIME	TS NOT NULL
START_MONITOR_TIME	TS
END_MONITOR_TIME	TS
SQLCODE	INT
SQLSTATE	CHAR(5)
NUM_ALERTS	INT NOT NULL
NUM_NOTIFICATIONS	INT NOT NULL
SUSPENSION_NAME	VCHAR(128)

  ```
  ALTER TABLE IBMSNAP_MONTRAIL
  ADD CONSTRAINT IBMSNAP_MONTRAIL_IBMSNAP_SUSPENDS_FK
  FOREIGN KEY (SUSPENSION_NAME)
  REFERENCES IBMSNAP_SUSPENDS (SUSPENSION_NAME) NOT ENFORCED
  ```

- `IBMSNAP_SUSPENDS`: This table stores information about temporary suspensions of the monitor program.

SUSPENSION_NAME	VCHAR(128) NOT NULL PRIMARY KEY
SERVER_NAME	CHAR(18) NOT NULL
SERVER_ALIAS	CHAR(8)
TEMPLATE_NAME	VCHAR(128)
START	TS NOT NULL
STOP	TS NOT NULL

  ```
  UNIQUE INDEX ASN.IBMSNAP_SUSPENDSX ON ASN.IBMSNAP_SUSPENDS(SERVER_
  NAME ASC, START ASC, TEMPLATE_NAME ASC)
  ALTER TABLE ASN.IBMSNAP_SUSPENDS VOLATILE CARDINALITY
  ALTER TABLE IBMSNAP_SUSPENDS
  ADD CONSTRAINT IBMSNAP_SUSPENDS_IBMSNAP_TEMPLATES_FK
  FOREIGN KEY (TEMPLATE_NAME)
  REFERENCES IBMSNAP_TEMPLATES (TEMPLATE_NAME) NOT ENFORCED
  ```

- IBMSNAP_TEMPLATES: This table stores information about how often and how long the monitor program is suspended. This information is called a **monitor suspension template**.

```
TEMPLATE_NAME                VCHAR(128) NOT NULL PRIMARY KEY
START_TIME                   TIME NOT NULL
WDAY                         SI DEFAULT null
DURATION                     INT NOT NULL

ALTER TABLE ASN.IBMSNAP_TEMPLATES VOLATILE CARDINALITY
```

Where do the control tables go

This section looks at where the Q replication control tables go for different source and target database types.

DB2 to DB2 replication

For DB2 to DB2 replication, the Q Capture control tables go on the server where Q Capture runs, and the Q Apply control tables go on the server where Q Apply runs. The placement of the Replication Alert Monitor tables is discussed in the *Monitoring using the Replication Alert Monitor* section of *Chapter 7, Monitoring and Reporting*.

DB2 to non-DB2 replication

In the scenario, where we are replicating from a DB2 source to a non-DB2 target (such as Oracle), the control tables are distributed as shown in the following figure:

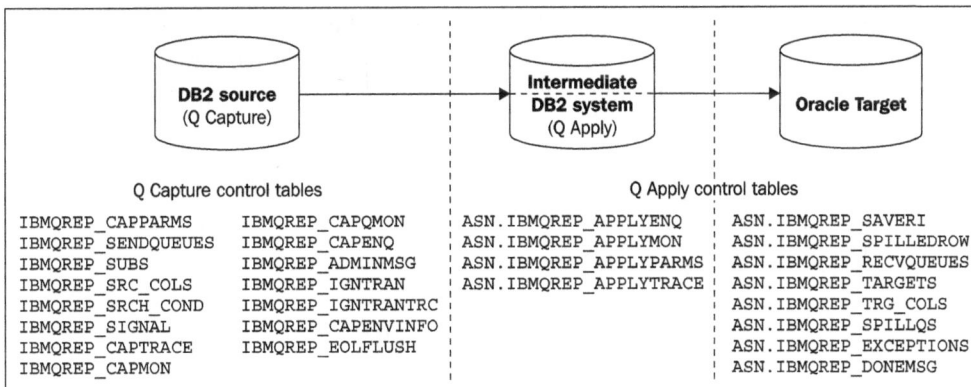

Non-DB2 to DB2 replication

In the scenario, where we are replicating from a non-DB2 source (such as Oracle) to a DB2 target, the control tables are distributed as shown in the following figure:

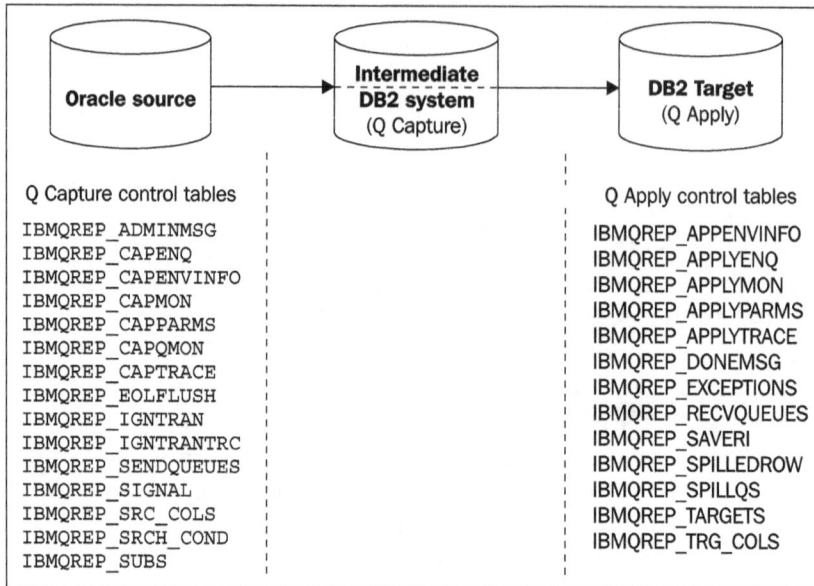

How are the Q replication control tables populated

The various tasks of creating the Q replication control tables, Replication Queue Maps, and Q subscriptions will populate a number of the control tables. The following figure shows which tables are populated for bidirectional replication:

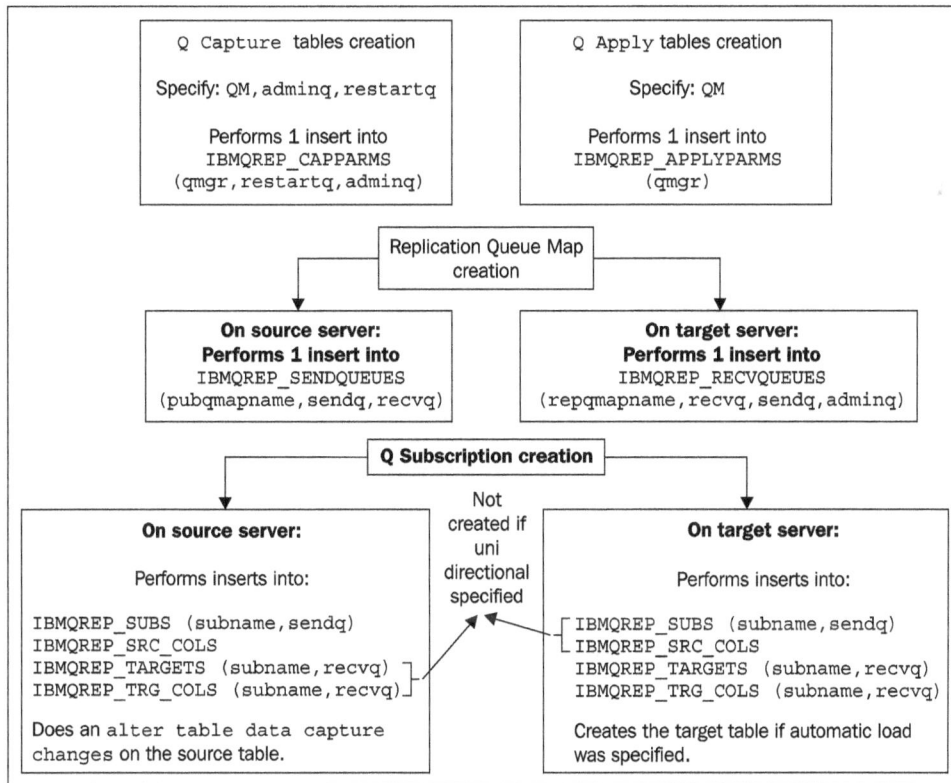

In addition to the control tables being populated at the Q replication definition stage, some are also populated during the normal operation of Q Capture and Q Apply.

Many of the control tables, for example IBMQREP_CAPMON and IBMQREP_APPLYMON are updated on a regular basis by Q Capture and Q Apply. For bidirectional replication, the IBMQREP_SIGNAL table can grow very large. There has to be some mechanism by which the amount of data in these tables is controlled. This mechanism is called **pruning** and is covered in the next section.

Pruning of the control tables

In the previous section, it was discussed how the control tables were populated. This section discusses how they are pruned. The control tables can be pruned automatically by Q Capture and Q Apply (and the Replication Alert Monitor) or can be pruned manually.

Let's first look at the tables that need to be pruned:

- **Q Capture**: IBMQREP_CAPMON, IBMQREP_CAPQMON, IBMQREP_CAPTRACE, and IBMQREP_SIGNAL.
- **Q Apply**: IBMQREP_APPLYMON and IBMQREP_APPLYTRACE.
- **The Replication Alert Monitor**: IBMSNAP_ALERTS and IBMSNAP_MONTRACE.

When it comes to dealing with data in these control tables, we have two questions:

- How long should the data stay in the tables?
- Once we have decided that data should be deleted, when is this done?

There are two parameters which manage the answer to both of these questions:

1. For the xxxMON and CAPQMON tables the answer to the first question is provided by the MONITOR_LIMIT parameter, which determines how long data should be kept in the tables.
2. The second question is answered by the PRUNE_INTERVAL parameter, which determines how often the tables should be checked for old data and then pruned. Both of these parameters are Q Capture and Q Apply startup parameters.

For tables IBMQREP_CAPTRACE and IBMQREP_APPLYTRACE, we can set up automatic pruning using the TRACE_LIMIT start up parameter.

For the RAM IBMSNAP_ALERTS table, we can set up automatic pruning by setting the AUTOPRUNE operational parameter to Y, which means that rows older than ALERT_PRUNE_LIMIT are pruned.

For the RAM IBMSNAP_MONTRACE table, we can set up automatic pruning using the TRACE_LIMIT parameter.

These *limit* and *interval* values are stored in the IBMQREP_CAPPARMS, IBMQREP_APPLYPARMS, and IBMSNAP_MONPARMS tables. The following queries show their current values (which are the defaults):

```
db2 "select monitor_interval, monitor_limit, prune_interval, trace_limit
from asn.ibmqrep_capparms"

MONITOR_INTERVAL MONITOR_LIMIT PRUNE_INTERVAL TRACE_LIMIT
---------------- ------------- -------------- -----------
          300000         10080            300       10080
```

```
db2 "select monitor_interval, monitor_limit, prune_interval, trace_limit
from asn.ibmqrep_applyparms "

MONITOR_INTERVAL MONITOR_LIMIT PRUNE_INTERVAL TRACE_LIMIT
---------------- ------------- -------------- -----------
          300000         10080            300       10080

db2 "select monitor_qual, monitor_interval, alert_prune_limit, trace_
limit from asn.ibmsnap_monparms "

MONITOR_QUAL          MONITOR_INTERVAL ALERT_PRUNE_LIMIT TRACE_LIMIT
------------------    ---------------- ----------------- -----------
MONAC1                             300             10080       10080
```

> The figure 10080 represents one week in minutes, and means that any records older than one week are pruned from the control tables when the tables are next up for pruning.

The following tables summarizes, which tables are automatically pruned by Q Capture, Q Apply, and the Replication Alert Monitor.

For Q Capture:

Control table	Startup parameter
IBMQREP_CAPMON	monitor_limit
IBMQREP_CAPQMON	monitor_limit
IBMQREP_CAPTRACE	trace_limit
IBMQREP_SIGNAL	Signal_limit

For Q Apply:

Control table	Startup parameter
IBMQREP_APPLYMON	monitor_limit
IBMQREP_APPLYTRACE	trace_limit

For the Replication Alert Monitor:

Control table	Startup parameter
IBMSNAP_ALERTS	alert_prune_limit
IBMSNAP_MONTRACE	trace_limit

The Q Capture control tables can be manually pruned using the following command:

```
$ asnqccmd CAPTURE_SERVER=db2a CAPTURE_SCHEMA=asn PRUNE
```

The Q Apply control tables can be manually pruned using the following command:

```
$ asnqacmd APPLY_SERVER=db2b APPLY_SCHEMA=asn PRUNE
```

There is no command to manually prune the Replication Alert Monitor tables.

> If we are using CCD tables, then these are not pruned automatically.

> The control tables are not cleared down when Q Capture is cold started.

> The size of the IBMQREP_EXCEPTIONS table is not controlled by any of the *limit* or *interval* values discussed previously. We have to delete from the table manually using SQL to delete unnecessary rows.

The IBMQREP_SIGNAL control table

The IBMQREP_SIGNAL table is a mechanism used to communicate with Q Capture. Remember that Q Capture reads from the DB2 logs, so if we insert data into the IBMQREP_SIGNAL table, then this will be picked up by Q Capture.

> The Q Capture does not read the IBMQREP_SIGNAL table, it detects when a row has been inserted into the table by reading the DB2 logs (it is the only control table that has DATA CAPTURE CHANGES set).

The following shows the structure of the IBMQREP_SIGNAL table:

```
SIGNAL_TIME          TS NNWD CURRENT TS
SIGNAL_TYPE          VCHAR(30) NOT NULL
SIGNAL_SUBTYPE       VCHAR(30)
SIGNAL_INPUT_IN      VCHAR(500)
SIGNAL_STATE         CHAR(1) NNWD 'P'
SIGNAL_LSN           CHAR(10) FOR BIT DATA
```

Let's look at each column in detail:

- SIGNAL_TIME: Timestamp that is used to uniquely identify the row. Q Capture uses this value to find the correct row in the signal table to indicate when it completed processing the Q Capture signal.

- SIGNAL_TYPE: This is a flag that indicates the type of signal that was posted:

  - CMD: This is a row that is inserted by the administrative commands, asnqccmd, the Replication Center, or another application. See the SIGNAL_SUBTYPE column for a list of the available signal subtypes.

  - USER: This is a signal posted by a user. Q Capture updates the SIGNAL_LSN column with the log sequence number of when the signal was inserted. Q Capture also updates the value in the SIGNAL_STATE column from pending (P) to received (R).

- SIGNAL_SUBTYPE: This is the type of action that a CMD-type signal is requesting that Q Capture performs:

  - ADDCOL: This adds one column to an active, unidirectional Q subscription, or to a publication.

  - CAPSTART: This starts capturing changes for a Q subscription or publication.

  - CAPSTOP: This stops capturing changes for a Q subscription or publication.

  - IGNORETRANS: This ignores the DB2 transaction that contains this signal.

  - LOADDONE: This acknowledges receipt of this signal from Q Apply or user application. The LOADDONE signal notifies Q Capture that the target table is loaded.

  - P2PLOADDONE: This is an internal signal that is used to initialize a peer-to-peer Q subscription. The signal is inserted at a new server.

  - P2PMEMB2INIT: This is an internal signal that is used to initialize a peer-to-peer Q subscription. The signal is inserted at active servers.

  - P2PMEMB2NEW: This is an internal signal that is used to initialize a peer-to-peer Q subscription. The signal is inserted at active servers.

  - P2PNEW2MEMB: This is an internal signal that is used to initialize a peer-to-peer Q subscription. The signal is inserted at a new server.

- ° P2PNORECAPTURE: This is a signal that is inserted by Q Apply to prevent Q Capture from recapturing changes. It is used in bidirectional replication.

- ° QINERROR: This executes the error action defined for the Send Queue in the IBMQREP_SENDQUEUES table.

- ° P2PREADYTOSTOP: This is an internal signal that is used to deactivate a peer-to-peer Q subscription. The signal is inserted at the server that is being deactivated.

- ° P2PSPOOLING: This is an internal signal that is used to initialize a peer-to-peer Q subscription. The signal is inserted at the server that initiated a new subscription.

- ° P2PSUBSTOP: This is an internal signal that is used to deactivate a peer-to-peer Q subscription. The signal is inserted at the server that is being deactivated.

- ° P2PSUBSTOPPING: This is an internal signal that is used to deactivate a peer-to-peer Q subscription. The signal is inserted at the remaining active servers.

- ° REINIT_SUB: This is used to deactivate and then activate one Q subscription or publication using the latest values in the IBMQREP_SUBS, IBMQREP_SRC_COLS, and IBMQREP_SENDQUEUES tables. This signal will not prompt a new load of targets.

- ° STARTQ: This starts putting messages on a specified queue or all inactive queues.

- ° STOP: This stops capturing changes and terminates.

- ° STOPQ: This stops putting messages on a specified queue or all inactive queues.

- • SIGNAL_INPUT_IN: If the SIGNAL_TYPE=USER, then this column contains user-defined input. If the SIGNAL_TYPE=CMD, then this value depends on the value of SIGNAL_SUBTYPE:

  - ° CMD + ADDCOL: It indicates the Q subscription or publication name and the column name, separated by a semicolon. For example, QSUB1; COL10.

  - ° CMD + CAPSTART: It indicates the Q subscription or publication name.

  - ° CMD + CAPSTOP: It indicates the Q subscription or publication name.

  - ° CMD + IGNORETRANS: NULL (no value is required).

- ○ CMD + LOADDONE: It indicates the Q subscription or publication name.

- ○ CMD + QINERROR: This indicates that for a user application, the name of the Send Queue that is in error. For Q Apply, the name of the Send Queue that is in error and the ASN message number and space-separated tokens.

- ○ CMD + REINIT_SUB: This indicates the Q subscription or publication name.

- ○ CMD + STARTQ: This indicates the queue name or ALL.

- ○ CMD + STOP: NULL (no value is required).

- ○ CMD + STOPQ: This indicates the queue name or ALL.

- SIGNAL_STATE: This is a flag that indicates the status of the signal:

  - ○ P: This is a default signal. It indicates that the signal is pending; Q Capture did not receive it yet.

  - ○ C: This indicates that Q Capture completed processing the signal.

  - ○ F: This indicates that the signal failed. For example, Q Capture cannot perform a CAPSTART because the Q subscription or publication is faulty.

  - ○ R: This indicates that Q Capture received the signal.

- SIGNAL_LSN: This is the logical log sequence number of the log record for the insert into the IBMQREP_SIGNAL table.

Sending signals using the IBMQREP_SIGNAL table

We have two methods for sending signals—we can either insert a record into the IBMQREP_SIGNAL table directly or we can issue an ASNCLP command, which issues the INSERT statement. Both of these methods are discussed next.

Sending signals using an INSERT statement

We can use the insert process into the IBMQREP_SIGNAL table to communicate with Q Capture. As a minimum, we need to insert a signal_subtype and a signal_input_in value (the signal_time column is optional).

Let's look at an example. Say we want Q Capture to stop the Q subscription T10001. We need to send a CAPSTOP signal or command. We will issue this when Q Capture is down, so we can see what is inserted into the IBMQREP_SIGNAL table. We issue the following commands:

```
db2 "INSERT INTO ASN.IBMQREP_SIGNAL (signal_type, signal_subtype, signal_
input_in) VALUES ('CMD', 'CAPSTOP', 'T10001') "
```

And let's see what fields are inserted into the IBMQREP_SIGNAL table:

```
db2 "select signal_time,substr(signal_type,1,10) as type, substr(signal_
subtype,1,10) as subtype, substr(signal_input_in,1,20) as input, signal_
state as S, signal_lsn from asn.ibmqrep_signal"

SIGNAL_TIME                 TYPE        SUBTYPE    INPUT      S SIGNAL_LSN
--------------------------- ----------  ---------- ---------- -----------------
2007-04-05-17.19.52.875000 CMD         CAPSTOP    T10001     P -
```

We can see the signal timestamp, the type of signal, and the affected Q subscription. Because Q Capture is not running, the SIGNAL_STATE is P, which means *pending*.

Let's look at another example. The signal command to inform Q Capture that a load has been done uses the LOADDONE type of action:

```
db2 "insert into asn.IBMQREP_SIGNAL(signal_time, signal_type, signal_
subtype, signal_input_in, signal_state) values (current timestamp,
'CMD','LOADDONE', 'T30001','P')"
```

In this example, we have included a timestamp in the insert statement. The timestamp is not always included when the SQL is generated through the Replication Center.

Sending signals using ASNCLP

We can also send signals using ASNCLP commands, which is covered in detail in the *Q subscription maintenance—Sending a signal using ASNCLP* section of *Chapter 5, The ASNCLP Command Interface*.

Using a signal to determine where Q Capture is up to

If we stop updating a source table, then how do we know when Q Capture has processed all the activity for that table? We can insert a record into the IBMQREP_SIGNAL table as follows:

```
db2 "INSERT INTO asn.ibmqrep_signal (signal_type, signal_subtype, signal_
state) VALUES ('USER', 'XXXXX','P')"
```

When Q Capture processes this insert command, it will change the SIGNAL_STATE from P to R, which means that Q Capture has passed the last activity to our table in the DB2 log. If we select from the IBMQREP_SIGNAL, we should see that the SIGNAL_STATE has changed its value to R.

Restricting access to IBMQREP_SIGNAL

We can see that being able to communicate with Q Capture using the IBMQREP_SIGNAL table can lead to problems, if anyone can insert into the table. Therefore, we should restrict who has access to this table. The following query lists who has access to the table:

```
db2 "select substr(tabschema,1,5) as schema, substr(tabname,1,10) as
tabname, substr(grantor,1,10) as grantor, substr(grantee,1,10)  as
grantee, insertauth as I, selectauth as S, updateauth as U, deleteauth as
D from syscat.tabauth where tabname = 'SIGNAL' "

SCHEMA TABNAME    GRANTOR    GRANTEE    I S U D

------ ---------- ---------- ---------- - - - -
```

Clearly, the DBA will have access to the table, so we need another mechanism to at least flag up that we are trying to insert into the table. One method is to create an insert trigger on the table to stop any inserts. Then, if we do really want to insert into the table we will first have to drop the trigger. This at least gives us a two step check for inserting data into the table. Here is an example of how to code such a trigger:

```
drop trigger DB2ADMIN.STOPINS #
CREATE TRIGGER DB2ADMIN.STOPINS
NO CASCADE
BEFORE  INSERT  ON ASN.IBMQREP_SIGNAL
REFERENCING  NEW AS t
FOR EACH ROW  MODE DB2SQL
WHEN ( t.signal_type = 'CMD' )
BEGIN ATOMIC
signal sqlstate '88888' ('Insert not allowed');
END #
```

If the preceding SQL is in a file called insert_trigger.sql, then the trigger can be created as follows:

```
$ db2 -td# -f insert_trigger.sql
```

So, when we try and insert into the ASN.IBMQREP_SIGNAL table:

```
db2 "INSERT INTO ASN.IBMQREP_SIGNAL (signal_type, signal_subtype, signal_
input_in) VALUES ('CMD', 'CAPSTOP', 'TAB1') "
```

We will get the error:

```
DB21034E  The command was processed as an SQL statement because it was
not a valid Command Line Processor command.  During SQL processing it
returned:
SQL0438N  Application raised error with diagnostic text: "Insert not
allowed".SQLSTATE=88888
```

Summary

In this chapter, we looked in detail at the DB2 database layer. We described the 15 Q Capture control tables, the 14 Q Apply control tables and the 12 Replication Alert Monitor control tables. We looked at where these control tables go, how they are pruned, and unveiled queries which can be run against the control tables to extract information about the current state of the Q replication set up. Finally, we looked at communicating with Q Capture using the IBMQREP_SIGNAL control table, and why it is important to restrict access to this table, to stop unauthorized users from compromising the Q replication environment.

We will now go on to look at the second component of a Q replication solution, namely the WebSphere MQ layer.

4
WebSphere MQ for the DBA

Continuing with the layers that make up Q replication, the second layer we will look at is the WebSphere MQ layer, as shown in the following diagram. After reading this section, you will not be a WebSphere MQ expert, but you will have brought your knowledge of MQ to a level where you can have a sensible conversation with your site's MQ administrator about what the Q replication requirements are.

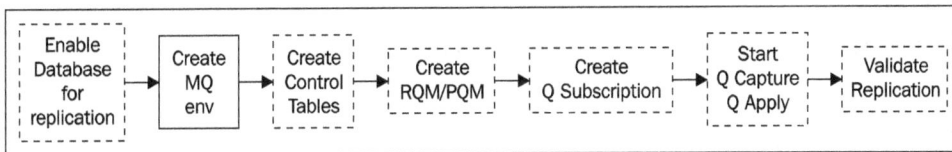

We will look at:

- How WebSphere MQ works
- How to set it up
- What to do when things go wrong

An introduction to MQ

In a nutshell, WebSphere MQ is an assured delivery mechanism, which consists of queues managed by Queue Managers. We can put messages onto, and retrieve messages from queues, and the movement of messages between queues is facilitated by components called Channels and Transmission Queues.

There are a number of fundamental points that we need to know about WebSphere MQ:

- All objects in WebSphere MQ are case sensitive
- We cannot read messages from a *Remote* Queue (only from a Local Queue)
- We can only put a message onto a *Local* Queue (not a Remote Queue)

It does not matter at this stage if you do not understand the above points, all will become clear in the following sections.

There are some standards regarding WebSphere MQ object names:

- Queue names, processes and Queue Manager names can have a maximum length of 48 characters
- Channel names can have a maximum length of 20 characters
- The following characters are allowed in names: A-Z, a-z, 0-9, and . / _ % symbols
- There is no implied structure in a name — dots are there for readability

Now let's move on to look at MQ queues in a little more detail.

MQ queues

MQ queues can be thought of as conduits to transport messages between Queue Managers.

There are four different types of MQ queues and one related object. The four different types of queues are: **Local Queue (QL)**, **Remote Queue (QR)**, **Transmission Queue (TQ)**, and **Dead Letter Queue**, and the related object is a **Channel (CH)**.

One of the fundamental processes of WebSphere MQ is the ability to move messages between Queue Managers. Let's take a high-level look at how messages are moved, as shown in the following diagram:

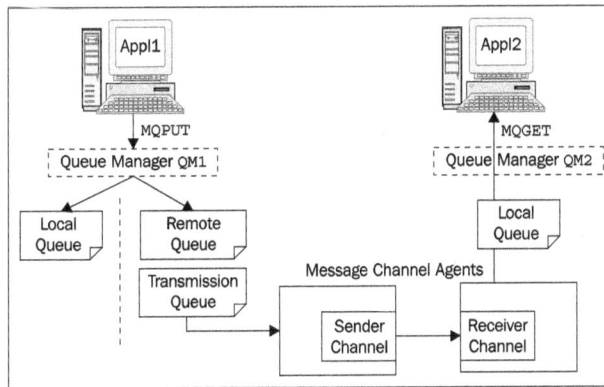

When the application `Appl1` wants to send a message to application `Appl2`, it opens a queue - the local Queue Manager (`QM1`) determines if it is a Local Queue or a Remote Queue. When `Appl1` issues an `MQPUT` command to put a message onto the queue, then if the queue is local, the Queue Manager puts the message directly onto that queue. If the queue is a Remote Queue, then the Queue Manager puts the message onto a Transmission Queue.

The Transmission Queue sends the message using the Sender Channel on `QM1` to the Receiver Channel on the remote Queue Manager (`QM2`). The Receiver Channel puts the message onto a Local Queue on `QM2`. `Appl2` issues a `MQGET` command to retrieve the message from this queue.

Now let's move on to look at the queues used by Q replication and in particular, unidirectional replication, as shown in the following diagram. What we want to show here is the relationship between Remote Queues, Transmission Queues, Channels, and Local Queues. As an example, let's look at the path a message will take from Q Capture on `QMA` to Q Apply on `QMB`.

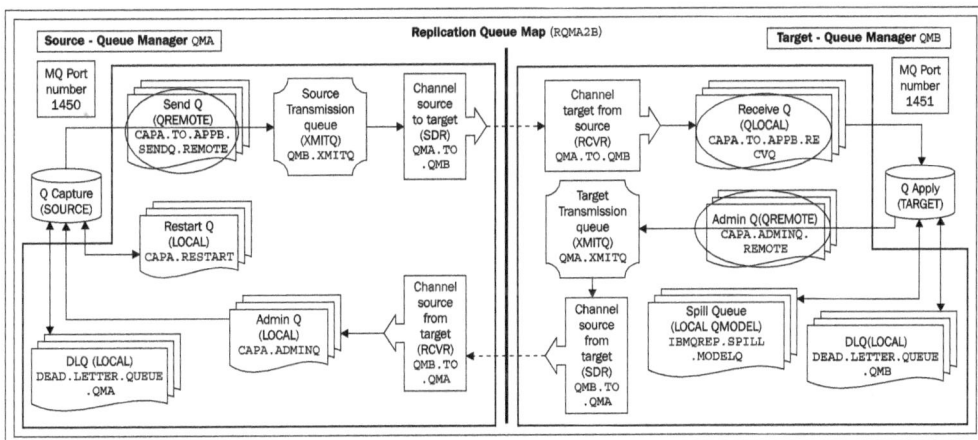

Note that in this diagram the Listeners are not shown.

Q Capture puts the message onto a remotely-defined queue on QMA (the local Queue Manager for Q Capture). This Remote Queue (CAPA.TO.APPB.SENDQ.REMOTE) is effectively a "place holder" and points to a Local Queue (CAPA.TO.APPB.RECVQ) on QMB and specifies the Transmission Queue (QMB.XMITQ) it should use to get there. The Transmission Queue has, as part of its definition, the Channel (QMA.TO.QMB) to use. The Channel QMA.TO.QMB has, as part of its definition, the IP address and Listening port number of the remote Queue Manager (note that we do not name the remote Queue Manager in this definition—it is specified in the definition for the Remote Queue).

The definition for unidirectional Replication Queue Map (circled queue names) is:

SENDQ: CAPA.TO.APPB.SENDQ.REMOTE on the source

RECVQ: CAPA.TO.APPB.RECVQ on the target

ADMINQ: CAPA.ADMINQ.REMOTE on the target

Let's look at the Remote Queue definition for CAPA.TO.APPB.SENDQ.REMOTE, shown next. On the left-hand side are the definitions on QMA, which comprise the Remote Queue, the Transmission Queue, and the Channel definition. The definitions on QMB are on the right-hand side and comprise the Local Queue and the Receiver Channel.

QMA (1450)	QMB (1451)
DEFINE QREMOTE (CAPA.TO.APPB.SENDQ.REMOTE) + REPLACE + PUT (ENABLED) + XMITQ (QMB.XMITQ) + RNAME (CAPA.TO.APPB.RECVQ) + RQMNAME (QMB) + DEFPSIST (YES)	DEFINE QLOCAL (CAPA.TO.APPB.RECVQ) + REPLACE + PUT (ENABLED) + GET (ENABLED) + DEFSOPT (SHARED) + DEFPSIST (YES)
DEFINE QLOCAL (QMB.XMITQ) + REPLACE + USAGE (XMITQ) + PUT (ENABLED) + GET (ENABLED) + TRIGGER + TRIGTYPE (FIRST) + TRIGDATA (QMA.TO.QMB) + INITQ (SYSTEM.CHANNEL.INITQ)	
DEFINE CHANNEL (QMA.TO.QMB) + CHLTYPE (SDR) + REPLACE + TRPTYPE (TCP) + DISCINT (0) + XMITQ (QMB.XMITQ) + CONNAME ('127.0.0.1(1451)')	DEFINE CHANNEL (QMA.TO.QMB) + CHLTYPE (RCVR) + REPLACE + TRPTYPE (TCP)

Let's break down these definitions to the core values to show the relationship between the different parameters, as shown next:

QMA[6] (1450)			QMB[1] 127.0.0.1[5] (1451[4])	
DEFINE QREMOTE (CAPA.TO.APPB.SENDQ.REMOTE) XMITQ (QMB.XMITQ)[3] RENAME (CAPA.TO.APPB.RECVQ)[2] RQMNAME (QMB)[1]	DEFINE QLOCAL (QMB.XMITQ)[3] USAGE (XMITQ) TRIGGER TRIGTYPE (FIRST) TRIGDATA (QMA.TO.QMB[9]) INITQ (SYSTEM.CHANNEL.IN ITQ)	DEFINE CHANNEL (QMA.TO.QMB[9]) CHLTYPE (SDR) XMITQ (QMB.XMITQ[3]) CONNAME ('127.0.0.1[5] (1451[4])')	DEFINE QLOCAL (CAPA.TO.APPB. RECVQ[2])	DEFINE CHANNEL (QMA.TO.QMB[9]) CHLTYPE (RCVR)

We define a Remote Queue by matching up the superscript numbers in the definitions in the two Queue Managers:

For definitions on QMA, QMA is the local system and QMB is the remote system.

For definitions on QMB, QMB is the local system and QMA is the remote system.

1. Remote Queue Manager name
2. Name of the queue on the remote system
3. Transmission Queue name
4. Port number that the remote system is listening on
5. The IP address of the Remote Queue Manager
6. Local Queue Manager name
7. Channel name

Queue names:

- QMB: Decide on the Local Queue name on QMB — CAPA.TO.APPB.RECVQ.
- QMA: Decide on the Remote Queue name on QMB — CAPA.TO.APPB.SENDQ.REMOTE.

Channels:

- QMB: Define a Receiver Channel on QMB, QMA.TO.QMB — make sure the channel type (CHLTYPE) is RCVR.
- The Channel names on QMA and QMB have to match: QMA.TO.QMB.
- QMA: Define a Sender Channel, which takes the messages from the Transmission Queue QMB.XMITQ and which points to the IP address and Listening port number of QMB. The Sender Channel name must be QMA.TO.QMB.

Let's move on from unidirectional replication to bidirectional replication. The bidirectional queue diagram is shown next, which is a cut-down version of the full diagram of the *The WebSphere MQ layer* section of *Chapter 2, Q Replication Components* and just shows the queue names and types without the details.

The principles in bidirectional replication are the same as for unidirectional replication. There are two Replication Queue Maps—one going from QMA to QMB (as unidirectional replication) and one going from QMB to QMA.

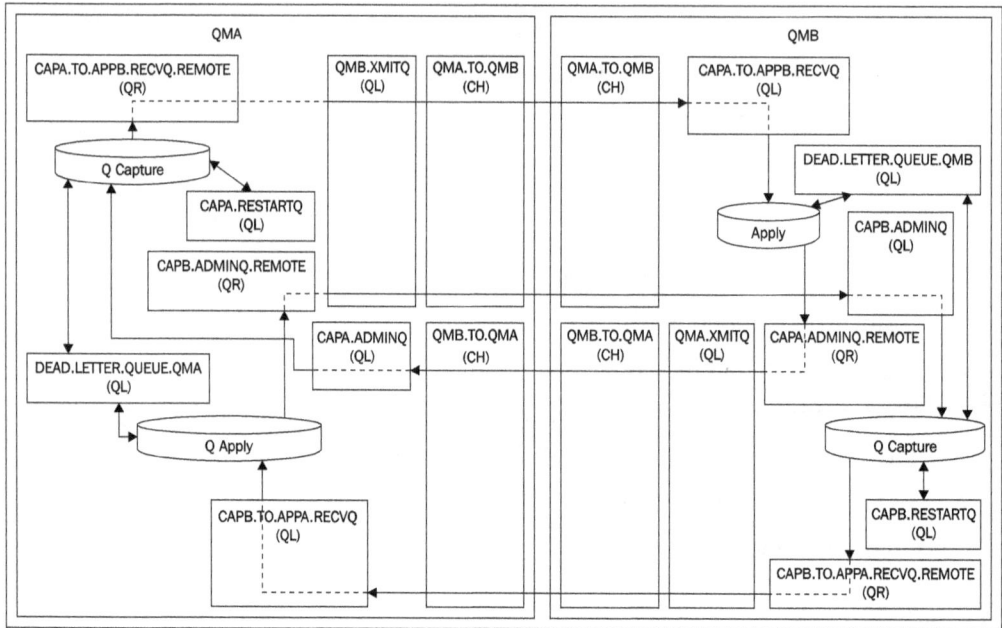

Dead Letter Queues are discussed in the *Dead Letter Queue handler (runmqdlq)* section.

MQ queue naming standards

The naming of the WebSphere MQ queues is an important part of Q replication setup. It may be that your site already has a naming standard for MQ queues, but if it does not, then here are some thoughts on the subject (WebSphere MQ naming standards were discussed in the *Introduction to MQ* section):

Queues are related to Q Capture and Q Apply programs, so it would be useful to have that fact reflected in the name of the queues.

- A Q Capture needs a local Restart Queue and we use the name `CAPA.RESTARTQ`.

- Each Queue Manager can have a Dead Letter Queue. We use the prefix `DEAD.LETTER.QUEUE` with a suffix of the Queue Manager name giving `DEAD.LETTER.QUEUE.QMA`.

- Receive Queues are related to Send Queues.

  For every Send Queue, we need a Receive Queue. Our Send Queue names are made up of where they are coming from, Q Capture on `QMA` (`CAPA`), and where they are going to, Q Apply on `QMB` (`APPB`), and we also want to put in that it is a Send Queue and that it is a remote definition, so we end up with `CAPA.TO.APPB.SENDQ.REMOTE`. The corresponding Receive Queue will be called `CAPA.TO.APPB.RECVQ`.

- Transmission Queues should reflect the names of the "to" Queue Manager.

  Our Transmission Queue on `QMA` is called `QMB.XMITQ`, reflecting the Queue Manager that it is going to, and that it is a Transmission Queue. Using this naming convention on `QMB`, the Transmission Queue is called `QMA.XMITQ`.

- Channels should reflect the names of the "from" and "to" Queue Managers.

  Our Sender Channel definition on `QMA` is `QMA.TO.QMB` reflecting that it is a channel from `QMA` to `QMB` and the Receiver Channel on `QMB` is also called `QMA.TO.QMB`. The Receiver Queue on `QMA` is called `QMB.TO.QMA` for a Sender Channel of the same name on `QMB`.

- A Replication Queue Map definition requires a local Send Queue, and a remote Receive Queue and a remote Administration Queue.

  The Send Queue is the queue that Q Capture writes to, the Receive Queue is the queue that Q Apply reads from, and the Administration Queue is the queue that Q Apply writes messages back to Q Capture with.

Throughout the examples in *Appendix A*, we use queue names which work—if you need to use different names because of the naming standards at your site, then try and map your queue names onto ours, to check that Send Queues go to Receive Queues, and so on. The examples also assume that there will only ever be one Q Capture and one Q Apply running per DB2 database.

MQ queues required for different scenarios

This section lists the number of Local and Remote Queues and Channels that are needed for each type of replication scenario.

The queues and channels required for unidirectional replication (including replicating to a Stored Procedure) and Event Publishing are shown in the following tables. Note that the queues and channels required for Event Publishing are a subset of those required for unidirectional replication, but creating extra queues and not using them is not a problem.

The queues and channels required for unidirectional (including replicating to a Stored Procedure) are shown in the following table:

QMA (7)	QMB (7)
3 Local Queues:	2 Local Queues:
`CAPA.ADMINQ`	`CAPA.TO.APPB.REVCQ`
`CAPA.RESTARTQ`	`DEAD.LETTER.QUEUE.QMB`
`DEAD.LETTER.QUEUE.QMA`	1 Remote Queue:
1 Remote Queue:	`CAPA.ADMINQ.REMOTE`
`CAPA.TO.APPB.SENDQ.REMOTE`	1 Transmission Queue:
1 Transmission Queue:	`QMA.XMITQ`
`QMB.XMITQ`	1 Sender Channel:
1 Sender Channel:	`QMB.TO.QMA`
`QMA.TO.QMB`	1 Receiver Channel:
1 Receiver Channel:	`QMA.TO.QMB`
`QMB.TO.QMA`	1 Model Queue:
	`IBMQREP.SPILL.MODELQ`

The queues required for Event Publishing are shown in the following table:

QMA (7)	QMB (7)
3 Local Queues: CAPA.ADMINQ CAPA.RESTARTQ DEAD.LETTER.QUEUE.QMA 1 Remote Queue: CAPA.TO.APPB.SENDQ.REMOTE 1 Transmission Queue: QMB.XMITQ 1 Sender Channel: QMA.TO.QMB 1 Receiver Channel: QMB.TO.QMA	2 Local Queues: CAPA.TO.APPB.REVCQ DEAD.LETTER.QUEUE.QMB 1 Receiver Channel: QMA.TO.QMB

The queues and channels required for bidirectional/P2P two-way replication are shown in the following table:

QMA (10)	QMB (10)
4 Local Queues: CAPA.ADMINQ CAPA.RESTARTQ DEAD.LETTER.QUEUE.QMA CAPB.TO.APPA.RECVQ 2 Remote Queues: CAPA.TO.APPB.SENDQ.REMOTE CAPB.ADMINQ.REMOTE 1 Transmission Queue: QMB.XMITQ 1 Sender Channel: QMA.TO.QMB 1 Receiver Channel: QMB.TO.QMA 1 Model Queue: IBMQREP.SPILL.MODELQ	4 Local Queues: CAPB.ADMINQ CAPB.RESTARTQ DEAD.LETTER.QUEUE.QMB CAPA.TO.APPB.RECVQ 2 Remote Queues: CAPB.TO.APPA.SENDQ.REMOTE CAPA.ADMINQ.REMOTE 1 Transmission Queue: QMA.XMITQ 1 Sender Channel: QMB.TO.QMA 1 Receiver Channel: QMA.TO.QMB 1 Model Queue: IBMQREP.SPILL.MODELQ

The queues and channels required for P2P three-way replication are shown in the following table:

QMA (16)	QMB (16)	QMC (16)
5 Local Queues:	5 Local Queues:	5 Local Queues:
CAPA.ADMINQ CAPA.RESTARTQ DEAD.LETTER.QUEUE.QMA CAPB.TO.APPA.RECVQ CAPC.TO.APPA.RECVQ	CAPB.ADMINQ CAPB.RESTARTQ DEAD.LETTER.QUEUE.QMB CAPA.TO.APPB.RECVQ CAPC.TO.APPB.RECVQ	CAPC.ADMINQ CAPC.RESTARTQ DEAD.LETTER.QUEUE.QMC CAPA.TO.APPC.RECVQ CAPB.TO.APPC.RECVQ
4 Remote Queues:	4 Remote Queues:	4 Remote Queues:
CAPA.TO.APPB.SENDQ.REMOTE CAPB.ADMINQ.REMOTE CAPA.TO.APPC.SENDQ.REMOTE CAPC.ADMINQ.REMOTE	CAPB.TO.APPA.SENDQ.REMOTE CAPA.ADMINQ.REMOTE CAPB.TO.APPC.SENDQ.REMOTE CAPC.ADMINQ.REMOTE	CAPC.TO.APPA.SENDQ.REMOTE CAPA.ADMINQ.REMOTE CAPC.TO.APPB.SENDQ.REMOTE CAPB.ADMINQ.REMOTE
2 Transmission Queues:	2 Transmission Queues:	2 Transmission Queues:
QMB.XMITQ QMC.XMITQ	QMA.XMITQ QMC.XMITQ	QMA.XMITQ QMB.XMITQ
2 Sender Channels:	2 Sender Channels:	2 Sender Channels:
QMA.TO.QMC QMA.TO.QMB	QMB.TO.QMA QMB.TO.QMC	QMC.TO.QMA QMC.TO.QMB
2 Receiver Channels:	2 Receiver Channels:	2 Receiver Channels:
QMC.TO.QMA QMB.TO.QMA	QMA.TO.QMB QMC.TO.QMB	QMA.TO.QMC QMB.TO.QMC
1 Model Queue:	1 Model Queue:	1 Model Queue:
IBMQREP.SPILL.MODELQ	IBMQREP.SPILL.MODELQ	IBMQREP.SPILL.MODELQ

WebSphere MQ commands

In this section, we look at the WebSphere MQ commands we need to set up and administer the MQ environment. The following table lists the V6 WebSphere MQ commands:

`amqccert` - Check certificate chains	`mqftrcv` - Receive file on server
`amqmdain` - WebSphere MQ services control	`mqftrcvc` - Receive file on client
`amqtcert` - Transfer certificates	`mqftsnd` - Send file from server
`crtmqm` - Create Queue Manager	`mqftsndc` - Send file from client
`dltmqm` - Delete queue manager	`rcdmqimg` - Record media image
`dmpmqaut` - Dump authority	`rcrmqobj` - Recreate object
`dmpmqlog` - Dump log	`rsvmqtrn` - Resolve transactions
`dspmq` - Display Queue Managers	`runmqchi` - Run channel initiator
`dspmqaut` - Display authority	`runmqchl` - Run channel
`dspmqcsv` - Display command server	`runmqdlq` - Run dead-letter queue handler
`dspmqfls` - Display files	`runmqdnm` - Run .NET monitor
`dspmqrte` - WebSphere MQ display route application	`runmqlsr` - Run listener
`dspmqtrc` - Display formatted trace output	`runmqsc` - Run MQSC commands
	`runmqtmc` - Start client trigger monitor
`dspmqtrn` - Display transactions	`runmqtrm` - Start trigger monitor
`dspmqver` - Display version information	`setmqaut` - Set or reset authority
`endmqcsv` - End command server	`setmqcrl` - Set certificate revocation
`endmqlsr` - End listener	`setmqscp` - Set service connection points
`endmqdnm` - Stop .NET monitor	`strmqcfg` - Start WebSphere MQ Explorer
`endmqm` - End Queue Manager	`strmqcsv` - Start command server
`endmqtrc` - End trace	`strmqm` - Start Queue Manager
`mqftapp` - Run File Transfer Application GUI	`strmqtrc` - Start trace

Only some of these commands are of real interest to us as database administrators! We will go through these relevant commands in the following sections.

Note that it is sometimes desirable to prefix these commands with the operating system START command, which opens a new window for the command to be executed in.

Create/start/stop a Queue Manager

To create a Queue Manager, our userID needs to be part of the mqm group. If we do not have the appropriate authority, then we need to ask our MQ administrator to issue this command.

The command to create a Queue Manager is CRTMQM and there are various parameters available with this command:

```
crtmqm [-z] [-q] [-c Text] [-d DefXmitQ] [-h MaxHandles]
[-g ApplicationGroup] [-t TrigInt]
[-u DeadQ] [-x MaxUMsgs] [-lp LogPri] [-ls LogSec]
[-lc | -ll] [-lf LogFileSize] [-ld LogPath] QMgrName
```

The only required parameter is the Queue Manager name (QMgrName), which can be up to 48 characters in length. The optional parameters are:

- -c <text>: Descriptive text (up to 64 characters) for this Queue Manager.

- -d <DefaultTransmissionQueue>: The name of the local Transmission Queue where remote messages are put if a Transmission Queue is not explicitly defined for their destination. There is no default.

- -g <ApplicationGroup>: The name of the group containing members allowed to: run MQI applications, update all IPCC resources, change the contents of some queue manager directories. This option applies only to WebSphere MQ for AIX, Solaris, HP-UX, and Linux. The default value is -g all, which allows unrestricted access. The -g ApplicationGroup value is recorded in the Queue Manager configuration file, qm.ini. The mqm userID and the user executing the command must belong to the specified ApplicationGroup.

- -h <MaximumHandleLimit>: (default 256). The maximum number of handles that any one application can have open at the same time. The range is 1 through 999,999,999.

- -lc: Use circular logging. This is the default logging method.

- -ll: Use linear logging.

- -ld <LogPath>: The directory used to hold log files. On Windows, the default is C:\Program Files\IBM\WebSphere MQ\log (assuming that C is the data drive). On UNIX systems, the default is /var/mqm/log. User ID mqm and group mqm must have full authority on these directories, which occurs automatically if the log files are in their default locations. If we change the locations of these files, we must give these authorities manually.

- -lf <LogFilePages>: The log data is held in a series of files called log files.

- -lp <LogPrimaryFiles>: The log files allocated when the Queue Manager is created.

- -ls <LogSecondaryFiles>: The log files allocated when the primary files are exhausted.

- -q: Makes this Queue Manager the default Queue Manager.

- -t <IntervalValue>: The trigger time interval in milliseconds for all queues controlled by this Queue Manager. This value specifies the time after receiving a trigger-generating message when triggering is suspended. That is, if the arrival of a message on a queue causes a trigger message to be put on the Initiation Queue, any message arriving on the same queue within the specified interval does not generate another trigger message.

- -u <DeadLetterQueue>: The name of the Local Queue that is to be used as the Dead Letter Queue. Messages are put on this queue if they cannot be routed to their correct destination. The default is no Dead Letter Queue.

- -x <MaxUMsgs>: The maximum number of uncommitted messages under any one syncpoint. The default value is 10,000 uncommitted messages.

- -z: Suppresses error messages. This flag is used within WebSphere MQ to suppress unwanted error messages. Because using this flag can result in loss of information, do not use it when entering commands through the command line.

The command to create a Queue Manager called QMA with a Dead Letter Queue called DEAD.LETTER.QUEUE.QMA is:

```
$ crtmqm  -u  DEAD.LETTER.QUEUE.QMA  QMA
```

You should see something similar to the following on your screen:

```
WebSphere MQ queue manager created.
Creating or replacing default objects for QMA.
Default objects statistics : 43 created. 0 replaced. 0 failed.
Completing setup.
Setup completed.
```

Note that this command just tells the Queue Manager that it can use a Dead Letter Queue called DEAD.LETTER.QUEUE.QMA, which is a Local Queue, and still has to be created, see the *MQ Queue management – to define a Local Queue* section. As we have not specified any logging options, we will be using **circular logging**.

> It is not possible to change the type of logging once the Queue Manager has been defined.

As can be seen from the command description, the CRTMQM command has only a small number of parameters that can be specified. A Queue Manager has many more attributes, and these are automatically set to default values. These default values can be changed using the ALTER QMGR MQSC command (discussed later). One such parameter that is assigned when a Queue Manager is created is the SCHINIT attribute, which controls channel initiators and is discussed next.

All Queue Managers need a channel initiator to monitor the system-defined initiation queue SYSTEM.CHANNEL.INITQ, which is the Initiation Queue for all Transmission Queues.

When we start a Queue Manager, a channel initiator is automatically started if the Queue Manager attribute SCHINIT is set to QMGR (which is the default value). Otherwise, it can be started using the START CHINIT MQSC command or the RUNMQCHI command.

Starting a Queue Manager

Before we can use a Queue Manager, we need to start it, using the STRMQM command. The command to start a Queue Manager called QMA is:

```
$ strmqm QMA
```

You should see output similar to the following on your screen:

```
WebSphere MQ queue manager 'QMA' starting.
2108 log records accessed on queue manager 'QMA' during the log
replay phase.
Log replay for queue manager 'QMA' complete.
Transaction manager state recovered for queue manager 'QMA'.
WebSphere MQ queue manager 'QMA' started.
```

Checking that the Queue Manager is running

To check that a Queue Manager is active, use the DSPMQ MQ command:

```
$ dspmq
```

If the Queue Manager is active it should have a status of "Running" as follows:

```
QMNAME(QMA)                                    STATUS(Running)
```

Stopping a Queue Manager

To stop (end) a Queue Manager, use the ENDMQM command. This command has four possible parameters:

- -c: Controlled/quiesced shutdown. This is the default. The queue manager stops, but only after all applications have disconnected. Any calls currently being processed are completed.

- -w: Wait shutdown. This type of shutdown is equivalent to a controlled shutdown except that control is returned to you only after the Queue Manager has stopped. You receive the message Waiting for Queue Manager qmName to end while shutdown progresses.

- -i: Immediate shutdown. The Queue Manager stops after it has completed all the calls currently being processed. Any MQI requests issued after the command has been issued fail. Any incomplete units of work are rolled back when the Queue Manager is next started. Control is returned after the Queue Manager has ended.

- -p: Preemptive shutdown—use this type of shutdown only in exceptional circumstances. For example, when a Queue Manager does not stop as a result of a normal endmqm command. The Queue Manager might stop without waiting for applications to disconnect or for MQI calls to complete.

If we want to suppress error messages, then we just have to add the -z parameter to the command.

An example of the command to stop Queue Manager QMA is shown next:

```
$ endmqm -i QMA
```

Deleting a Queue Manager

The command to delete/drop a Queue Manager is DLTMQM, but before we can issue that command we need to stop all the Listeners for the Queue Manager and then stop (end) the Queue Manager.

The following command will stop all the Listeners associated with Queue Manager pointed to by the `-m` flag (QMA in this example). The `-w` flag means the command will wait until all the Listeners are stopped before returning control:

```
$ endmqlsr  -w  -m  QMA
```

The command to stop (end) the Queue Manager is:

```
$ endmqm  QMA
```

And finally the command to delete the Queue Manager is:

```
$ dltmqm  QMA
```

The Queue Manager configuration file

The Queue Manager configuration file is called `qm.ini` on UNIX systems. On Windows the configuration information is stored in the Windows Registry.

On UNIX, the `qm.ini` file is in directory `/var/mqm/qmgrs/<QMname>/`. This name may not be unique, so the name is generated.

On Windows, we can access the Windows Registry by typing `regedit` from a windows line command. Then navigate down through: **HKEY_LOCAL_MACHINE | SOFTWARE | IBM | MQSeries**, as shown in the following screenshot:

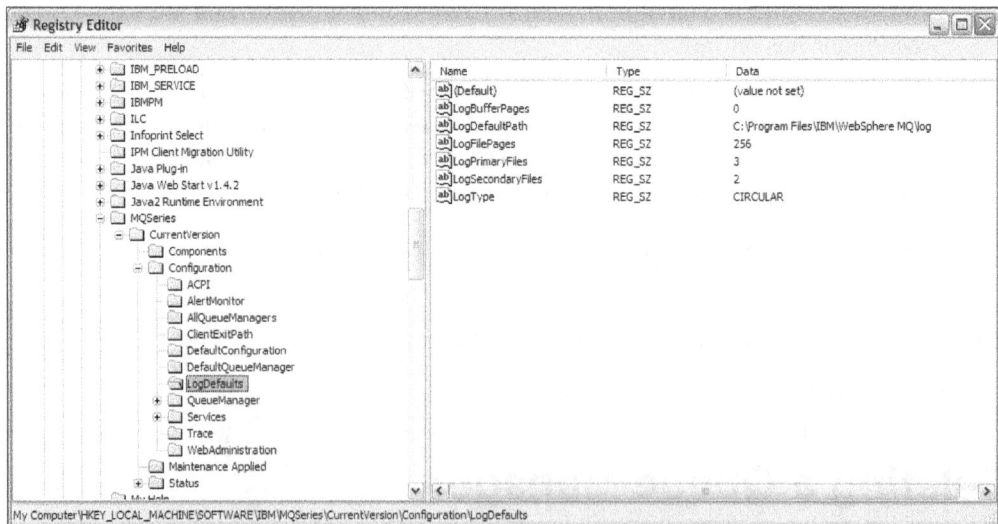

MQ logging

The default logging option (circular) can be found in the qm.ini file on UNIX or the Windows Registry on Windows. The alternative is linear logging (which DB2 people call *archive logging*). The type of logging is determined at Queue Manager creation time and cannot be altered afterwards. See the *WebSphere MQ Commands – Create/ start/stop a Queue Manager* section for information on the crtmqm command.

Issuing commands to a Queue Manager (runmqsc)

Once we have created a Queue Manager, we will want to perform administrative tasks, such as creating queues, among others. To enable us to communicate with our Queue Manager, we use the RUNMQSC MQ command, which opens the MQSC (MQ Script Center) environment.

After entering the MQSC environment, we can issue one of the following MQSC commands: ALTER, CLEAR, DEFINE, DELETE, DISPLAY, END, PING, REFRESH, RESET, RESOLVE, RESUME, START, STOP, or SUSPEND. Each of these commands has it's own options, which are shown in the following table:

ALTER	CLEAR	DEFINE	DELETE	DISPLAY	END	PING
AUTHINFO	QLOCAL	AUTHINFO	AUTHINFO	AUTHINFO		CHANNEL
CHANNEL		CHANNEL	CHANNEL	QREMOTE		QMGR
PROCESS		PROCESS	PROCESS	CHANNEL QUEUE		
NAMELIST		NAMELIST	NAMELIST	CHSTATUS		
QALIAS		QALIAS	QALIAS	QSTATUS		
QLOCAL		QLOCAL	QLOCAL	CLUSQMGR		
QMGR		QMODEL	QMODEL	CONN		
QMODEL		QREMOTE	QREMOTE	PROCESS SERVICE		
QREMOTE		SERVICE	SERVICE	NAMELIST		
SERVICE		LISTENER	LISTENER	LISTENER		
LISTENER				QALIAS SVSTATUS		
				QCLUSTER LSSTATUS		
				QLOCAL QMSTATUS		
				QMGR		
				QMODEL		

REFRESH	RESET	RESOLVE	RESUME	START	STOP	SUSPEND
CLUSTER	CHANNEL	CHANNEL	QMGR CLUSTER	CHANNEL	CHANNEL	QMGR CLUSTER
SECURITY	CLUSTER			CHINIT	LISTENER	
	QMGR		QMGR CLUSNL	LISTENER	SERVICE	QMGR CLUSNL
				SERVICE	CONN	

We can either enter the these MQSC commands interactively or pipe the commands into the MQSC environment.

To invoke the MQSC environment for Queue Manager QMA, issue the RUNQMSC command as follows:

```
$ runmqsc QMA
```

You should see something similar to the following on your screen:

```
5724-H72 (C) Copyright IBM Corp. 1994, 2004.  ALL RIGHTS RESERVED.
Starting MQSC for queue manager QMA.
```

And then enter the command we want. For example, to define a Local Queue called CAPA.ADMINQ, we would enter:

```
DEFINE QLOCAL(CAPA.ADMINQ) REPLACE PUT(ENABLED) GET(ENABLED) SHARE
DEFSOPT(SHARED) DEFPSIST(YES)
     1 : DEFINE QLOCAL(CAPA.ADMINQ) REPLACE PUT(ENABLED) GET(ENABLED)
SHARE DEFSOPT(SHARED) DEFPSIST(YES)
AMQ8006: WebSphere MQ queue created.
end
     2 : end
One MQSC command read.
No commands have a syntax error.
All valid MQSC commands were processed.
```

Note that the end command exits the MQSC environment.

Alternatively, and more usually, we can create a text file containing the commands to execute, and then pipe this text file into the MQSC environment:

```
$ runmqsc  QMA  <  <input-text-file>
```

```
: alter qmgr maxumsgs(10001)

    3 : alter qmgr maxumsgs(10001)
AMQ8005: WebSphere MQ queue manager changed.
: dis qmgr maxumsgs

    4 : dis qmgr maxumsgs
AMQ8408: Display Queue Manager details.
    QMNAME(QMA)                          MAXUMSGS(10001)
```

We can see that the value has been changed from the default value of 10,000 to the value we specified in the command.

MQ Listener management

Before a local Queue Manager can send messages to a remote Queue Manager, we need to start a Listener for the remote Queue Manager. The **default MQ Listener port** number is 1414, and if we use this port, then we do not have to specify a port number when we issue the start listener command, but in our examples, we use port numbers other than the default. This section looks at how we manage the MQ Listeners. We will look at the different ways of defining, starting, and stopping a Listener.

Defining/Starting an MQ Listener

There are two ways of defining and starting an MQ Listener:

The first method uses the run Listener RUNMQLSR command. The parameters for the command are the type of connectivity (-t), the Queue Manager name (-m), and the port number to be started (-p). So if we want to start a TCP listener on port 1450 for Queue Manager QMA, we would issue:

```
$ runmqlsr  -t  tcp  -m  QMA  -p  1450
```

This command can be put into a batch file (SYSA_QMA_START_RUNMQLSR.BAT) and in UNIX can be run with the nohup and & options:

```
$ nohup runmqlsr  -t  tcp  -m  QMA  -p  1450  &
```

The command to start a TCP listener on port 1451 for Queue Manager QMB is:

```
$ nohup runmqlsr  -t  tcp  -m  QMB  -p  1451  &
```

This command can be put into a SYSB_QMB_START_RUNMQLSR.BAT batch file.

The second method creates the Listener from the MQSC environment, using the following RUNMQSC command file:

```
DEFINE LISTENER (QMA1450) +
TRPTYPE (TCP) +
PORT (1450) +
CONTROL(QMGR)
```

In this text file, we have given the Listener a name (QMA1450), and assigned a port number to that Listener. The last parameter shown is CONTROL, which determines how the Listener is started, with the possible options being MANUAL, QMGR, and STARTONLY, which mean:

- MANUAL: (default) The Listener is not to be started automatically or stopped automatically. It is to be controlled by use of the START LISTENER and STOP LISTENER commands.
- QMGR: The Listener being defined is to be started and stopped at the same time as the Queue Manager is started and stopped.
- STARTONLY: The Listener is to be started at the same time as the Queue Manager is started, but is not requested to stop when the Queue Manager is stopped.

If a Listener is to be controlled manually, then it can be started using the following command issued from the MQSC environment:

```
: start listener(QMA1450)
```

So to recap, if we use an MQ command (RUNMQLSR) to start a Listener, then we cannot give it a name, and we have to start it manually every time the Queue Manager is started. If we use a text file from the MQSC environment, then we can name the Listener and have it start when the Queue Manager starts.

In the examples in *Appendix A*, we define the Listeners following the first method we described. We do this to reinforce the fact that WebSphere MQ needs Listeners and Channels to be active. To start the Listeners, issue the following commands on QMA and QMB respectively:

```
start runmqlsr -t tcp -m  QMA    -p  1450
start runmqlsr -t tcp -m  QMB    -p  1451
```

Both of these commands can be contained in batch files SYSA_QMA_START_RUNMQLSR.BAT and SYSB_QMB_START_RUNMQLSR.BAT respectively.

Depending on the standards at your site, you can create Listeners according to the second method.

Displaying an MQ Listener

What we mean by "displaying" an MQ Listener is firstly checking if the Listener is actually running and secondly displaying the attributes of the Listener.

Let's first look at checking if the Listener is running.

If the Listener was started using the RUNMQLSR MQ command:

```
$ runmqlsr -t tcp -m  QMA   -p  1450  &
```

Then this creates a Listener, whose name is of the form SYSTEM.LISTENER.TCP.<n>. We can check if this listener is running by issuing the DISPLAY LSSTATUS MQSC command:

```
: display lsstatus(*)
```

And you'll see:

```
AMQ8631: Display listener status details.
   LISTENER(SYSTEM.LISTENER.TCP.3)          STATUS(RUNNING)
   PID(12912)
```

We can see that the status is RUNNING.

And the PID corresponds to the output from the UNIX ps -ef command:

```
$ ps -ef | grep -i "runmqlsr"
mqm    12912  1   0 14:14 pts/1 00:00:00 runmqlsr -t tcp -m QMA -p 1450
db2instp 15937 10695  0 14:43 pts/1  00:00:00 grep -i runmqlsr
```

If the Listener had been created using the MQSC commands in a file (as shown previously), then we could have given the Listener a name (QMA1450). And now we can check if the Listener is running using the DISPLAY LSSTATUS MQSC command:

```
: display lsstatus(*)
```

And you'll see:

```
AMQ8631: Display listener status details.
   LISTENER(QMA1450)                        STATUS(RUNNING)
   PID(2360)
```

We could of course have specified our Listener name in place of the asterisk:

```
: display lsstatus(QMA1450)
AMQ8631: Display listener status details.
```

```
LISTENER(QMA1450)                    STATUS(RUNNING)
PID(2360)                            STARTDA(2009-02-19)
STARTTI(16.41.41)                    DESCR( )
TRPTYPE(TCP)                         CONTROL(QMGR)
IPADDR(*)                            PORT(1450)
BACKLOG(100)
```

If the Listener was created using an MQSC command file, then its properties can be displayed using the DISPLAY LISTENER MQSC command and specifying a name:

```
: display listener(QMA1450)
AMQ8630: Display listener information details.
LISTENER(QMA1450)                    CONTROL(QMGR)
TRPTYPE(TCP)                         PORT(1450)
IPADDR( )                            BACKLOG(100)
DESCR( )                             ALTDATE(2009-02-19)
ALTTIME(16.41.41)
```

If the Listener was started using the RUNMQLSR command, then to display its attributes we need to append the parameter ALL to the DISPLAY LSSTATUS command:

```
: display lsstatus(*) all
AMQ8631: Display listener status details.
LISTENER(SYSTEM.LISTENER.TCP.3)      STATUS(RUNNING)
PID(8256)                            STARTDA(2010-01-07)
STARTTI(16.54.54)                    DESCR( )
TRPTYPE(TCP)                         CONTROL(MANUAL)
IPADDR(*)                            PORT(1450)
BACKLOG(100)
```

Stopping an MQ Listener

There are two ways of stopping a Listener. The first method uses the ENDMQLSR MQ command, and the second method uses the STOP LISTENER MQSC command.

In the following example, we want to stop the Listener for Queue Manager QMA using the ENDMQLSR MQ command (The flags were discussed in the previous section *Create/ start/stop a Queue Manager – Stopping a Queue Manager*):

```
$ endmqlsr  -w  -m  QMA
```

In the following example we are using the STOP LISTENER MQSC command to stop a Listener:

```
: stop listener(QMA1450)
```

MQ Channel management

This section looks at how we define, stop, start, and display the status of WebSphere MQ Channels. For each local Queue Manager, we need a Sender Channel and a Receiver Channel, both of which need a matching pair on a remote Queue Manager.

To define a Channel

In the following figure, on the left-hand side, we are on QMA and define two Channels:

- A Sender Channel called QMA.TO.QMB, which uses the Transmission Queue QMB.XMITQ and points to the remote WebSphere MQ system at IP address 127.0.0.1, which is listening on port number 1451 (which is QMB).

- A Receiver Channel called QMB.TO.QMA, which is used to receive messages (from QMB in this case).

There are corresponding Sender and Receiver Channels defined on QMB. Note that the pair of Sender and Receiver Channel names on both QMA and QMB must be the same, so the Receiver Channel on QMB must have the same name as the Sender Channel on QMA.

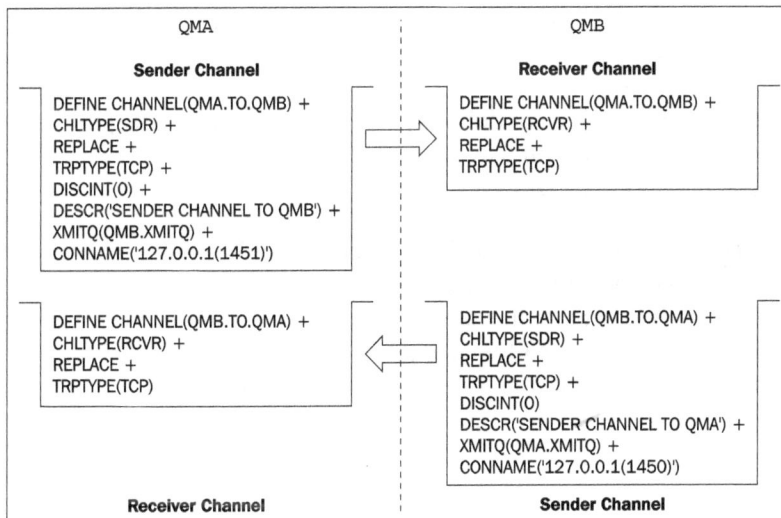

To start a Channel

There are four ways of starting a Channel, the choice depending on your site standards. The following examples are for the Sender Channel QMA.TO.QMB, defined on QMA. Note that we always start a Sender Channel, never a Receiver Channel.

- **By issuing the** RUNMQCHL **MQ command on** QMA: Using the RUNMQCHL MQ command, shown next (which can be stored in a file called SYSA_QMA_START_RUNMQCHL_AB.BAT):

```
start runmqchl -m  QMA -c QMA.TO.QMB
```

- **By issuing the** START CHANNEL **MQSC command on** QMA: We can use the START CHANNEL MQSC command on QMA as follows:

```
: start channel(QMA.TO.QMB)
```

- **By defining and starting a Service**: A Service is used to define the user programs that are to be started and stopped when a Queue Manager is started and stopped. We can start a Channel by defining an MQ Service for it and then starting the Service. So let's define a Service called STSYSACH, to start the Sender Channel QMA.TO.QMB defined on Queue Manager QMA. The Service calls the program RUNMQCHL, and we know what the parameters for this program are, because we covered them in the first method. These values are passed to the command through the STARTARG parameter. The DEFINE SERVICE MQSC command is:

```
: DEFINE SERVICE(STSYSACH) +

CONTROL(QMGR) +

SERVTYPE(COMMAND) +

STARTARG('-c QMA.TO.QMB -m QMA') +

STARTCMD(RUNMQCHL)
```

Once the service has been defined, we need to start it, using the START SERVICE MQSC command on QMA:

```
: start service(STSYSACH)
```

- **As part of the Transmission Queue definition**: We may not want the Channel to be continuously active, and only want it activated when there is a message to process. In this situation, we can initiate a Channel start when the Transmission Queue is used. For more details, see the *MQ Queue management – To define a Transmission Queue* section.

To display a list of Channels

We use the DISPLAY CHANNEL MQSC command to list out the Channels for a Queue Manager:

```
: dis channel(*)
```

To display the status of a Channel

To check that a Channel is running, issue the DISPLAY CHSTATUS MQSC command:

```
: dis chstatus(*)
AMQ8417: Display Channel Status details.
    CHANNEL(QMA.TO.QMB)              CHLTYPE(SDR)
    CONNAME(127.0.0.1(1450))            CURRENT
    RQMNAME( )                          STATUS(RUNNING)
    SUBSTATE( )                         XMITQ(QMB.XMITQ)
```

We are looking for a status of RUNNING.

To stop a Channel

As an example, let's say we want to stop the Sender Channel QMB.TO.QMA defined on QMB. We can stop it by using the STOP CHANNEL MQSC command:

```
$ runmqsc QMB
: stop channel(QMB.TO.QMA)
     1 : stop channel(QMB.TO.QMA)
AMQ8019: Stop WebSphere MQ Channel accepted.
```

If we now display the Channels, we can see that the QMB.TO.QMA Channel has a status of STOPPED.

```
: dis chstatus(*)
     2 : dis chstatus(*)
AMQ8417: Display Channel Status details.
    CHANNEL(QMA.TO.QMB)              CHLTYPE(RCVR)
    CONNAME(127.0.0.1)                  CURRENT
    RQMNAME(QMA)                        STATUS(RUNNING)
    SUBSTATE(RECEIVE)
AMQ8417: Display Channel Status details.
    CHANNEL(QMB.TO.QMA)              CHLTYPE(SDR)
```

```
CONNAME(127.0.0.1 (1450))          CURRENT
RQMNAME(QMA)                        STATUS(STOPPED)
SUBSTATE( )                         XMITQ(QMA.XMITQ)
```

MQ Queue management

This section looks at how we manage WebSphere MQ queues once a Queue Manager has been created and started. We cover defining, displaying, and deleting Local Queues.

To define a Local Queue

The following table shows all the possible parameters, and their possible values, which can be specified when creating a Local Queue. The example following the table shows a typical definition of a Local Queue

DEFINE QLOCAL(<qname>)		
CMDSCOPE(' '/<qmgr-name>/*)	DEFBIND(OPEN/NOTFIXED)	QDPMAXEV(ENABLED/ENABLED)
QSGDISP(QMGR/COPY/	DEFSOPT(SHARED/EXCL)	QSVCIEV(NONE/HIGH/OK)
GROUP/SHARED)		
LIKE (<qlocalname>)	DISTL(NO/YES)	QSVCINT(999,999,999/<int>)
NOREPLACE/REPLACE	GET(ENABLED/DISABLED)	RETINTVL(999,999,999/<int>)
DEFPRTY(0/<int>)	NOHARDENBO/HARDENBO	SCOPE(QMGR/CELL)
DEFPSIST(NO/YES)	INDXTYPE(NONE/MSGID/	SHARE/NOSHARE
	CORRELID/GROUPID/	
	MSGTOKEN)	
DESCR('<desc>')	INITQ(' '/<string>)	STATQ(QMGR/OFF/ON)
PUT(ENABLED/DISABLED)	**MAXDEPTH**(5000/<int>)	STGCLASS('DEFAULT'/<string>)
ACCTQ(QMGR/ON/OFF)	**MAXMSGL**(4,194,304/<int>)	TRIGDATA(' '/<string>)
BOQNAME(' '/<string>)	MONQ(QMGR/OFF/LOW/	TRIGDPTH(1/<int>)
	MEDIUM/HIGH)	
BOTHRESH(0/<int>)	MSGDLVSQ(PRIORITY/FIFO)	NOTRIGGER/TRIGGER

DEFINE QLOCAL(<qname>)		
CFSTRUCT(' '/<name>)	NPMCLASS(NORMAL/ HIGH)	TRIGMPRI(0/<int>)
CLUSNL(' '/<name>)	PROCESS(' '/<string>)	TRIGTYPE(FIRST/EVERY/ DEPTH/NONE)
CLUSTER(' '/<name>)	QDEPTHHI(80/<int>)	USAGE(NORMAL/XMITQ)
CLWLPRTY(0/<int>)	QDEPTHLO(40/<int>)	
CLWLRANK(0/<int>)	QDPHIEV(DISABLED/ ENABLED)	
CLWLUSEQ(QMGR/ ANY/	QDPLOEV(DISABLED/ ENABLED)	
LOCAL)		

The content of the text file that we pipe into the MQSC environment to create a Local Queue is shown next. This example shows how to create the Administration Queue for Q Capture:

```
DEFINE QLOCAL(CAPA.ADMINQ) +
REPLACE +
DESCR('LOCAL DEFN OF ADMINQ FOR CAPA CAPTURE') +
PUT(ENABLED) +
GET(ENABLED) +
SHARE +
DEFSOPT(SHARED) +
DEFPSIST(YES)
```

Two attributes for which we are accepting the default values are:

- **MAXMSGL**: The Maximum Message Length. This value specifies the maximum message length of messages (in bytes) allowed in queues for this Queue Manager. The default value is 4,194,304 bytes.
- **MAXDEPTH**: The Maximum queue depth. This value specifies the maximum number of messages allowed in the Queue. The default value is 5,000.

The definition of a Dead Letter Queue follows this format, as it is just a Local Queue. So to define a Dead Letter Queue for Queue Manager QMA we would code:

```
DEFINE QLOCAL(DEAD.LETTER.QUEUE.QMA) +
REPLACE +
DESCR('LOCAL DEAD LETTER QUEUE QMA') +
PUT(ENABLED) +
GET(ENABLED) +
```

```
SHARE +
DEFSOPT(SHARED) +
DEFPSIST(YES)
```

Remember that the name of the Dead Letter Queue is the name that was specified when the Queue Manager was created, see the *Create/start/stop a Queue Manager* section.

To display the attributes of a Local Queue

We use the DIS QLOCAL MQSC command to display the attributes of a Local Queue. If we want to display the value of one attribute, then we just have to append that attribute name to the command. For example, to check the current depth of the Receive Queue issue the DIS QLOCAL (DIS QL) MQSC command with the CURDEPTH option:

```
: dis ql(CAPA.TO.APPB.RECVQ) CURDEPTH
```

To check if there are any messages in the Dead Letter Queue issue the following MQSC command:

```
: dis ql(DEAD.LETTER.QUEUE.QMA) CURDEPTH
```

To alter the attributes of a Queue

There are two ways of altering the attributes of a Queue, which are shown next:

- **Using the** ALTER QLOCAL (ALTER QL) **MQSC command**: The following command changes a single attribute, that of the maximum message length (MAXMSGL) - all the other attributes remain the same:

  ```
  : alter ql(CAPA.ADMINQ) MAXMSGL(10000)
  ```

- **Using the** DEFINE QLOCAL **MQSC command with the** REPLACE **option**:

  ```
  : define ql(CAPA.ADMINQ) MAXMSGL(10000) replace
  ```

To empty a Local Queue

To delete messages from a queue (clear it down), use the CLEAR QLOCAL MQSC command:

```
: clear qlocal(CAPA.ADMINQ)
```

To delete a Local Queue

To delete a Local Queue, use the DELETE QLOCAL MQSC command:

```
: delete qlocal(CAPA.ADMINQ) purge
```

One of the options of the command is NOPURGE (default) / PURGE. This option
specifies whether any existing committed messages on the queue are to be purged
for the command to work: NOPURGE means that the deletion is not to go ahead if there
are any committed messages on the queue. PURGE means that the deletion is to go
ahead even if there are committed messages in the queue, and these messages
are also to be purged.

To define a Remote Queue

An example of creating a Remote Queue on QMA is shown next. Pipe the following
text into the MQSC environment on QMA:

```
DEFINE QREMOTE (CAPA.TO.APPB.SENDQ.REMOTE) +

REPLACE +

DESCR('REMOTE DEFN OF SEND QUEUE FROM CAPA TO APPB') +

PUT(ENABLED) +

XMITQ(QMB.XMITQ)   +

RNAME(CAPA.TO.APPB.RECVQ) +

RQMNAME(QMB)  +

DEFPSIST(YES)
```

The parameters for the command are discussed in the core values figure in the
MQ Queues section.

To define a Model Queue

An example of creating a Model Queue on QMA is shown next. Pipe the following
text into the MQSC environment on QMA:

```
DEFINE QMODEL (IBMQREP.SPILL.MODELQ) +

REPLACE +

DEFSOPT(SHARED) +

MAXDEPTH(500000) +

MSGDLVSQ(FIFO) +

DEFTYPE(PERMDYN)
```

To define a Transmission Queue

A Transmission Queue is a form of Local Queue which has its USAGE attribute set to MQUS_TRANSMISSION rather than MQUS_NORMAL.

When sending messages to a Remote Queue defined in a local WebSphere MQ server, we need to create a **Sender Channel** and a **Transmission Queue**. A Transmission Queue can be defined to start automatically. The following definition would be defined on QMA and is a Transmission Queue to Queue Manager QMB:

```
DEFINE QLOCAL(QMB.XMITQ) +

REPLACE +

DESCR('TRANSMISSION QUEUE TO QMB') +

USAGE(XMITQ) +

PUT(ENABLED) +

GET(ENABLED) +

TRIGGER +

TRIGTYPE(FIRST) +

TRIGDATA(QMA.TO.QMB) +

INITQ(SYSTEM.CHANNEL.INITQ)
```

To start the Sender Channel automatically when a message shows up the Transmission Queue, triggering control of the Transmission Queue must be configured properly — this is what the last four lines of code achieve.

To list Queues

We use the DISPLAY QLOCAL and DISPLAY QREMOTE MQSC commands to list out the Local and Remote Queues for a Queue Manager:

```
: dis ql(*)

: dis qr(*)
```

WebSphere MQ sample programs—server

There is a whole set of sample programs available to the WebSphere MQ administrator. We are interested in only a couple of them: the program to put a message onto a queue and a program to retrieve a message from a queue. The names of these sample programs depend on whether we are running WebSphere MQ as a server or as a client.

There is a server sample program called amqsput, which puts messages onto a queue using the MQPUT call. This sample program comes as part on the WebSphere MQ samples installation package, not as part of the base package—see the *Q replication constituent components* section of *Chapter 1, Q Replication Overview*.

> The maximum length of message that we can put onto a queue using the amqsput sample program is 100 bytes.

There is a corresponding server sample program to retrieve messages from a queue called amqsget.

> Use the sample programs only when testing that the queues are set up correctly—do NOT use the programs once Q Capture and Q Apply have been started. This is because Q replication uses dense numbering between Q Capture and Q Apply, and if we insert or retrieve a message, then the dense numbering will not be maintained and Q Apply will stop. The usual response to this is to cold start Q Capture!

To put a message onto a Queue (amqsput)

The amqsput utility can be invoked from the command line or from within a batch program.

If we are invoking the utility from the command line, the format of the command is:

```
$ amqsput  <Queue>  <QM name>   <   <message>
```

We would issue this command from the system on which the Queue Manager sits. We have to specify the queue (<Queue>) that we want to put the message on, and the Queue Manager (<QM name>) which controls this queue. We then pipe (<) the message (<message>) into this. An example of the command is:

```
$ amqsput CAPA.TO.APPB.SENDQ.REMOTE  QMA  < hello
```

In the scenarios in *Appendix A*, we put these commands into an appropriately named batch file (say SYSA_QMA_TESTP_UNI_AB.BAT), which would contain the following:

Batch file—Windows example:

```
call "C:\Program Files\IBM\WebSphere MQ\bin\amqsput"  CAPA.TO.APPB.
SENDQ.REMOTE  QMA  < QMA_TEST1.TXT
```

Batch file—UNIX example:

```
"/opt/mqm/samp/bin/amqsput" CAPA.TO.APPB.SENDQ.REMOTE  QMA  < QMA_
TEST1.TXT
```

Where the `QMA_TEST1.TXT` file contains the message we want to send.

Once we have put a message onto the Send Queue, we need to be able to retrieve it (which is discussed in the next section).

To retrieve a message from a Queue (amqsget)

The `amqsget` utility can be invoked from the command line or from within a batch program. The utility takes 15 seconds to run. We need to specify the Receive Queue that we want to read from and the Queue Manager that the queue belongs to:

```
$ amqsget  <Queue>  <QM name>
```

As example of the command is shown here:

```
$ amqsget  CAPA.TO.APPB.RECVQ  QMB
```

If we have correctly set up all the queues, and the Listeners and Channels are running, then when we issue the preceding command, we should see the message we put onto the Send Queue in the previous section.

If you do not get the message back, then please refer to the trouble shooting in the *The WebSphere MQ layer* section of *Chapter 7, Monitoring and Reporting*.

We can put the `amqsget` command into a batch file, as shown next:

Batch file—Windows example:

```
@ECHO This takes 15 seconds to run
call "C:\Program Files\IBM\WebSphere MQ\bin\amqsget"  CAPA.TO.APPB.
RECVQ   QMB
@ECHO You should see: test1
```

Batch file—UNIX example:

```
echo This takes 15 seconds to run
"/opt/mqm/samp/bin/amqsget"  CAPA.TO.APPB.RECVQ   QMB
echo You should see: test1
```

Using these examples and putting messages onto the queues in a unidirectional scenario, then the "get" message batch file for QMA (SYSA_QMA_TESTG_UNI_BA.BAT) contains:

```
@ECHO This takes 15 seconds to run
call "C:\Program Files\IBM\WebSphere MQ\bin\amqsget"  CAPA.ADMINQ  QMA
@ECHO You should see: test2
```

From CLP-A, run the file as:

$ SYSA_QMA_TESTG_UNI_BA.BAT

The "get" message batch file for QMB (SYSB_QMB_TESTG_UNI_AB.BAT) contains:

```
@ECHO This takes 15 seconds to run
call "C:\Program Files\IBM\WebSphere MQ\bin\amqsget"  CAPA.TO.APPB.
RECVQ    QMB
@ECHO You should see: test1
```

From CLP-B, run the file as:

$ SYSB_QMB_TESTG_UNI_AB.BAT

To browse a message on a Queue

It is useful to be able to browse a queue, especially when setting up Event Publishing. There are three ways to browse the messages on a Local Queue. We can use the rfhutil utility, or the amqsbcg sample program, both of which are WebSphere MQ entities, or we can use the asnqmfmt Q replication command.

- **Using the WebSphere MQ** rfhutil **utility**: The rfhutil utility is part of the WebSphere MQ support pack available to download from the web — to find the current download website, simply type rfhutil into an internet search engine. The installation is very simple — unzip the file and run the rfhutil.exe file.

See the *Some what happens if… scenarios – If Q Apply is not running* section of *Chapter 7, Monitoring and Reporting* for an example of how to use this command.

- **Using the WebSphere MQ** amqsbcg **sample program**: The **amqsbcg** sample program displays messages including message descriptors.

  $ amqsbcg CAPA.TO.APPB.RECVQ QMB

See the *Event Publishing – Test publication* from *Appendix A* for an example of the output from this command.

- **Using the asnqmfmt Q replication command**: See the *Administration Tasks – Viewing messages using asnqmfmt* section of *Chapter 6, Administration Tasks* for an example of how to use this command.

WebSphere MQ sample programs—client

The sample program used to put messages onto a queue using the MQPUT call is amqsputc.

The sample program used to retrieve messages onto a queue using the MQPUT call is amqsgetc.

Dead Letter Queue handler (runmqdlq)

This section looks at the WebSphere **MQ Dead Letter Queue** (**DLQ**), what it is, and how to handle messages that are put on this queue.

Firstly, let's look at what a DLQ actually does. In one sentence, a DLQ is a queue that stores messages that cannot be routed to their correct destination(s). This occurs when, for example, the destination queue is full.

In our examples, we always define a DLQ called DEAD.LETTER.QUEUE.<QMgr-name>.

We can check that we have a DLQ defined by displaying the attributes of the Queue Manager. So for Q Apply running on CLP-B, we would issue:

```
$ runmqsc QMB
```

```
: dis qmgr
```

The output from this command can be seen in the *Issuing commands to a Queue Manager (runmqsc) - Displaying the attributes of a Queue Manager* section.

To handle messages in the DLQ, we use the WebSphere MQ DLQ message handler utility called runmqdlq. Note that we cannot simply read the messages off the DLQ and put them somewhere else, because then we would change the message header information.

As part of the WebSphere MQ samples package, the source of a Dead Letter Queue handler program is provided and is called amqsdlq. We can customize this program if the provided handler does not meet our requirements.

So let's look at how we handle messages on the DLQ using the provided handler.

The first thing we need is a DLQ rule handler file. This is a text file and tells the utility what type of messages to look for in the DLQ and then what to do with them. The contents of such a file is as follows:

```
WAIT (NO) REASON(MQRC_Q_FULL) ACTION (RETRY) RETRY (1)
```

This says for any messages that are in the DLQ because the queue they were supposed to go to was full, retry putting the message onto that original queue. Try this once and then stop. We will run the utility only when we have sorted out any problems, so we do not think specifying a retry value of 1 is a problem.

Create a file in the `c:\temp` directory called `dlqrule.txt` and put the preceding code line into it.

Now we can run the DLQ handler utility as:

```
C:\TEMP> runmqdlq  DEAD.LETTER.QUEUE.QMB  QMB < dlqrule.txt
```

WebSphere MQ message format

Each WebSphere MQ message consists of two parts: a header and the application data.

There are five types of header, as shown in the following table

MQMD	The message descriptor. Created by the application at message create time.
MQXQH	The Transmission Queue header, which contains delivery information in remote queuing.
MQDLH	The dead letter header, which identifies conditions that prevent delivery to a destination queue.
MQRMH	Reference message header, which contains information to assist in delivery of reference messages.
IMSrtm	Information header (MQIIH), which is carried with the message using the IMS hierarchical database bridge facility.

Let's look at the MQMD header in more detail. The following figure shows how the MQMD is made up:

MQMD								Appl Data
1	2	3	4	5	6	7	8	
Reply to Q	DLQ or discard	Persistence	Msg type	Context – 8 fields	Priority	Group id	Sequence Number	Just a series of bytes

The following table shows the meaning of each MQMD entry in the preceding figure:

1	The queue name for reply messages.
2	If we cannot deliver this message, put it in the DLQ or discard (DLQ is the default).
3	Is the message persistent or non-persistent.
4	Message type – Request, Reply, Report, Datagram (broadcast message).
5	The context is 8 fields that travel with the MQMD which can be used for security. It gets filled in automatically, but we can change it with the appropriate authority.
6	Priority 0 to 9, with 9 being the highest.
7	Used for authentication. This contains the userid and other security information (does the user have the authority to access the queue).
8	Used to identify which physical message this segment belongs to if the original message had to be split.

WebSphere MQ messages have the concept of **persistence**:

- If a message is defined as persistent then its delivery is assured.
- If a message is defined as *non-persistent*, then if WebSphere MQ cannot deliver the message it is discarded.

Persistence is decided at message creation time by the application program creating the message and is a property of a message, not a queue. Non-persistent messages get deleted at Queue Manager start-up time.

Prior to DB2 9.7, Q replication had to use persistent WebSphere MQ messages. Starting with DB2 9.7, we have the option of using non-persistent WebSphere MQ messages. To specify non-persistent messages, start Q Capture with the `msg_persistence=n` parameter.

MQ error messages

The current WebSphere MQ error log is called AMQERR01.LOG. The two previous copies of the log are called AMQERR02.LOG and AMQERR03.LOG. The log directories are called:

On UNIX: var/mqm/errors

On Windows: C:\Program Files\IBM\WebSphere MQ\errors

We can see the MQ error messages in the Q Capture and Q Apply logs. Some common errors are shown in the following table:

AMQ2053	A queue is full. We need to stop the Channel before clearing the queue using the MQSC command clear qlocal <queue-name>.
AMQ2058	We have specified an invalid Queue Manager name.
AMQ2059	We have specified a Queue Manager name which is not available (it knows it exists, but is unavailable – perhaps there are authorization problems or it has not been started).
AMQ2080	The length of the message we are trying to retrieve using amqsget is greater than 100 bytes.
AMQ2085	The queue name does not exist in the Queue Manager where we told it that the queue existed.
AMQ2101	Damaged disks.

Summary

In this chapter, we introduced you to WebSphere MQ in terms of how it is used in Q replication to achieve assured delivery of messages once and only once. We covered the MQ queues required for the various scenarios, which are covered in later chapters, and gave some guidelines on naming standards. We then went on to cover the MQ commands that we would usually come across, such as creating, starting, and stopping a Queue Manager and issuing commands to a Queue Manager. We covered the MQ sample programs that can be used to check that MQ has been set up correctly and then looked at the Dead Letter Queue handler. We finally listed some of the common MQ error messages that occur with Q replication.

We will now move on to looking at the ASNCLP command interface, which is our choice for setting up a Q replication environment.

5

The ASNCLP Command Interface

In this chapter, we look at the ASNCLP command interface in some detail. We cover:

- What the ASNCLP interface is
- The required setup work
- How to use ASNCLP scripts to perform some common Q replication tasks

The ASNCLP environment

Let's start by looking at what ASNCLP is. In a nutshell, it is a command-line interface for administering Q replication, Event Publishing, and SQL replication.

We can set up the ASNCLP environment on the replication servers, or alternatively we can set it up on another server, which is shown in the following diagram:

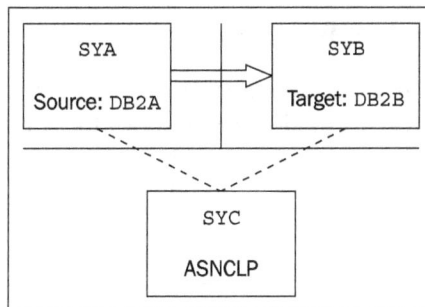

If we are replicating from DB2A on a system called SYA to DB2B on a system called SYB, then we can administer the replication scenario from a system called SYC by cataloguing the DB2A and DB2B databases on SYC as DB2A and DB2B. We need to use the same database names because ASNCLP on SYC will use the database alias names and not the actual database names.

The examples in *Appendix A*, use ASNCLP commands to set up various Q replication scenarios.

The ASNCLP interface can also be used to set up InfoSphere *Classic* replication (say IMS to Oracle), but this is outside the scope of this book.

In DB2 V8, we had to alter the operating system PATH setting on the machine we wanted ASNCLP on—this all changed in DB2 V9, where we generally do not have to add anything to the PATH settings in a 32-bit environment, we can just use ASNCLP out of the box. However, if we get the following error:

```
>asnclp
The java class could not be loaded. java.lang.
UnsupportedClassVersionError: (com/ibm/db2/tools/repl/replapis/cmdline/
Asnclp) bad major version at offset=6
```

Then we have to add the Java JDK BIN library path to our PATH variable (note that the library we are adding is specified first). On a Windows system, the command is:

```
set PATH=C:\Program Files\IBM\SQLLIB\java\jdk\bin;%PATH%
```

If we are running on a 64-bit operating system, then we need to add the 64-bit JDK library to the PATH variable. We can do this using the command:

```
set PATH=C:\Program Files\IBM\SQLLIB\java\jdk64\bin;%PATH%
```

The equivalent UNIX command would be:

```
$ export PATH=:/data/home/db2inst1/sqllib/java/jdk64/bin:$PATH
```

On UNIX systems, we can edit our operating system user profile to include the preceding command, so it is executed every time we log on. The profile file name is dependent on which shell we are running. One way of checking which shell we are using is to issue the echo $SHELL command. Now let's move on to look at the ASNCLP commands.

ASNCLP commands can be issued at the ASNCLP prompt or combined into a file and run that way.

The ASNCLP prompt is obtained by typing ASNCLP on the command-line. In this book, we focus on combining ASNCLP commands into a file, and then running this file from a command prompt as:

```
asnclp -f <ASNCLP-script-file-name>
```

The ASNCLP commands

A complete set of ASNCLP commands for Q replication and Event Publishing is shown in the following table (a list of ASNCLP command-line programs can be found in the DB2 Information Center at `http://publib.boulder.ibm.com/infocenter/db2luw/v9r7/topic/com.ibm.swg.im.iis.db.repl.asnclp.intro.doc/topics/iiyrccncasnclpovu.html`):

> An important point to note is that ASNCLP parameters are positional.

ASNCLP commands	Description
ALTER ADD COLUMN	Adds a column to a Q subscription or Publication
ALTER CAPTURE PARAMETERS (Classic)	Updates the IBMQREP_CAPPARMS table when you replicate from a Classic source
ALTER PUB	Changes a publication
ALTER PUBQMAP	Changes a Publishing Queue Map
ALTER QSUB	Changes a Q subscription
ALTER REPLQMAP	Changes a Replication Queue Map
ASNCLP SESSION SET TO	Establishes a session for Q replication
CREATE CONTROL TABLES FOR	Creates the control tables for Q Capture and Q Apply
CREATE PUB	Creates a publication
CREATE PUBQMAP	Creates a Publishing Queue Map
CREATE QSUB	Creates a Q subscription
CREATE REPLQMA	Creates a Replication Queue Map
DROP CONTROL TABLES ON	Drops the control tables for Q Capture and Q Apply
DROP PUB	Deletes a publication
DROP PUBQMAP	Deletes a Publishing Queue Map
DROP QSUB	Deletes a Q subscription

ASNCLP commands	Description
DROP REPLQMAP	Deletes a Replication Queue Map
DROP SUBGROUP	Deletes the subgroup that was set using the SET SUBGROUP command.
DROP SUBTYPE	Deletes a Q subscription for multi-directional replication
LIST APPLY SCHEMA	Lists Q Apply schemas
LIST CAPTURE SCHEMA	Lists Q Capture schemas
LIST PUBQMAPS	Lists Publishing Queue Maps
LIST PUBS	List publications
LIST QSUB	Lists Q subscriptions
LOAD MULTIDIR REPL SCRIPT	Invokes ASNCLP program scripts used to set up multidirectional replication
LIST REPLQMAP	Lists Replication Queue Maps
LOAD DONE	Signals that a manual load of the target table is complete
PROMOTE PUB	Promotes a publication
PROMOTE PUBQMAP	Promotes a Publishing Queue Map
PROMOTE QSUB	Promotes a Q subscription
PROMOTE REPLQMAP	Promotes a Replication Queue Map
SET APPLY SCHEMA	Sets the Q Apply schema for all task commands
SET CAPTURE SCHEMA	Sets the Q Capture schema for all task commands
SET CONNECTION	Connects the servers that are used for multi-directional replication
SET DROP	Specifies whether to drop the target table or table space when a Q subscription is deleted, and whether to drop the table space when the control tables are dropped
SET ENFORCE MATCHING CONSTRAINTS	Specifies whether the ASNCLP will enforce matching constraints between the source and target tables
SET LOG	Defines the log file for ASNCLP
SET MULTIDIR SCHEMA	Specifies the Q Capture and Q Apply schema on a server that is used for multi-directional replication

ASNCLP commands	Description
SET OUTPUT	Defines output files that contain SQL statements to set up unidirectional Q replication
SET PROFILE	Specifies custom parameters for database objects to be created implicitly
SET QMANAGER	Sets the WebSphere MQ Queue Manager
SET REFERENCE TABLE	Sets a reference table to identify a Q subscription that is to be changed or deleted
SET RUN SCRIPT	Specifies whether to automatically run each task command from an input file before the ASNCLP program processes the next task command
SET SERVER	Specifies the Q Capture server and/or Q Apply server to use in the ASNCLP session for unidirectional replication.
SET SUBGROUP	Specifies the name of the subgroup, a collection of Q subscriptions between servers that are used for multidirectional replication
SET TABLES	Specifies the tables that participate in a multi-bidirectional configuration
SET TRACE	Enables and disable the trace for the ASNCLP commands
SHOW SET ENV	Displays the environment set during the session
START PUB	Starts a publication
START QSUB	Starts a Q subscription
STOP PUB	Stops a publication
STOP QSUB	Stops a Q subscription
VALIDATE WSMQ ENVIRONMENT FOR	Verifies that the required WebSphere MQ objects exist and have the correct properties for schemas, queue maps, and Q subscriptions
VALIDATE WSMQ MESSAGE FLOW FOR REPLQMAP	Sends test messages that validate the message flow between the WebSphere MQ queues that are specified for a Replication Queue Map

Some, but not all of these commands are discussed in more detail in the following sections.

Setting up the administration environment

In an ASNCLP script, we can set various environment settings to define things such as what the script output files are called, whether to run the script now or just generate the SQL in the output files to be run later. The following is a list of the administration environment commands:

- SET APPLY SCHEMA: Sets a Q Apply schema.
- SET CAPTURE SCHEMA: Sets a Q Capture schema.
- SET DROP: Sets table or table space drop options.
- SET LOG: Sets logging options.
- SET OUTPUT: Sets SQL output script options.
- SET PROFILE: Sets DDL profile options.
- SET QMANAGER: Sets the Queue Manager name.
- SET RUN SCRIPT: Sets script execution options. The options are LATER or NOW STOP ON SQL ERROR [ON|OFF].
- SET SERVER: Sets replication server options.
- SET TRACE: Sets tracing options.

When we run an ASNCLP command, we create or append to three default work files:

- qreplapp.sql: A script file containing the SQL executed on the Apply server.
- qreplcap.sql: A script file containing the SQL executed on the Capture server.
- qreplmsg.log: The message log.

It is possible to change the names of these work files using the SET LOG and SET OUTPUT commands. For example, to change the name of the message log, we would issue:

```
SET LOG "<log-filename>"
```

To change the name of the script files, we use the SET OUTPUT command, as follows:

```
SET OUTPUT CAPTURE SCRIPT "<log-filename>"
SET OUTPUT TARGET  SCRIPT "<log-filename>"
```

There are a couple of other options for the SET OUTPUT command, we can specify CONTROL SCRIPT and MONITOR SCRIPT.

> If we do not need an output file, then we should specify "" for the filename. The double quotation marks in the command syntax are required.
> If a script file already exists, the new script appends to the current file.

Setting the environment session

In an ASNCLP script, we need to tell ASNCLP whether we are administering a Q replication (including Event Publishing) or a SQL Replication environment, which we do using the ASNCLP SESSION SET TO <sess> command, where <sess> is SQL Replication for SQL Replication and Q Replication for Q replication.

Comments in an ASNCLP script

A **comment** is a hash symbol (#).

```
#set run script now stop on SQL error on;
set server capture to db db2a id db2admin password "db2admin";
set server target  to db db2b id db2admin password "db2admin";
set server control to db db2b id db2admin password "db2admin";
```

To comment out multiple lines, enclose those lines between /* and */.

Possible header lines in a script

To stop a script from running accidentally (such as in a drop situation), we could put the following lines at the beginning of such scripts:

```
-

# =======================================================================
# To run this script you first need to delete the above line containing a
single dash(-)

# =======================================================================
```

The dash in the first line causes the script to fail with the following message:

```
ASN1950E  ASNCLP :  An unexpected token "-" was found. Valid
tokens include "SET, CREATE, DROP, ALTER, LIST, PROMOTE, OFFLINE,
SUBSTITUTE, DELEGATE, QUIT".
```

```
ASN1954E  ASNCLP :  Command failed.
```

Common Q replication tasks

This section goes through some of the common Q replication tasks that we need to perform and the corresponding ASNCLP command. The following table lists some of the common tasks that we may need to perform:

If we want to...	Use this ASNCLP command
Create control tables for Q Capture or Q Apply	CREATE CONTROL TABLES FOR
Drop control tables for Q Capture or Q Apply	DROP CONTROL TABLES ON
Create a Replication Queue Map	CREATE REPLQMAP
Change a Replication Queue Map	ALTER REPLQMAP
Delete a Replication Queue Map	DROP REPLQMAP
Start a Q subscription	START QSUB
Stop a Q subscription	STOP QSUB
Verify that the required WebSphere MQ objects exist and have the correct properties for schemas, Queue Maps, and Q subscriptions	VALIDATE WSMQ ENVIRONMENT FOR
Send test messages that validate the message flow between the WebSphere MQ queues that are specified for a Replication Queue Map	VALIDATE WSMQ MESSAGE FLOW FOR REPLQMAP
Insert a LOADDONE signal into the IBMQREP_SIGNAL table for a manual load	LOAD DONE
Add a column to a Q subscription	ALTER ADD COLUMN

Following is the sample setup we will use. We have four systems called SYSA, SYSB, SYSC, and SYSD. The Queue Manager on each of these systems is called QMA, QMB, QMC, and QMD respectively with Listener ports of **1450**, **1451**, **1452**, and **1453**. The four databases are called DB2A, DB2B, DB2C, and DB2D, and each system or database has an appropriately named Command Line Processor (CLP) session:

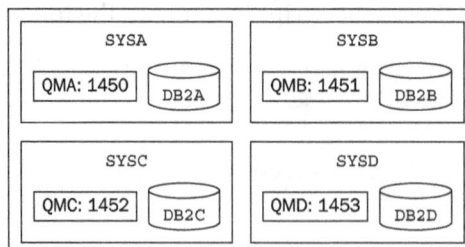

The monitor data will be written to a separate database called MONDB on the SYSE system (not shown).

Creating or dropping Q Capture control tables on DB2A

This section describes how to create and drop the Q Capture control tables on SYSA in database DB2A with a schema of ASN for Queue Manager QMA.

The structure of the Q Capture control tables is described in the *The control tables – The Q Capture control tables* section of *Chapter 3, The DB2 Database Layer*.

When we create the Q Capture control tables, we can specify a number of parameters. As stated previously, ASNCLP parameters are positional, so the following is an ordered list (downwards then across) of all parameters required for setting up the Q Capture control tables using the CREATE CONTROL TABLES command:

```
IN              MONITOR INTERVAL   LOGREUSE
RESTARTQ        MONITOR LIMIT      LOGSTDOUT
ADMINQ          TRACE LIMIT        CAPTURE PATH
STARTMODE       SIGNAL LIMIT       RELEASE
MEMORY LIMIT    PRUNE INTERVAL
AUTOSTOP        SLEEP INTERVAL
```

There are only three required parameters — the Restart Queue name (CAPA.RESTARTQ) and the Administration Queue name (CAPA.ADMINQ), which are both Local Queues in the QMA Queue Manager, and the third parameter is the CAPTURE PATH parameter (the location where the Q Capture log gets written to), which depends on whether we are running on UNIX or Windows, so for example the value could be C:\TEMP on Windows or /home/db2inst1/qrep_logs on UNIX.

The following example shows an ASNCLP command file to create the Q Capture control tables (stored in SYSA_db2a_crt_capture.asnclp file):

```
ASNCLP SESSION SET TO Q REPLICATION;
SET RUN SCRIPT NOW STOP ON SQL ERROR ON;

SET SERVER CAPTURE TO DB DB2A;
SET QMANAGER QMA FOR CAPTURE SCHEMA;
SET CAPTURE SCHEMA SOURCE ASN;

CREATE CONTROL TABLES FOR CAPTURE SERVER
USING
RESTARTQ "CAPA.RESTARTQ"
ADMINQ "CAPA.ADMINQ"
STARTMODE WARMSI
```

```
MEMORY LIMIT 4
AUTOSTOP N
MONITOR INTERVAL 5
MONITOR LIMIT 30
TRACE LIMIT 30
SIGNAL LIMIT 30
PRUNE INTERVAL 180
SLEEP INTERVAL 20
LOGREUSE N
LOGSTDOUT N
TERM Y
CAPTURE PATH c:\temp;
```

The AUTOSTOP parameter determines if Q Capture terminates after retrieving the last transaction from the DB2 log (Y) or not (N).

The SLEEP INTERVAL parameter specifies the number of seconds that Q Capture sleeps, when it finishes processing the active log, and determines that the buffer is empty.

The MONITOR INTERVAL parameter specifies how frequently (in seconds) Q Capture inserts rows into the Q Capture monitor tables. We are setting this value to five seconds.

The MONITOR LIMIT parameter specifies how long (in minutes) a row can remain in the Q Capture monitor tables (IBMQREP_CAPMON and IBMQREP_CAPQMON) before it becomes eligible for pruning. All rows that are older than the value of the MONITOR LIMIT parameter are pruned at the next pruning cycle. Pruning was discussed in the *Pruning of the control tables* section of *Chapter 3*.

From CLP-A, run the file as:

```
$ asnclp -f SYSA_db2a_crt_capture.asnclp
```

```
====
CMD: ASNCLP SESSION SET TO Q REPLICATION;
====
CMD: SET SERVER CAPTURE TO DB DB2A;
====
CMD: SET QMANAGER QMA FOR CAPTURE SCHEMA;
====
CMD: SET CAPTURE SCHEMA SOURCE ASN;
====
CMD: SET RUN SCRIPT NOW STOP ON SQL ERROR ON;
```

```
====
CMD: CREATE CONTROL TABLES FOR CAPTURE SERVER USING RESTARTQ "CAPA.
RESTARTQ" ADMINQ "CAPA.ADMINQ" STARTMODE WARMSI MEMORY LIMIT 4
MONITOR INTERVAL 30;

====

<ClpInfo2Log:: Now running SQL...>

ASN2000I  The action "Create Capture Control Tables" started at "15
October 2004 23:37:04 o'clock BST".  The Q Capture server is "DB2A" ,
and the Q Capture schema is "ASN".

ASN2006I  The action "Create Capture Control Tables" ended
successfully at "15 October 2004 23:37:05 o'clock BST" for the Q
Capture server "DB2A"  and Q Capture schema "ASN".

ASN1514I  The replication action ended at "15 October 2004 23:37:05
o'clock BST" with "1" successes, "0" errors, and "0" warnings.

<ClpInfo2Log:: The SQL command completed successfully.>

ASN1953I  ASNCLP :  Command completed.
```

We can list the tables created as follows:

```
$ db2 LIST TABLES FOR SCHEMA asn
```

We can see what is inserted into the catalog table IBMQREP_CAPPARMS, using the SQL commands as shown in the *The control tables – The Q Capture control tables* section of *Chapter 3*.

To drop the Q Capture control tables on DB2A, use the DROP CONTROL TABLES command. Create a text file called SYSA_db2a_drop_capture.asnclp, which should specify the database name (DB2A), the Queue Manager name (QMA), and the table schema (ASN). The following file shows this:

```
ASNCLP SESSION SET TO Q REPLICATION;
SET RUN SCRIPT NOW STOP ON SQL ERROR ON;

SET SERVER CAPTURE TO DB DB2A;
SET QMANAGER QMA FOR CAPTURE SCHEMA;
SET CAPTURE SCHEMA SOURCE ASN;

DROP CONTROL TABLES ON CAPTURE SERVER;
```

This file can be run as:

```
$ asnclp -f SYSA_db2a_drop_capture.asnclp
```

Creating or dropping Q Apply control tables on DB2B

This section describes how to create the Q Apply control tables on SYSB in database DB2B, with a schema of ASN for Queue Manager QMB.

The structure of the Q Apply control tables is described in the *The control tables – The Q Apply control tables* section of *Chapter 3*.

Following is an ordered list (downwards and across) of all possible parameters required for setting up the Q Apply control tables:

```
IN                  AUTOSTOP        TERM
MONITOR LIMIT       SLEEP INTERVAL  PWDFILE
TRACE LIMIT         LOGREUSE        DEADLOCK RETRIES
MONITOR INTERVAL    LOGSTDOUT       SIGNAL LIMIT
PRUNE INTERVAL      APPLY PATH      RELEASE
```

In the following file (SYSB_db2a_crt_apply.asnclp), the apply path will be c:\temp and we will use a password file called asnpwd.aut in the same directory as the logs:

```
ASNCLP SESSION SET TO Q REPLICATION;
SET RUN SCRIPT NOW STOP ON SQL ERROR ON;

SET SERVER TARGET TO DB DB2B;
SET QMANAGER QMB FOR APPLY SCHEMA;
SET APPLY SCHEMA ASN;

CREATE CONTROL TABLES FOR APPLY SERVER
USING
MONITOR LIMIT 30
TRACE LIMIT 9
MONITOR INTERVAL 30
PRUNE INTERVAL 30
AUTOSTOP N
LOGREUSE N
LOGSTDOUT N
APPLY PATH c:\temp
TERM Y
PWDFILE asnpwd.aut
DEADLOCK RETRIES 5;
```

From CLP-B, run the file as:

```
$ asnclp -f SYSB_db2b_crt_apply.asnclp
```

```
====
CMD: ASNCLP SESSION SET TO Q REPLICATION;
====
CMD: SET SERVER TARGET TO DB DB2B;
====
CMD: SET QMANAGER QMA FOR APPLY SCHEMA;
====
CMD: SET APPLY SCHEMA ASN;
====
CMD: SET RUN SCRIPT NOW STOP ON SQL ERROR ON;
====
CMD: CREATE CONTROL TABLES FOR APPLY SERVER USING MONITOR LIMIT 3
TRACE LIMIT 9;
====

<ClpInfo2Log:: Now running SQL...>

ASN2001I  The action "Create Apply Control Tables" started at "15
October 2004 23:32:57 o'clock BST".  The Q Apply server is "DB2B",
and the Q Apply schema is "ASN".

ASN2007I  The action "Create Apply Control Tables" ended successfully
at "15 October 2004 23:32:59 o'clock BST" for the Q Apply server
"DB2B" and Q Apply schema "ASN".

ASN1514I  The replication action ended at "15 October 2004 23:32:59
o'clock BST" with "1" successes, "0" errors, and "0" warnings.

<ClpInfo2Log:: The SQL command completed successfully.>

ASN1953I  ASNCLP :  Command completed.
```

We can list the tables created as follows:

```
$ db2 list tables for schema asn
```

We can see what is inserted into the IBMQREP_APPLYPARMS table, when the Q Apply
control tables are created using the query shown in the *The control tables – The Q
Apply control tables* section of *Chapter 3*.

To drop the Q Apply control tables with a schema of ASN on DB2B, create a text file
called SYSB_db2b_drop_apply.asnclp containing:

```
ASNCLP SESSION SET TO Q REPLICATION;
SET RUN SCRIPT NOW STOP ON SQL ERROR ON;

SET SERVER TARGET TO DB DB2B;
SET APPLY SCHEMA ASN;
DROP CONTROL TABLES ON APPLY SERVER;
```

Run this file as:

```
$ asnclp -f SYSB_db2b_drop_apply.asnclp
```

Creating Q Capture and Q Apply control tables in the same database

For multi-directional replication, we need to create the Q Capture and Q Apply control tables in the same database (for example **DB2C**). They need to have the same schema name (ASN in our example). We combine the Q Apply create and Q Capture create files and delete the second SESSION line, as shown in the following file (SYSC_db2c_crt_capture_and_apply_tables.asnclp):

```
ASNCLP SESSION SET TO Q REPLICATION;
SET RUN SCRIPT NOW STOP ON SQL ERROR ON;

SET SERVER CAPTURE TO DB DB2C;
SET SERVER TARGET  TO DB DB2C;

SET CAPTURE SCHEMA SOURCE ASN;
SET APPLY   SCHEMA         ASN;

SET QMANAGER QMC FOR CAPTURE SCHEMA;
SET QMANAGER QMC FOR APPLY   SCHEMA;

CREATE CONTROL TABLES FOR APPLY SERVER
USING
MONITOR LIMIT 30
TRACE LIMIT 9;

CREATE CONTROL TABLES FOR CAPTURE SERVER
USING
RESTARTQ "CAPC.RESTARTQ"
ADMINQ "CAPC.ADMINQ"
STARTMODE WARMSI
MEMORY LIMIT 4
MONITOR INTERVAL 30;
```

From CLP-C, run the file as:

```
$ asnclp -f SYSC_db2c_crt_capture_apply.asnclp

====

CMD: ASNCLP SESSION SET TO Q REPLICATION;

====

CMD: SET SERVER CAPTURE TO DB DB2C;

====
```

CMD: SET QMANAGER QMA FOR CAPTURE SCHEMA;

====

CMD: SET CAPTURE SCHEMA SOURCE ASN;

====

CMD: SET RUN SCRIPT NOW STOP ON SQL ERROR ON;

====

CMD: CREATE CONTROL TABLES FOR CAPTURE SERVER USING RESTARTQ "restartq" ADMINQ "adminq" STARTMODE WARMSI MEMORY LIMIT 4 MONITOR INTERVAL 3;

====

<ClpInfo2Log:: Now running SQL...>

ASN2000I The action "Create Capture Control Tables" started at "15 October 2004 23:50:00 o'clock BST". The Q Capture server is "

DB2C" , and the Q Capture schema is "ASN".

ASN2006I The action "Create Capture Control Tables" ended successfully at "15 October 2004 23:50:01 o'clock BST" for the Q Capture server "DB2C" and Q Capture schema "ASN".

ASN1514I The replication action ended at "15 October 2004 23:50:02 o'clock BST" with "1" successes, "0" errors, and "0" warnings.

<ClpInfo2Log:: The SQL command completed successfully.>

====

CMD: SET SERVER TARGET TO DB DB2C;

====

CMD: SET QMANAGER QMA FOR APPLY SCHEMA;

====

CMD: SET APPLY SCHEMA ASN;

====

CMD: SET RUN SCRIPT NOW STOP ON SQL ERROR ON;

====

CMD: CREATE CONTROL TABLES FOR APPLY SERVER USING MONITOR LIMIT 3 TRACE LIMIT 9;

====

<ClpInfo2Log:: Now running SQL...>

ASN2001I The action "Create Apply Control Tables" started at "15 October 2004 23:50:07 o'clock BST". The Q Apply server is "DB2C ", and the Q Apply schema is "ASN".

ASN2007I The action "Create Apply Control Tables" ended successfully at "15 October 2004 23:50:07 o'clock BST" for the Q Apply server "DB2C" and Q Apply schema "ASN".

```
ASN1514I  The replication action ended at "15 October 2004 23:50:07
o'clock BST" with "1" successes, "0" errors, and "0" warnings.
<ClpInfo2Log:: The SQL command completed successfully.>
ASN1953I  ASNCLP :  Command completed.
```

Queue Map maintenance

Once we have created the control tables, we can continue to create the other required Q replication objects. The first of these is a Queue Map.

This section discusses how we manage Replication and Publication Queue Maps.

Creating a Replication Queue Map

The ASNCLP command to create a **Replication Queue Map (RQM)** is CREATE REPLQMAP, and has the following parameters (defaults in brackets):

```
CREATE REPLQMAP <qmapname>
DESC "<description>"
USING ADMINQ "<admnqname>"
RECVQ "<recvqname>"
SENDQ "<sendqname>"
NUM APPLY AGENTS <num> (16)
MAXAGENTS CORRELID <num>
MEMORY LIMIT <limit> (2MB)
ERROR ACTION [S|Q]
HEARTBEAT INTERVAL <interval> (60 seconds)
MAX MESSAGE SIZE <size> (64KB)
```

The important parameters from the previous list are: MAX MESSAGE SIZE and ERROR ACTION:

- MAX MESSAGE SIZE: Clearly, if we think the messages are going to be larger than 64 KB then we will need to increase this value.

- ERROR ACTION: The default is Stop Q Capture program with an alternative of Stop Q subscriptions. Which one to choose depends on many factors such as how many other Replication Queue Maps are using this Q Capture and do we want Q Capture to stop functioning if just one of the Replication Queue Maps fails. Another factor to consider is how sophisticated is our monitoring setup? It is a lot easier to monitor for a Q Capture abend than it is to monitor for a stopped Q subscription. Also, remember that a stopped subscription will force a reload when it is restarted, which can take a long time for large tables.

Let us assume, we want to create a Replication Queue Map to perform unidirectional replication from DB2A to DB2B, with the Q Capture tables on DB2A and the Q Apply tables on DB2B, both having a schema of ASN and the following Administration, Receive, and Send Queues:

Queue	Tables
Administration Queue on QMB	CAPA.ADMINQ.REMOTE
Receive Queue on QMB	CAPA.TO.APPB.RECVQ
Send Queue on QMA	CAPA.TO.APPB.SENDQ.REMOTE

We then create a text file called SYSA_crt_rqma2b.asnclp containing:

```
ASNCLP SESSION SET TO Q REPLICATION;
SET RUN SCRIPT NOW STOP ON SQL ERROR ON;

SET SERVER CAPTURE TO DB DB2A;
SET SERVER TARGET  TO DB DB2B;

SET CAPTURE SCHEMA SOURCE ASN;
SET APPLY    SCHEMA ASN;

CREATE REPLQMAP "RQMA2B"
USING
ADMINQ "CAPA.ADMINQ.REMOTE"
RECVQ "CAPA.TO.APPB.RECVQ"
SENDQ "CAPA.TO.APPB.SENDQ.REMOTE"
NUM APPLY AGENTS 3
MEMORY LIMIT 9
ERROR ACTION S
HEARTBEAT INTERVAL 5
MAX MESSAGE SIZE 4;
```

From CLP-A, run the file as:

```
$ asnclp -f SYSA_crt_rqma2b.asnclp

====

CMD: ASNCLP SESSION SET TO Q REPLICATION;

====

CMD: SET SERVER CAPTURE TO DB DB2A;

====

CMD: SET SERVER TARGET TO DB DB2B;

====

CMD: SET CAPTURE SCHEMA SOURCE ASN;
```

```
====

CMD: SET APPLY SCHEMA ASN;

====

CMD: SET RUN SCRIPT NOW STOP ON SQL ERROR ON;

====

CMD: CREATE REPLQMAP"RQMA2B"

====

CMD: USING

====

CMD: ADMINQ "CAPA.ADMINQ.REMOTE"

====

CMD: RECVQ "CAPA.TO.APPB.RECVQ"

====

CMD: SENDQ "CAPA.TO.APPB.SENDQ.REMOTE";

====
```

ASN1956I ASNCLP : The program now generates the script for action: "CREATE REPLICATION QUEUE MAP".

ASN1955I ASNCLP : The program will use the following files: "qreplcap.sql" for the Capture SQL script, "replctl.sql" for the control SQL script, "qreplapp.sql" for the target SQL script, and "qreplmsg.log" for the log file.

<ClpInfo2Log:: Now running SQL...>

ASN2005I The action "Create Replication Queue Map" started at "16 October 2004 00:16:42 o'clock BST". The replication queue map name is "RQMA2B", the Q Capture server is "DB2A", the Q Capture schema is "ASN", the Q Apply server is "DB2B", and the Q Apply schema is "ASN".

ASN2011I The action "Create Replication Queue Map" ended successfully at "16 October 2004 00:16:42 o'clock BST" for the replication queue map name "RQMA2B". The Q Capture server is "DB2A" and the Q Capture schema is "ASN". The Q Apply Server is "DB2B" and the Q Apply schema is "ASN".

ASN1514I The replication action ended at "16 October 2004 00:16:42 o'clock BST" with "1" successes, "0" errors, and "0" warnings.

<ClpInfo2Log:: The SQL command completed successfully.>

ASN1953I ASNCLP : Command completed.

To create a Replication Queue Map for the queues going from DB2B to DB2A, we use the following queues:

Queues	Tables
Administration Queue on QMA	CAPB.ADMINQ.REMOTE
Receive Queue on QMA	CAPB.TO.APPB.RECVQ
Send Queue on QMB	CAPB.TO.APPA.SENDQ.REMOTE

We then create a text file called `SYSB_crt_rqmb2a.asnclp` containing:

```
ASNCLP SESSION SET TO Q REPLICATION;
SET RUN SCRIPT NOW STOP ON SQL ERROR ON;

SET SERVER CAPTURE TO DB DB2B;
SET SERVER TARGET  TO DB DB2A;
SET CAPTURE SCHEMA SOURCE ASN;
SET APPLY SCHEMA ASN;

CREATE REPLQMAP "RQMB2A" USING
ADMINQ  "CAPB.ADMINQ.REMOTE"
RECVQ   "CAPB.TO.APPA.RECVQ"
SENDQ   "CAPB.TO.APPA.SENDQ.REMOTE";
```

From CLP-B, run the file as:

```
$ asnclp -f SYSA_crt_rqmb2a.asnclp
```

We can check that the RQM has been created by running the queries against the tables IBMQREP_SENDQUEUES and IBMQREP_RECVQUEUES in the *The control tables – The Q Capture control tables* section of *Chapter 3*.

Creating a Publication Queue Map

The parameters for the CREATE PUBQMAP ASNCLP command are:

```
CREATE PUBQMAP <qmapname>
DESC "<desc>"
USING SENDQ "<queue-name>"
MESSAGE FORMAT [XML|DELIMITED]
MESSAGE CONTENT TYPE [T|R]
ERROR ACTION [S|Q]
HEARTBEAT INTERVAL <interval>
MAX MESSAGE SIZE <size>
HEADER [NONE|MQ RFH2]
ON CODEPAGE ERROR[SEND NO DATA| SEND RAW DATA]
```

Some of the important parameters are discussed next:

- MESSAGE FORMAT: This specifies whether we want to publish messages in XML format or delimited format.

- MESSAGE CONTENT TYPE: This specifies whether messages put on the queue will contain an entire database transaction or only a row operation:
  - ○ T: It is the default type. Messages contain all of the row operations (update, insert, or delete) within a DB2 transaction and information about the transaction.
  - ○ R: Messages contain a single update, insert, or delete operation and information about the DB2 transaction to which it belongs.

- ERROR ACTION: The action that Q Capture takes when the Send Queue stops accepting messages:
  - ○ S: Q Capture stops.
  - ○ Q: Q Capture stops putting messages on any Send Queues that are in error and continues putting messages on other Send Queues.

- HEADER: This specifies whether we want a JMS-compliant MQ RFH2 header added to all messages that use the Send Queue that is specified in this Publishing Queue Map. This keyword is not supported for delimited message format:
  - ○ NONE: This specifies to send only the publication message with no special headers.
  - ○ MQ RFH2: This specifies to attach a special header to the message, which will contain the topic name that we specify as part of a publication.

If we have two Queue Managers called QMA and QMB, with Q Capture running on the QMA server in a database called DB2A, and with the control tables having a schema of ASN, then to create a Publication Queue Map called PQMA2B, we would use the following ASNCLP commands:

```
ASNCLP SESSION SET TO Q REPLICATION;

SET RUN SCRIPT NOW STOP ON SQL ERROR ON;

SET SERVER CAPTURE TO DB DB2A;

SET CAPTURE SCHEMA SOURCE ASN;

SET QMANAGER QMA FOR CAPTURE SCHEMA;
```

```
CREATE PUBQMAP "PQMA2B"

USING

SENDQ "CAPA.TO.APPB.SENDQ.REMOTE"

MESSAGE CONTENT TYPE T

ERROR ACTION S

HEARTBEAT INTERVAL 0

HEADER NONE;
```

Dropping a Queue Map

The ASNCLP command to drop a RQM is DROP REPLQMAP <RQM-name>. For example, to drop a RQM called RQMA2B, the commands would be as follows in the SYSA_db2a_drop_rqma2b.asnclp file:

```
ASNCLP SESSION SET TO Q REPLICATION;
SET RUN SCRIPT NOW STOP ON SQL ERROR ON;

SET SERVER CAPTURE TO DB DB2A;

SET CAPTURE SCHEMA SOURCE ASN;

DROP REPLQMAP RQMA2B;
```

A Publication Queue Map is dropped in a similar manner, but with the REPLQMAP keyword replaced with PUBQMAP.

Altering a Replication Queue Map

We can alter the attributes of a Replication Queue Map using the ALTER REPLQMAP ASNCLP command:

```
ALTER REPLQMAP <qmapname> USING DESC "<description>"

   ADMINQ "<admnqname>"

   RECVQ "<recvqname>"

   SENDQ "<sendqname>"

   NUM APPLY AGENTS <num>

   MAXAGENTS CORRELID <num>

   MEMORY LIMIT <limit>

   ERROR ACTION [S|Q]

   HEARTBEAT INTERVAL <interval>

   MAX MESSAGE SIZE <size>
```

So, to alter the memory limit of a RQM called RQMA2B to 8 KB, we would code:

```
ASNCLP SESSION SET TO Q REPLICATION;

SET RUN SCRIPT NOW STOP ON SQL ERROR ON;

SET SERVER CAPTURE TO DB DB2A;

SET CAPTURE SCHEMA SOURCE ASN;

ALTER REPLQMAP RQMA2B USING MEMORY LIMIT 8;
```

Creating Q subscriptions and Publications

In this section, we first look at how to create a Q subscription in unidirectional and multi-directional environments using the CREATE QSUB command. We then look at creating Publications for Event Publishing.

For unidirectional replication, we can place all the ASNCLP commands we need to define a Q subscription into a single command file.

In a multi-directional replication environment, the structure of the ASNCLP command to create a Q subscription changes. Rather than having just one command file, we need two command files—the first file being called a **load** script file, which is run from the ASNCLP command-line and which calls the second **content** file. Both files need to be in the same directory.

There are certain operations we can and cannot perform when creating a unidirectional and multi-directional Q subscription, which are shown in the following table, and are explained in the following sections.

The permissible operations in Q subscription creation are:

What we want to do...	Unidirectional	Multi-directional
Can we give our Q subscription a name we want?	Y	N
Can we specify different source and target table names?	Y	Y
Can we specify a Spill Queue to use?	Y	N
Can we specify the type of target table?	Y	N
Can we specify what columns to use as the key?	Y	N
Can we specify the conflict action?	Y	Y
Can we specify a load type?	Y	Y

For unidirectional replication, the Q subscription name is the name specified with the SUBNAME parameter of the CREATE QSUB SUBTYPE U command. For multi-directional replication, each Q subscription name of a subscription group is made up of the table name followed by an increasing numeric string starting with 0001.

Q subscription for unidirectional replication

The following code shows the major options of the CREATE QSUB command for unidirectional replication:

```
CREATE QSUB SUBTYPE U USING REPLQMAP <mapname> SUBNAME <subname>
DESC "<description>" REPLQMAP <mapname> src-clause | trg-clause
```

src-clause:

```
<source_owner>.<source_name>|SRC OWNER LIKE | SRC NAME LIKE | SRC ALL
OPTIONS
SEARCH CONDITION "<search_condition>"
ALL CHANGED ROWS [N|Y]
HAS LOAD PHASE [I|E|N]
CAPTURE_LOAD [W|R]
SPILL_MODELQ <name>
SUPPRESS DELETES [N|Y]
START AUTOMATICALLY [YES|NO]
```

trg-clause:

```
EXIST TARGET NAME <owner>.<name>
TABLE OWNER [<target_owner> | NAMING PREFIX <prefix> | SAME AS SOURCE
| SAME AS USERID]
TABLE NAME [<target_name> | NAMING PREFIX <prefix> | SAME AS SOURCE]
FEDERATED | fed-clause |
IN <tsname>
TYPE [USERTABLE targetcolumns | STOREDPROC | NICKNAME | CCD ccd-
clause]
KEYS
NICKNAME [<owner>.<nickname> | NAMING PREFIX—prefix ]
NEW NICKNAME RMT SERVERNAME <srvname> <owner>.<nickname>
CONFLICT ACTION [I|F|D|S|Q]
ERROR ACTION [S|D|Q]
OKSQLSTATES "<sqlstates>"
LOAD TYPE [0|1|2|3|4|104|5|104]
```

ccd-clause:

```
CONDENSED [ON|OFF]
COMPLETE  [ON|OFF]
```

The default values for a unidirectional Q subscription are:

Commands	Default values
all_changed_rows	n
changed_cols_only	y
state	n
before_values	n
has_loadphase	i

Let's assume, we want to create a Q subscription called TAB1 (specified with the subname keyword) with a source table name ERIC.T1 and a target user table called FRED.T1. Following is an example of an ASNCLP command file to create such a Q subscription (SYSA_crt_qsub_uni_AB.asnclp). Note that we have defined that the target table has c1 as a key column.

```
ASNCLP SESSION SET TO Q REPLICATION;
SET RUN SCRIPT NOW STOP ON SQL ERROR ON;

SET SERVER CAPTURE TO DB DB2A;
SET SERVER TARGET  TO DB DB2B;

SET CAPTURE SCHEMA SOURCE ASN;
SET APPLY   SCHEMA         ASN;

SET QMANAGER QMA FOR CAPTURE SCHEMA;
SET QMANAGER QMB FOR APPLY   SCHEMA;

CREATE QSUB
USING REPLQMAP RQMA2B
(SUBNAME TAB1 ERIC.T1
OPTIONS
HAS LOAD PHASE I
SPILL_MODELQ "IBMQREP.SPILL.MODELQ"
TARGET NAME FRED.T1
TYPE USERTABLE
KEYS (C1)
CONFLICT ACTION F
LOAD TYPE 0);
```

From CLP-A, issue:

```
$ asnclp -f SYSA_crt_qsub_uni_AB.asnclp
```

We can check that the Q subscription has been created by querying the IBMQREP_SUBS table as discussed in the *The control tables – The Q Capture control tables* section of *Chapter 3*. The columns in the table map to the ASNCLP command parameters as follows:

In IBMQREP_SUBS table	In Command	In IBMQREP_SUBS table	In Command
ALL_CHANGED_ROWS	all changed rows	CONFLICT_ACTION	conflict action
CHANGED_COLS_ONLY	changed cols only	CONFLICT_RULE	conflict rule
HAS_LOADPHASE	has load phase	ERROR_ACTION	error action
BEFORE_VALUES	before values		

The following shows a cut down query to see if a Q subscription is active:

```
db2 "SELECT SUBSTR(subname,1,20) AS subname, state AS s, state_time FROM
asn.ibmqrep_subs "
```

In unidirectional replication, we can specify some simple transformation processing in the Q subscription. One such example is to create a target table which contains a **computed column** (COM), which is the result of concatenating two source columns (c1 and c2).

```
ASNCLP SESSION SET TO Q REPLICATION;
SET RUN SCRIPT NOW STOP ON SQL ERROR ON;

SET SERVER CAPTURE TO DB DB2A;
SET SERVER TARGET TO DB DB2B;
SET CAPTURE SCHEMA SOURCE ASN;
SET APPLY SCHEMA ASN;

CREATE QSUB USING REPLQMAP RQMA2B
(SUBNAME TAB1 ERIC.T1 TARGET NEW NAME FRED.T1
TRGCOLS ALL EXPRESSION ("CONCAT(:C1,:C2)" TARGET COM);
```

This usage of computed columns is not available in multi-directional replication.

In unidirectional replication, we can also filter rows. Filtering conditions are stored in the SEARCH_CONDITION column of the IBMQREP_SUBS table. In an ASNCLP script, we use the SEARCH CONDITION keyword to specify a WHERE condition:

```
CREATE QSUB USING REPLQMAP RQMA2B

(SUBNAME tab1 eric.t1 OPTIONS
```

```
SEARCH CONDITION
"WHERE :C3 > 1000")
```

In the WHERE clause, any source table columns that are referenced must be prefixed with a colon (:).

Now let's move on to ask the question: Why do we have to worry about conflict detection in a unidirectional scenario? Let's look at the situation where the target table is updated outside of Q replication, and see what the CONFLICT ACTION possibilities are. We have set up unidirectional replication between a source table ERIC.T1 and a target table FRED.T1. We have CONFLICT_ACTION set to F. What happens if a row is inserted into FRED.T1 outside of Q replication? We start off with both tables empty.

We start on DB2A, and insert a row into ERIC.T1:

```
db2 "insert into eric.t1 values (1,1,'H')"
```

This row gets replicated to FRED.T1 on DB2B.

On DB2B, we insert a row into FRED.T1 outside of Q replication:

```
db2 "insert into fred.t1 values(2,2,'A')"
```

```
C1             C2             C3
-----------   -----------   ----------
          1             1 H
          2             2 A
```

The table FRED.T1 now has two rows in it.

Now on DB2A, insert a row into ERIC.T1, which has the same key as the row we manually inserted on DB2B:

```
db2 "insert into eric.t1 values(2,2,'H')"
```

And check the result on DB2B:

```
db2 "select * from fred.t1"
```

```
C1             C2             C3
-----------   -----------   ----------
          1             1 H
          2             2 H
```

We can see that our manually inserted row (which had a c3 value of A) has been overwritten with the row which was inserted into eric_t1 (which has a c3 value of H). This fact is recorded in the IBMQREP_EXCEPTIONS table on DB2B:

```
EXCEPTION_TIME              REC
VQ                                            SRC_COMMIT_LSN
SRC_TRANS_TIME             SUBNAME


REASON         SQLCODE     SQLSTATE SQLERRMC
OPERATION          TEXT
2010-01-23-13.45.20.975000 CAPA.TO.APPB.REC
VQ                              x'000000000000039086A2'
2010-01-23-13.45.17.000001 TAB1


DUPLICATE              -803 23505     x'31FF465245442E5431'

INSERT INSERT INTO "FRED"."T1"( "C1", "C2", "C3") VALUES (2, 2, 'H')
```

We can see that a conflict was recorded for the INSERT statement into FRED.T1, and because the CONFLICT_ACTION was set to F, then this value is forced into the table. Note that the original value is not recorded in the IBMQREP_EXCEPTIONS table.

If CONFLICT_ACTION had been set to S, then if we try to replicate a row and the insert fails due to a duplicate key, then Q Apply will stop and the TEXT value in IBMQREP_EXCEPTIONS is INSERT INTO "FRED"."T1"("C1", "C2", "C3") VALUES (2, 2, 'A'), which is the row that we tried (unsuccessfully) to insert into FRED. T1. The message will remain on the Receive Queue, so we have to alter the Q subscription to add the SQLSTATE 23505 to the OKSLQSTATES parameter, and only then restart Q Apply.

If CONFLICT_ACTION had been set to I, then if we try to replicate a row and the insert fails due to a duplicate key (the original row remains in the target table), then the TEXT value in IBMQREP_EXCEPTIONS is INSERT INTO "FRED"."T1"("C1", "C2", "C3") VALUES (2, 2, 'H'), which is the row that we tried (unsuccessfully) to insert into FRED.T1. The message does not remain on the Receive Queue and we do not have to do anything to the Receive Queue.

Q subscription for bidirectional replication

The introduction to Q subscriptions mentioned that for multi-directional replication, we need two files to create a Q subscription, a load file and a content file.

Here is an example of a load file called SYSA_loadbidi.asnclp:

```
ASNCLP SESSION SET TO Q REPLICATION;
```

```
SET RUN SCRIPT NOW STOP ON SQL ERROR ON;

LOAD MULTIDIR REPL SCRIPT "SYSA_contbidi.txt";
```

The key to this file is the LOAD MULTIDIR REPL SCRIPT line—it calls the content file (SYSA_contbidi.txt).

From CLP-A, issue:

```
$ asnclp -f SYSA_loadbidi.asnclp
```

The following screenshot shows the content file:

`set subgroup "TABT1";`	A subgroup name is NOT a Q subscription name, but the name for the collection of Q subscriptions in the file.
`set server multidir to db "DB2A";` `set server multidir to db "DB2B";`	Specify to set the database as a bidirectional or peer-to-peer replication server.
`set multidir schema "DB2A".ASN;` `set multidir schema "DB2B".ASN;`	Set the same schema for the Q Capture and Q Apply control tables
`set connection SOURCE "DB2A".ASN` `TARGET "DB2B".ASN replqmap "RQMA2B";`	These statements connect the two servers that are used for bidirectional or peer-to-peer replication.
`set connection SOURCE "DB2B".ASN` `TARGET "DB2A".ASN replqmap "RQMB2A";`	
`set tables("DB2A".ASN.ERIC.T1,` `  "DB2B".ASN.FRED.T1);`	This specifies the tables that participate in a single multi-directional subscription (each listed table is both a source and a target).

`create qsub subtype b`	We are creating a bidirectional Q subscription
`from node db2a.asn`	We need a "FROM NODE" statement because we want to specify options for our Q subscription going from DB2A to DB2B.
`SOURCE`	SOURCE refers to the source table on DB2A.
`all changed rows Y` `has load phase E`	We say how we want to filter on source row selection, and how the Q Apply program on the other side will handle the initial load.
`TARGET`	TARGET refers to the target table as seen from DB2A (so it's DB2B).

`conflict rule C`
`conflict action F`
`error action S`
`load type 0`
`oksqlstates "000"`
	Here we define the parameters that Q Apply on DB2B will use.

`from node db2b.asn`
`SOURCE`
`all changed rows Y`
`has load phase N`
`TARGET`
`conflict rule A`
`conflict action I`
`error action S`
`load type 0`
`oksqlstates "000";`
	This is the section for replication from DB2B back to DB2A. The has loadphase value of "N" means that Q Apply on DB2A will not perform an initial load.

In the following section, the parameters are explained in more detail.

The FROM NODE statement (FROM NODE <servername>.<schemaname>) is required because we want to specify options for both of our Q subscriptions. If we omit FROM NODE, both Q subscriptions will be created with the following default options:

ALL_CHANGED_ROWS (C) = N	BEFORE_VALUES (B) = N	ERROR_ACTION = Q
HAS_LOADPHASE (L) = I	CONFLICT_ACTION = K	
CHANGED_COLS_ONLY (H) = Y	CONFLICT_RULE = I	

In the preceding commands, the letters in brackets cross reference to the columns of the query to list out the attributes of a Q subscription in the *Issuing commands to a Queue Manager – Displaying the attributes of a Q subscription* section of *Chapter 4, WebSphere MQ for the DBA*.

The FROM NODE statement has two sections, a Source section and a Target section. Note that the order of tables in the set tables ("DB2A".ASN.ERIC.T1, "DB2B".ASN.FRED.T1) statement does not affect which table is treated as the source and which as the target, or the state of the Q subscription.

In the Source section, we specify the following:

- ALL CHANGED ROWS: This specifies the data sending option. It has the following values:
  - N: This is a default value. It sends a row only if a subscribed column in the source table changes.
  - Y: This sends a row when any column in the source table changes.
- HAS LOAD PHASE: This specifies whether the target table for the Q subscription will be loaded with data from the source. If the FROM NODE statement specifies DB2A, then this parameter points to Q Apply on DB2B. It has the following values:
  - N: This is a default value. It does not have a load phase at the target.
  - I: This specifies an automatic load. Q Apply calls the EXPORT and IMPORT utilities or EXPORT and LOAD utilities, depending on the type of load that is specified in the LOAD_TYPE keyword and on the platform of the Q Apply server and Q Capture server.

- E: This specifies a manual load. An application other than Q Apply loads the target table. In this case, we insert the LOADDONE signal (using the LOADDONE command) into the IBMQREP_SIGNAL table at the Q Capture server to inform Q Capture once the application is done loading.

In the Target section, we specify the following:

- CONFLICT RULE:

  - K: This is a default value. It checks only key values.

  - C: This checks changed non-key values in addition to key values.

  - A: This checks all values for updates.

- CONFLICT ACTION: This value determines the action to take when a row change is invalid. For example, the row to DELETE/UPDATE is not found. It has the following values:

  - I: This is a default value. Q Apply does not apply the conflicting row but applies other rows in the transaction.

  - F: Q Apply tries to force the change. This requires that Q Capture sends all columns, so the CHANGED_COLS_ONLY value must be set to N (no) in the IBMQREP_SUBS table. Note that this is the default value while a target table is being loaded.

  - D: Q Apply does not apply the conflicting row but applies other rows in the transaction. Then it disables the Q subscription (set it to I), stops applying transactions to the target, and sends an error report to Q Capture on the Administration Queue.

  - S: Q Apply rolls back the transaction, commits, and then stops.

  - Q: Q Apply stops reading from the queue. All conflicting rows are inserted into the IBMQREP_EXCEPTIONS table.

- ERROR ACTION: This specifies what action to take if an error occurs. It has the following values:

  - Q: This is a default value. It stops reading from the Receive Queue.

  - D: This disables the Q subscription and notifies Q Capture.

  - S: This stops Q Apply without applying the transaction.

- OKSQLSTATES: This specifies a list of SQL statements within double quotation marks that are not to be considered as errors when applying changes to this table.
- LOAD TYPE: This specifies the utilities that Q Apply uses to load the target. It has the following values:
  - ○ 0: This is a default value. Choose the best type automatically.
  - ○ 1: Use LOAD FROM CURSOR only. Not valid for Classic sources or federated targets.
  - ○ 2: Use SELECT/IMPORT only. Not valid for Classic sources.
  - ○ 3: Use SELECT/LOAD only. Not valid for Classic sources or for federated targets.
  - ○ 4/104/5/105: Only used in Classic replication.

> If Q Apply is to load the target table, then if the target table is already populated, the contents will get overwritten without warning.

> In multi-directional replication, the LOAD TYPE can only be 0 or 3

Q subscription for P2P two-way replication

The only difference between the Q subscription definition for bidirectional and peer-to-peer replication is the value of the subtype parameter. For bidirectional replication, the value is b and for peer-to-peer the value is p.

An example of the content file for peer-to-peer two-way replication is SYSA_contp2p2w.txt containing the following ASNCLP commands:

```
set subgroup "TABT1";

set server multidir to db "DB2A";
set server multidir to db "DB2B";

set multidir schema "DB2A".ASN;
set multidir schema "DB2B".ASN;

set connection SOURCE "DB2A".ASN
TARGET "DB2B".ASN replqmap "RQMA2B";

set connection SOURCE "DB2B".ASN
TARGET "DB2A".ASN replqmap "RQMB2A";

set tables("DB2A".ASN.ERIC.T1, "DB2B".ASN.FRED.T1);
create qsub subtype p;
```

Here is the associated load file called `SYSA_loadp2p2w.asnclp`:

```
ASNCLP SESSION SET TO Q REPLICATION;
SET RUN SCRIPT NOW STOP ON SQL ERROR ON;

LOAD MULTIDIR REPL SCRIPT "SYSA_contp2p2w.txt";
```

From CLP-A, issue:

```
$ asnclp -f SYSA_loadp2p2w.asnclp
```

Q subscription for P2P three-way replication

For Peer-to-peer three-way replication, an example of a content file is
`SYSA_contp2p3w.txt` containing the following ASNCLP commands:

```
set subgroup "3Nodes";

set output multidir;

set server multidir to db DB2A;
set multidir schema DB2A.ASN;
set server multidir to db DB2B;
set multidir schema DB2B.ASN;
set server multidir to db DB2C;
set multidir schema DB2C.ASN;

SET CONNECTION SOURCE DB2A.ASN TARGET DB2B.ASN REPLQMAP RQMA2B;
SET CONNECTION SOURCE DB2A.ASN TARGET DB2C.ASN REPLQMAP RQMA2C;
SET CONNECTION SOURCE DB2B.ASN TARGET DB2A.ASN REPLQMAP RQMB2A;
SET CONNECTION SOURCE DB2B.ASN TARGET DB2C.ASN REPLQMAP RQMB2C;
SET CONNECTION SOURCE DB2C.ASN TARGET DB2A.ASN REPLQMAP RQMC2A;
SET CONNECTION SOURCE DB2C.ASN TARGET DB2B.ASN REPLQMAP RQMC2B;

set tables(
 DB2A.ASN.ERIC.T1
,DB2B.ASN.FRED.T1
,DB2C.ASN.HEAT.T1 );
create qsub subtype p;
```

The associated load file is as `SYSA_loadp2p2w.asnclp`, but with
`SYSA_contp2p2w.txt` replaced with `SYSA_contp2p3w.txt`.

Publication for Event Publishing

An example of the ASNCLP commands to create a Publication for Event Publishing is in a file called `SYSA_crt_xmlpub.asnclp` containing the following ASNCLP commands:

```
ASNCLP SESSION SET TO Q REPLICATION;
SET RUN SCRIPT NOW STOP ON SQL ERROR ON;

SET SERVER CAPTURE TO DB DB2A;
SET CAPTURE SCHEMA SOURCE ASN;

SET QMANAGER QMA FOR CAPTURE SCHEMA;
SET QMANAGER QMB FOR APPLY   SCHEMA;

CREATE XML PUB (PUBNAME PUBA2B
PUBQMAP "PQMA2B"
ERIC.T1
COLS ALL
ALL CHANGED ROWS Y
BEFORE VALUES Y
CHANGED COLS ONLY N
HAS LOAD PHASE N
SUPPRESS DELETES N);
```

Q subscription maintenance

This section looks at how we can stop or drop or alter a Q subscription using ASNCLP commands and how we can issue a CAPSTART command.

Checking the state of a Q subscription

The state of a Q subscription is recorded in the IBMQREP_SUBS table, and can be queried as follows:

```
db2 "SELECT SUBSTR(subname,1,10) AS subname, state FROM asn.ibmqrep_subs"

SUBNAME     STATE
----------  -----
DEPT0001    A
XEMP0001    A
```

The meaning of each column was covered in the *The control tables – The Q Capture control tables* section of *Chapter 3*.

Stopping a Q subscription

The command to stop a Q subscription is STOP QSUB SUBNAME <qsubname>.

Note that if Q Capture is not running, then the command will not take effect until Q Capture is started, because the STOP QSUB command generates an INSERT command into the IBMQREP_SIGNAL table:

```
INSERT INTO ASN.IBMQREP_SIGNAL
(signal_type, signal_subtype, signal_input_in)
 VALUES
('CMD', 'CAPSTOP', 'T10001');
```

In a unidirectional setup, to stop a Q subscription called T10001 where the Q Capture and Q Apply control tables have a schema of ASN, create a text file called SYSA_qsub_stop_uni.asnclp containing the following ASNCLP commands:

```
ASNCLP SESSION SET TO Q REPLICATION;
SET RUN SCRIPT NOW STOP ON SQL ERROR ON;

SET SERVER CAPTURE TO DB DB2A;
SET SERVER TARGET  TO DB DB2B;
SET CAPTURE SCHEMA SOURCE ASN;
SET APPLY   SCHEMA ASN;

stop qsub subname T10001;
```

In bidirectional or peer-to-peer two-way replication, we have to specify both Q subscriptions (T10001 and T10002) for the subscription group:

```
ASNCLP SESSION SET TO Q REPLICATION;
SET RUN SCRIPT NOW STOP ON SQL ERROR ON;

SET CAPTURE SCHEMA SOURCE ASN;
SET APPLY SCHEMA ASN;

SET SERVER CAPTURE TO DB DB2A;
SET SERVER TARGET  TO DB DB2B;

stop qsub subname T10001;

SET SERVER CAPTURE TO DB DB2B;
SET SERVER TARGET  TO DB DB2A;

stop qsub subname T10002;
```

In a Peer-to-peer four-way setup, the commands would be in a file called qsub_stop_p2p4w.asnclp containing the following ASNCLP commands:

```
ASNCLP SESSION SET TO Q REPLICATION;
SET RUN SCRIPT NOW STOP ON SQL ERROR ON;
```

```
SET CAPTURE SCHEMA SOURCE ASN;
SET APPLY   SCHEMA ASN;

SET SERVER CAPTURE TO DB DB2A;
SET SERVER TARGET  TO DB DB2B;

stop qsub subname T10001;

SET SERVER CAPTURE TO DB DB2A;
SET SERVER TARGET  TO DB DB2C;

stop qsub subname T10002;

SET SERVER CAPTURE TO DB DB2A;
SET SERVER TARGET  TO DB DB2D;

stop qsub subname T10003;
```

Dropping a Q subscription

The ASNCLP command to drop a Q subscription is:

```
DROP QSUB (SUBNAME <qsubname> USING REPLQMAP <repqmapname>);
```

In a unidirectional setup, to drop a Q subscription called T10001, which uses a Replication Queue Map called RQMA2B, create a file called drop_qsub_uni.asnclp containing the following ASNCLP commands:

```
ASNCLP SESSION SET TO Q REPLICATION;
SET RUN SCRIPT NOW STOP ON SQL ERROR ON;

SET SERVER CAPTURE TO DB DB2A;
SET SERVER TARGET  TO DB DB2B;

SET CAPTURE SCHEMA SOURCE ASN;
SET APPLY   SCHEMA ASN;

drop qsub (subname TAB1 using replqmap RQMA2B);
```

We can use the SET DROP command to specify whether for unidirectional replication the target table and its table space are dropped when a Q subscription is deleted:

```
SET DROP TARGET [NEVER|ALWAYS]
```

The default is not to drop the target table.

In a multi-directional setup, there are three methods we can use:

- In the first method, we need to issue the DROP QSUB command twice, once for the Q subscription from DB2A to DB2B and once for the Q subscription from DB2B to DB2A. In this method, we need to know the Q subscription and Replication Queue Map names, which is shown in the qsub_drop_bidi0.asnclp file:

```
ASNCLP SESSION SET TO Q REPLICATION;
SET RUN SCRIPT NOW STOP ON SQL ERROR ON;

SET CAPTURE SCHEMA SOURCE ASN;
SET APPLY    SCHEMA ASN;

SET SERVER CAPTURE TO DB DB2A;
SET SERVER TARGET  TO DB DB2B;

drop qsub (subname T10001 using replqmap RQMA2B);

SET SERVER CAPTURE TO DB DB2B;
SET SERVER TARGET  TO DB DB2A;

drop qsub (subname T10002 using replqmap RQMB2A);
```

- In the second method, we use the DROP SUBTYPE command, which is used to delete the multi-directional Q subscriptions for a single logical table. We use the DROP SUBTYPE command with the SET REFERENCE TABLE construct, which identifies a Q subscription for multi-directional replication. An example of using these two is shown in the following content file, which drops all the Q subscriptions for the source table eric.t1. This content file needs to be called from a load script file.

```
SET SUBGROUP "TABT1";

SET SERVER MULTIDIR TO DB "DB2A";
SET SERVER MULTIDIR TO DB "DB2B";

SET REFERENCE TABLE USING SCHEMA "DB2A".ASN
USES TABLE eric.t1;

DROP SUBTYPE B QSUBS;
```

The USING SCHEMA part of the SET REFERENCE TABLE command identifies the server that contains the table (DB2A) and the schema (ASN) of the control tables in which this table is specified as a source and target. The USES TABLE part specifies the table schema (eric) and table name (t1) to which the Q subscription applies.

When we use this command, no tables or table spaces are ever dropped.

The SUBGROUP name must be the valid for the tables whose Q subscriptions we want to drop. We can find the SUBGROUP name for a table using the following query:

```
db2 "SELECT SUBSTR(subgroup,1,10) AS subsgroup, SUBSTR(source_
owner,1,10) as schema, SUBSTR(source_name,1,10) as name FROM asn.
ibmqrep_subs"
```

```
SUBSGROUP   SCHEMA      NAME

---------- ---------- ----------

TABT2       DB2ADMIN    DEPT

TABT2       DB2ADMIN    XEMP
```

The preceding ASNCLP command generates the following SQL:

```
-- CONNECT TO DB2B USER XXXX using XXXX;
DELETE FROM ASN.IBMQREP_TRG_COLS WHERE subname = 'T10001' AND
recvq =
'CAPA.TO.APPB.RECVQ';
DELETE FROM ASN.IBMQREP_TARGETS WHERE subname = 'T10001' AND recvq
=
'CAPA.TO.APPB.RECVQ';
DELETE FROM ASN.IBMQREP_SRC_COLS WHERE subname = 'T10002';
DELETE FROM ASN.IBMQREP_SUBS WHERE subname = 'T10002';

-- CONNECT TO DB2A USER XXXX using XXXX;
DELETE FROM ASN.IBMQREP_SRC_COLS WHERE subname = 'T10001';
DELETE FROM ASN.IBMQREP_SUBS WHERE subname = 'T10001';
DELETE FROM ASN.IBMQREP_TRG_COLS WHERE subname = 'T10002' AND
recvq =
'CAPB.TO.APPA.RECVQ';
DELETE FROM ASN.IBMQREP_TARGETS WHERE subname = 'T10002' AND recvq
=
'CAPB.TO.APPA.RECVQ';
```

- A third method uses the DROP SUBGROUP command, as shown:

```
SET SUBGROUP "TABT2";

SET SERVER MULTIDIR TO DB "DB2A";
SET SERVER MULTIDIR TO DB "DB2B";

SET MULTIDIR SCHEMA "DB2A".ASN ;

DROP SUBGROUP;
```

With this command, we just need to specify the Q subscription group name (SUBGROUP).

The preceding ASNCLP command generates the following SQL:

```
-- CONNECT TO DB2A USER XXXX using XXXX;
DELETE FROM ASN.IBMQREP_TRG_COLS WHERE subname = 'T10002' AND
recvq =
'CAPB.TO.APPA.RECVQ';
DELETE FROM ASN.IBMQREP_TARGETS WHERE subname = 'T10002' AND recvq
=
'CAPB.TO.APPA.RECVQ';
DELETE FROM ASN.IBMQREP_SRC_COLS WHERE subname = 'T10001';
DELETE FROM ASN.IBMQREP_SUBS WHERE subname = 'T10001';

-- CONNECT TO DB2B USER XXXX using XXXX;
DELETE FROM ASN.IBMQREP_SRC_COLS WHERE subname = 'T10002';
DELETE FROM ASN.IBMQREP_SUBS WHERE subname = 'T10002';
DELETE FROM ASN.IBMQREP_TRG_COLS WHERE subname = 'T10001' AND
recvq =
'CAPA.TO.APPB.RECVQ';
DELETE FROM ASN.IBMQREP_TARGETS WHERE subname = 'T10001' AND recvq
=
'CAPA.TO.APPB.RECVQ';
```

In a peer-to-peer three-way scenario, we would add a third SET SERVER
MULTIDIR TO DB line pointing to the third server.

If we use the second or third method, then we do not need to know the Q subscription
names, just the table name in the second method and the Q subscription group name
in the third method.

Altering a Q subscription

We can only alter Q subscriptions which are inactive. The following query shows the
state of all Q subscriptions:

```
db2 "SELECT SUBSTR(subname,1,10) AS subname, state FROM asn.ibmqrep_subs"

SUBNAME     STATE
---------- -----
DEPT0001    I
```

At the time of writing, if we try and alter an active Q subscription, we will get the
following error when we run the ASNCLP commands:

```
ErrorReport :
```

```
ASN2003I  The action "Alter Subscription" started at "Friday, 22
January 2010 12:53:16 o'clock GMT". Q subscription name: "DEPT0001".
Q Capture server: "DB2A". Q Capture schema: "ASN". Q Apply server:
"DB2B". Q Apply schema: "ASN". The source table is "DB2ADMIN.DEPT".
The target table or stored procedure is "DB2ADMIN.DEPT".
ASN0999E  "The attribute "erroraction" cannot be updated." : "The
Subscription cannot be updated because it is in active state" : Error
condition "*", error code(s): "*", "*",  "*".
```

This should be resolved in a future release.

So now let's move on and look at the command to alter a Q subscription.

To alter a Q subscription, we use the ALTER QSUB ASNCLP command.

The parameters for the command depend on whether we are running unidirectional or multi-directional replication. We can change attributes for both the source and target tables, but what we can change depends on the type of replication (unidirectional, bidirectional, or peer-to-peer), as shown in the following table:

Parameter	Uni	Bi	P2P
Source table:			
ALL CHANGED ROWS [N | Y]	Y	Y	
HAS LOAD PHASE [N | I |E]	Y	Y	Y
Target table:			
CONFLICT RULE [K | C | A]		Y	
CONFLICT ACTION [I | F | D | S | Q]		Y	
ERROR ACTION [Q | D | S]	Y	Y	Y
LOAD TYPE [0 | 2 | 3 | 4 | 104 | 5 | 105]	Y	Y	Y
OKSQLSTATES ["sqlstates "]	Y	Y	Y

For unidirectional replication, the format of the command is:

```
ALTER QSUB <subname> REPLQMAP <mapname>
USING REPLQMAP <mapname> DESC <description>
MANAGE TARGET CCD [CREATE SQL REGISTRATION|DROP SQL REGISTRATION|ALTER
SQL REGISTRATION FOR Q REPLICATION]
USING OPTIONS [other-opt-clause|add-cols-clause]
```

other-opt-clause:

```
    SEARCH CONDITION "<search_condition>"
    ALL CHANGED ROWS [N|Y]
    HAS LOAD PHASE--  [N|I|E]
    SUPPRESS DELETES [N|Y]
```

```
CONFLICT ACTION [I|F|D|S|Q]
ERROR ACTION [S|D|Q]
OKSQLSTATES "<sqlstates>"
LOAD TYPE [0|1|2|3|4|104|5|105]
```

add-cols-clause:

```
ADD COLS (<trgcolname1> <srccolname1>,<trgcolname2> <srccolname2>)
```

An example of altering a Q subscription to add a search condition is:

```
ASNCLP SESSION SET TO Q REPLICATION;
SET RUN SCRIPT NOW STOP ON SQL ERROR ON;

SET CAPTURE SCHEMA SOURCE ASN;
SET APPLY    SCHEMA ASN;

SET SERVER CAPTURE TO DB DB2A;
SET SERVER TARGET  TO DB DB2B;

ALTER QSUB tab1 REPLQMAP rqma2b
  USING OPTIONS
  SEARCH CONDITION
  "WHERE :c1 > 1000" ;
```

In multi-directional replication, the format of the command is:

```
ALTER QSUB SUBTYPE B
FROM NODE <svn.schema> SOURCE [src-clause] TARGET [trg-clause]
FROM NODE <svn.schema> SOURCE [src-clause] TARGET [trg-clause]
```

src-clause:

```
ALL CHANGED ROWS [N/Y] HAS LOAD PHASE [N/I/E]
```

trg-clause:

```
CONFLICT RULE [K/C/A] +-' '-CONFLICT ACTION [I/F/D/S/Q]
ERROR ACTION [Q/D/S] LOAD TYPE [0/2/3]
OKSQLSTATES <"sqlstates">
```

If we are altering a Q subscription in a multi-directional environment, then we can use the SET REFERENCE TABLE construct, discussed in the previous section. We need to specify the SUBTYPE parameter as follows:

- Bidirectional replication: ALTER QSUB SUBTYPE B

- Peer-to-peer replication: ALTER QSUB SUBTYPE P

Let's look at a bidirectional replication example, where we want to change the ERROR ACTION to D for a Q subscription where the source table name is db2admin.dept. The content file (SYSA_cont_alter02.txt) will contain:

```
SET SUBGROUP "TABT2";

SET SERVER MULTIDIR TO DB "DB2A";
SET SERVER MULTIDIR TO DB "DB2B";

SET REFERENCE TABLE USING SCHEMA "DB2A".ASN
  USES TABLE db2admin.dept;

ALTER QSUB SUBTYPE B
  FROM NODE DB2A.ASN SOURCE    TARGET ERROR ACTION D
  FROM NODE DB2B.ASN SOURCE    TARGET ERROR ACTION D;
```

We have to specify the SOURCE keyword even though we are only changing the target attributes.

The ALTER QSUB statement spans the three last lines of the file.

Starting a Q subscription

An example of the ASNCLP command START QSUB to start a Q subscription can be found in the SYSA_qsub_start_db2ac.asnclp file. We just have to plug in the Q subscription name (T10002 in our example).

```
ASNCLP SESSION SET TO Q REPLICATION;
SET RUN SCRIPT NOW STOP ON SQL ERROR ON;

SET CAPTURE SCHEMA SOURCE ASN;
SET APPLY SCHEMA ASN;

SET SERVER CAPTURE TO DB DB2A;
SET SERVER TARGET  TO DB DB2C;
START QSUB SUBNAME T10002;
```

Run the file as:

```
asnclp -f SYSA_qsub_start_db2ac.asnclp
```

> We cannot put two START QSUB statements in the same file (as shown), even if they have their own section.

So, we cannot code:

```
ASNCLP SESSION SET TO Q REPLICATION;

SET RUN SCRIPT NOW STOP ON SQL ERROR ON;

SET SERVER CAPTURE TO DB DB2A;

SET SERVER TARGET TO DB DB2D;

SET CAPTURE SCHEMA SOURCE ASN;
```

```
SET APPLY SCHEMA ASN;
START QSUB SUBNAME T10003;
SET SERVER CAPTURE TO DB DB2A;
SET SERVER TARGET TO DB DB2C;
START QSUB SUBNAME T10002;
```

Sending a signal using ASNCLP

For signals such as CAPSTART, CAPSTOP, and LOADDONE to be picked up, Q Capture needs to be running. Note that Q Capture does not have to be up for the signals to be issued, just picked up. As they are written to the DB2 log, Q Capture will see them when it reads the log and will action them in the order they were received.

An example of an ASNCLP script to send a CAPSTART command was shown in the previous section.

We can use the query in the *Sending signals using the IBMQREP_SIGNALS table* section of *Chapter 3*, to see what is inserted into the IBMQREP_SIGNALS table.

Validating the WebSphere MQ environment

We can validate the WebSphere MQ environment in two ways. We can use the native WebSphere MQ amqsput and amqsget commands to put messages onto a queue and retrieve them, or we can use some Q replication commands. In the examples in *Appendix A*, we use the latter method, so in this chapter we will look at this method.

The two Q replication commands, we can use to check the WSMQ environment are:

VALIDATE WSMQ ENVIRONMENT FOR

And:

VALIDATE WSMQ MESSAGE FLOW FOR REPLQMAP

Use the VALIDATE WSMQ ENVIRONMENT FOR command to verify that the required WebSphere MQ objects exist and have the correct properties for Q replication schemas, queue maps, and Q subscriptions.

Use the VALIDATE WSMQ MESSAGE FLOW FOR REPLQMAP command to send test messages that validate the message flow between the WebSphere MQ queues that are specified for a Replication Queue Map.

Both of these commands require a supplied stored procedure. Prior to DB2 9.5, the stored procedure was called ASN.ADMINIF and was created automatically in each database that is taking part in the replication process. From DB2 9.5 onwards, the stored procedure name has changed to SYSPROC.ASN_ADMIN_UTIL.

[We should only send test messages when Q Apply and Q Capture are stopped.]

We run the following tests when Q Capture and Q Apply are stopped. The Queue Managers need to be running. The Listeners and Channels only need to be running when we are checking the Replication Queue Map (the VALIDATE WSMQ MESSAGE FLOW FOR REPLQMAP command). So let's look at each of the commands.

Validating WSMQ for the Capture schema

The first option we are going to look at is to validate the WSMQ environment for the Q Capture schema VALIDATE WSMQ ENVIRONMENT FOR CAPTURE SCHEMA. The following is a table of the different Q replication components and what needs to be running as a minimum for the test command to work:

Component	Running/Stopped/Doesn't matter
Q Capture	Doesn't matter
Q Apply	Stopped
QMA	Running
QMB	Running
Listeners	Doesn't matter
Channels	Doesn't matter

We can use the wsmq_validate_capture.asnclp file containing:

```
ASNCLP SESSION SET TO Q REPLICATION;
SET RUN SCRIPT NOW STOP ON SQL ERROR ON;

SET SERVER CAPTURE TO DB DB2A;
SET SERVER TARGET  TO DB DB2B;

SET CAPTURE SCHEMA SOURCE ASN;
SET APPLY   SCHEMA ASN;

VALIDATE WSMQ ENVIRONMENT FOR CAPTURE SCHEMA;
```

The file is run as:

```
asnclp -f wsmq_validate_capture.asnclp
```

The following is an example output for unidirectional replication:

```
====
CMD: ASNCLP SESSION SET TO Q REPLICATION;
====
CMD: SET RUN SCRIPT NOW STOP ON SQL ERROR ON;
====
CMD: SET SERVER CAPTURE TO DB DB2A;
====
CMD: SET SERVER TARGET  TO DB DB2B;
====
CMD: SET CAPTURE SCHEMA SOURCE ASN;
====
CMD: SET APPLY   SCHEMA ASN;
====
CMD: VALIDATE WSMQ ENVIRONMENT FOR CAPTURE SCHEMA;
====
ASN2291I  "11" tests were executed to validate the WebSphere MQ
objects. "11" tests passed and "0" tests failed.
ASN1953I  ASNCLP :  Command completed.
```

We are looking for the ASN2291I message—the command does not generate any SQL.

Validating WSMQ for the Apply schema

The next option is to validate the WSMQ environment for the Q Apply schema using the VALIDATE WSMQ ENVIRONMENT FOR APPLY SCHEMA command. The following is a table of the different Q replication components and what needs to be running as a minimum for the test command to work:

Component	Running/Stopped/Doesn't matter
Q Capture	Doesn't matter
Q Apply	Stopped
QMA	Running
QMB	Running
Listeners	Doesn't matter
Channels	Doesn't matter

We can use the `wsmq_validate_apply.asnclp` file containing:

```
ASNCLP SESSION SET TO Q REPLICATION;
SET RUN SCRIPT NOW STOP ON SQL ERROR ON;

SET SERVER CAPTURE TO DB DB2A;
SET SERVER TARGET  TO DB DB2B;
SET CAPTURE SCHEMA SOURCE ASN;
SET APPLY   SCHEMA ASN;

VALIDATE WSMQ ENVIRONMENT FOR APPLY SCHEMA;
```

The file is run as:

```
asnclp -f wsmq_validate_apply.asnclp
```

The following is an example output for unidirectional replication:

```
ASN2291I  "9" tests were executed to validate the WebSphere MQ
objects.  "8" tests passed and "1" tests failed.
```

Validating a Replication Queue Map

The next option is to validate the WSMQ environment for a Replication Queue Map using the `VALIDATE WSMQ ENVIRONMENT FOR REPLQMAP` command. The following is a table of the different Q replication components and what needs to be running as a minimum for the test command to work:

Component	Running/Stopped/Doesn't matter
Q Capture	Doesn't matter
Q Apply	Stopped
QMA	Running
QMB	Running
Listeners	Running
Channels	Running

We can use the `wsmq_validate_rqm.asnclp` file containing:

```
ASNCLP SESSION SET TO Q REPLICATION;
SET RUN SCRIPT NOW STOP ON SQL ERROR ON;

SET SERVER CAPTURE TO DB DB2A;
SET SERVER TARGET  TO DB DB2B;
SET CAPTURE SCHEMA SOURCE ASN;
SET APPLY   SCHEMA ASN;

VALIDATE WSMQ ENVIRONMENT FOR REPLQMAP RQMA2B;
```

The file is run as:

```
asnclp -f wsmq_validate_rqm.asnclp
```

```
ASN2291I  "22" tests were executed to validate the WebSphere MQ
objects. "22" tests passed and "0" tests failed.
```

Validating a Publication Queue Map

The next option is to validate the WSMQ environment for a Publication Queue Map using the `VALIDATE WSMQ ENVIRONMENT FOR PUBQMAP` command. The following is a table of the different Q replication components and what needs to be running as a minimum for the test command to work:

Component	Running/Stopped/Doesn't matter
Q Capture	Doesn't matter
Q Apply	n/a
QMA	Running
QMB	Running
Listeners	Running
Channels	Running

We can use the `wsmq_validate_pqm.asnclp` file containing:

```
ASNCLP SESSION SET TO Q REPLICATION;
SET RUN SCRIPT NOW STOP ON SQL ERROR ON;

SET SERVER CAPTURE TO DB DB2A;
SET SERVER TARGET  TO DB DB2B;

SET CAPTURE SCHEMA SOURCE ASN;
SET APPLY    SCHEMA ASN;

VALIDATE WSMQ ENVIRONMENT FOR PUBQMAP PQMA2B;
```

The file is run as:

```
asnclp -f wsmq_validate_pqm.asnclp
```

Validating a Q subscription

The next option is to validate the WSMQ environment for a Q subscription using the `VALIDATE WSMQ ENVIRONMENT FOR QSUB` command. The following is a table of the different Q replication components and what needs to be running as a minimum for the test command to work:

Component	Running/Stopped/Doesn't matter
Q Capture	Doesn't matter
Q Apply	Stopped
QMA	Running
QMB	Running
Listeners	Doesn't matter
Channels	Doesn't matter

We can use the `wsmq_validate_qsub.asnclp` file containing:

```
ASNCLP SESSION SET TO Q REPLICATION;
SET RUN SCRIPT NOW STOP ON SQL ERROR ON;

SET SERVER CAPTURE TO DB DB2A;
SET SERVER TARGET  TO DB DB2B;

SET CAPTURE SCHEMA SOURCE ASN;
SET APPLY   SCHEMA ASN;

VALIDATE WSMQ ENVIRONMENT FOR QSUB T1001 USING REPLQMAP RQMA2B;
```

The file is run as:

```
asnclp -f wsmq_validate_qsub.asnclp
```

```
ASN2291I  "9" tests were executed to validate the WebSphere MQ
objects.  "9" tests passed and "0" tests failed.
```

Validation error messages

The following are some of the common validation messages that you may get:

Error name	Error messages
ASN2266E	An error occurred while accessing the WebSphere MQ queue manager `host_name-queue_manager_name`. The WebSphere MQ reason code is `reason_code`.
ASN2267E	The WebSphere MQ queue `queue_name` does not exist in the queue manager `host_name-queue_manager_name`.
ASN2268E	The action action failed on WebSphere MQ queue `host_name-queue_manager_name-queue_name`. The WebSphere MQ reason code is `reason_code`.

Error name	Error messages
ASN2270E	The stored procedure schema_stored_ procedure_name in database database_name is not authorized to access the WebSphere MQ Queue Manager queue_manager_name because the operating system user ID user_ID, which is the DB2 fenced user of the instance that contains this database, is not a member of the operating system group for WebSphere MQ applications (usually mqm) at the host host_name.
ASN2271W	The WebSphere MQ Queue Manager host_ name-queue_manager_name has the version version_number that is older than the minimum supported version version_number.
ASN2272W	The WebSphere MQ queue host_name-queue_ manager_name-queue_name has an invalid definition and cannot be opened. The internal WSMQ error code is error_code.
ASN2273W	The WebSphere MQ base queue (BASE_Q) queue_name1 that is referenced by the alias queue host_name-queue_manager_name- queue_name2 does not exist.
ASN2274W	The WebSphere MQ transmission queue queue_ name for the remote queue host_name-queue_ manager_name-queue_name does not exist.
ASN2275W	The maximum message size (MAXMSGL) size1 of the WebSphere MQ queue host_name- queue_manager_name-queue_name is greater than the maximum message size (MAXMSGL) size2 of its queue manager host_name-queue_ manager_name.
ASN2276W	The maximum message size (MAXMSGL) size1 of the WebSphere MQ queue host_name-queue_ manager_name-queue_name that sends data is greater than the maximum message size (MAXMSGL) size2 of the queue host_name- queue_manager_name-queue_name that is receiving this data.
ASN2277W	The WebSphere MQ queue host_name-queue_ manager_name-queue_name cannot be used as a Q_replication_queue_type because it is neither a Local Queue nor an alias queue referencing a Local Queue.

Error name	Error messages
ASN2278W	The WebSphere MQ queue host_name-queue_manager_name-queue_name cannot be used as a Send Queue because it is not a Local Queue, a Remote Queue, or an Alias Queue referencing directly or indirectly a Local or Remote Queue.
ASN2279W	The maximum message size (MAX_MESSAGE_SIZE) size1 of the Publication Queue Map publishing_queue_map_name is greater than the maximum message size (MAXMSGL) size2 of the WebSphere MQ queue host_name-queue_manager_name-queue_name that is used as the Send Queue.
ASN2280W	The maximum message size (MAX_MESSAGE_SIZE) size1 of the Replication Queue Map replication_queue_map_name is greater than the maximum message size (MAXMSGL) size2 of the WebSphere MQ queue host_name-queue_manager_name-queue_name that is used as the Send Queue.
ASN2281W	The WebSphere MQ queue host_name-queue_manager_name-queue_name cannot be used as a Q_replication_queue_type. Although the Q Capture and Q Apply programs use the same Queue Manager, the specified queue is neither a Local Queue nor an alias queue referencing a Local Queue directly or indirectly.
ASN2282W	Although the Q Capture and Q Apply programs use the same Queue Manager host_name-queue_manager_name, the queue queue1 that is used as a Q_replication_queue_type1 and the queue queue2 that is used as a Q_replication_queue_type2 are not identical or are not alias queues referring to the same local queue.
ASN2283W	The WebSphere MQ queue host_name-queue_manager_name-queue_name cannot be used as a Receive Queue in the Replication Queue Map replication_queue_map_name. Although the Q Capture and Q Apply programs use different Queue Managers, the specified queue is neither a Local Queue nor an alias queue referencing a Local Queue directly or indirectly.

Error name	Error messages
ASN2284W	The WebSphere MQ queue host_name-queue_manager_name-queue_name cannot be used as Q_replication_queue_type in the Replication Queue Map replication_queue_map_name. Although the Q Capture and Q Apply programs use different Queue Managers, the specified queue is neither a Remote Queue nor an alias queue referencing a Remote Queue directly or indirectly.
ASN2285W	The WebSphere MQ model queue queue_name does not exist in Queue Manager host_name-queue_manager_name, although the Q subscription specifies a load phase.
ASN2286W	The value of the parameter_name parameter of the WebSphere MQ Model Queue host_name-queue_manager_name-queue_name is incorrect. The value is set to value1 but the required value is value2.
ASN2287W	The WebSphere MQ queue host_name-queue_manager_name-queue_name cannot be used as Q_replication_queue_type because the value value1 of the attribute parameter_name does not match the required value value2.
ASN2288W	The test message put on WebSphere MQ queue host_name1-queue_manager_name1-queue_name1 did not arrive at the queue host_name2-queue_manager_name2-queue_name2.
ASN2289W	The test message put on WebSphere MQ queue host_name1_queue_manager_name1_queue_name1 was received at the queue host_name2_queue_manager_name2_queue_name2, but the content has been distorted.
ASN2290I	The test message put on WebSphere MQ queue host_name1-queue_manager_name1-queue_name1 was received at the queue host_name2-queue_manager_name2-queue_name2 used as Q_replication_queue_type.
ASN2291I	number1 tests were executed to validate the WebSphere MQ objects. number2 tests passed and number3 tests failed.

Summary

In this chapter, we introduced the ASNCLP interface and how to use it to set up and perform tests in a Q replication environment. We took you through some of the Q replication setup tasks and showed you how to perform them using ASNCLP commands.

In the next chapter, we will cover common administration tasks and show how they can be performed using the ASNCLP commands covered in this chapter or by using the Replication Center GUI.

6

Administration Tasks

In this chapter, we discuss:

- Q replication administration tasks, which cover setting up the Q replication environment (as shown in the following diagram)
- Administration of a running system

These tasks are represented by the various boxes, and will be highlighted as we go through the chapter:

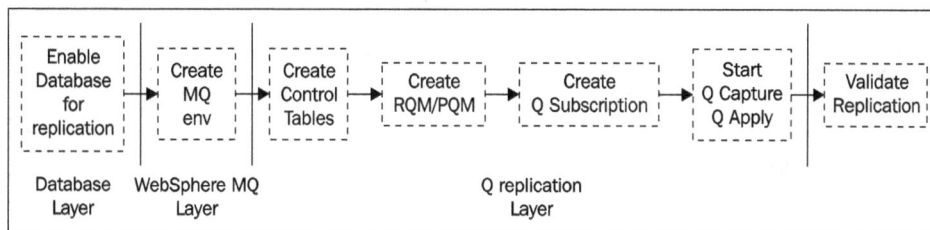

Many of the administration tasks that we need to perform can be achieved using either the Replication Center (only on Linux and Windows) or ASNCLP commands.

The Replication Center can be started either by typing db2rc from a command prompt, or on Windows through the **Start** menu:

Start | All Programs | IBM DB2 | DB2COPY1 | General Administration Tools | Replication Center

Many of the Replication Center fields have an *eclipse* button next to them:

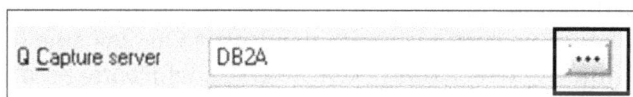

If we are unsure as to the correct value for a field, we can press this button and a list of possible values to choose from will be displayed.

The final step of any task that we perform through the Replication Center takes us to the **Run Now or Save SQL** screen. On this screen, we can either run the generated SQL immediately or we can save the SQL to a file to run later. Note that if we save the SQL to run later, then we need to edit the file to put in the correct passwords for the DB2 CONNECT commands.

Defining the MQ queues

The mechanics of defining WebSphere MQ queues are covered in the *WebSphere MQ for the DBA – MQ Queue management* section of *Chapter 4, WebSphere MQ for the DBA*.

Create/drop the Q replication control tables

This is the first stage in the Q replication layer.

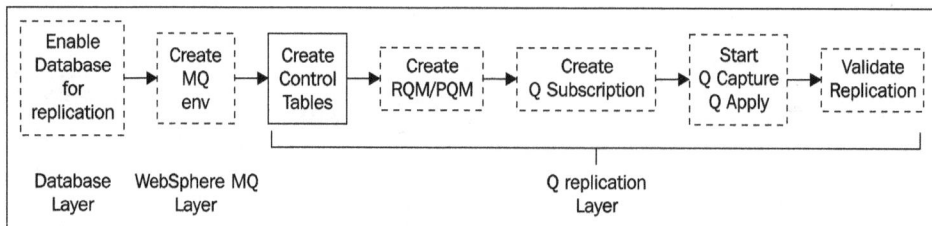

Q replication has three sets of control tables: the Q Capture control tables, the Q Apply control tables, and the Replication Alert Monitor tables. The structure of these tables was discussed in the *The DB2 Database Layer – The control tables* section of *Chapter 3, The DB2 Database Layer*.

Create/drop the Q Capture control tables

We can create the Q Capture control tables using the Replication Center or an ASNCLP command.

To create the Q Capture control tables in database DB2A with a schema of ASN and a Queue Manager of QMA, we need to specify the Restart Queue name (CAPA.RESTARTQ) and the Administration Queue name (CAPA.ADMINQ), which are both Local Queues in the QMA Queue Manager.

We can create the Q Capture control tables using the Replication Center, as shown next:

1. Start the **Replication Center**.

2. Navigate down the folders to **Q Replication | Definitions | Q Capture Servers**.

3. Right-click on **Q Capture Servers** and select **Create Q Capture Control Tables**.

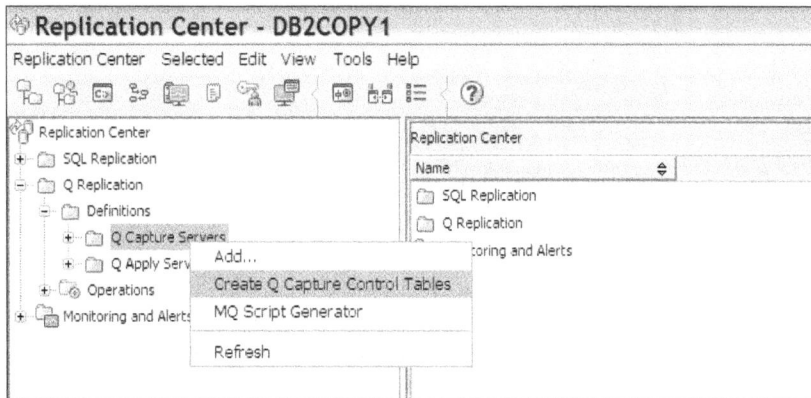

4. This brings up the **Create Q Capture Control Tables Wizard** screen:

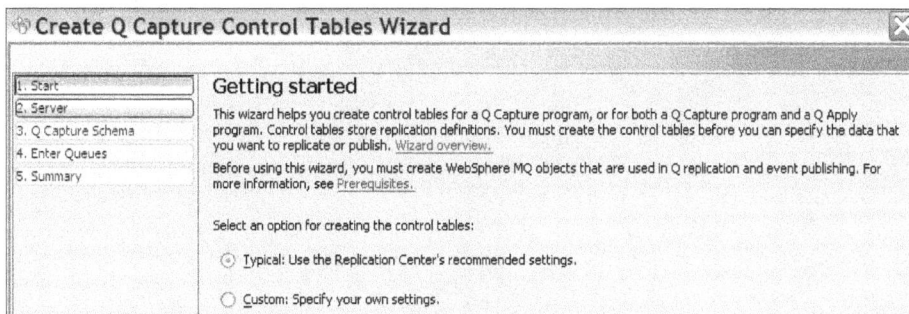

5. Accept the default radio button of **Typical: Use the Replication Center's recommended settings**.

    If we choose the **Custom** radio button, then we can specify the table space where the control tables will go, and so on.

6. Click **Next**.

7. Fill in the next screen as shown in the following screenshot. It is on this screen that we decide on which DB2 server we want to create the control tables in (DB2A), the **User ID** and **Password** that the Replication Center needs to access the database, and finally the **Q Capture schema** (ASN).

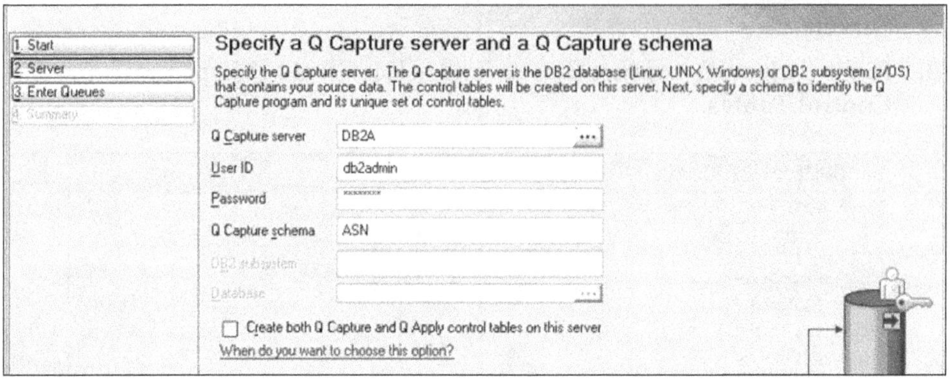

Note that if we are setting up multi-directional replication, then we can create the Q Capture and Q Apply control tables at the same time by ticking the box, which says **Create both Q Capture and Q Apply control tables on this server**.

8. Click **Next**.

9. On the next screen is where we specify the **Queue Manager** name (QMA), the **Restart queue** name (CAPA.RESTARTQ), and the **Administration queue** name (CAPA.ADMINQ).

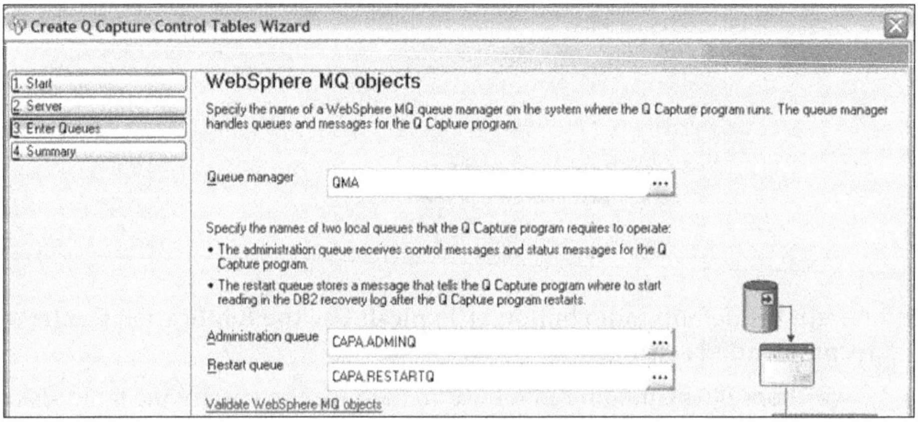

10. Click on **Next**.

This brings up the **Summary** screen:

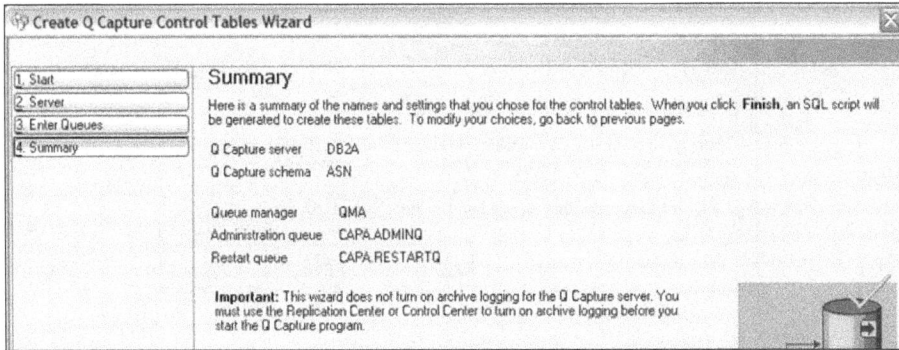

11. Click **Finish**.

12. This takes us to the **Run Now or Save SQL** screen from where we click on **OK** and go through the process to run the SQL.

To drop the Q Capture control tables using the Replication Center, we need to navigate to the **Q Capture Servers** folder, right-click on the **Q Capture schema** that is to be dropped and select **Drop**.

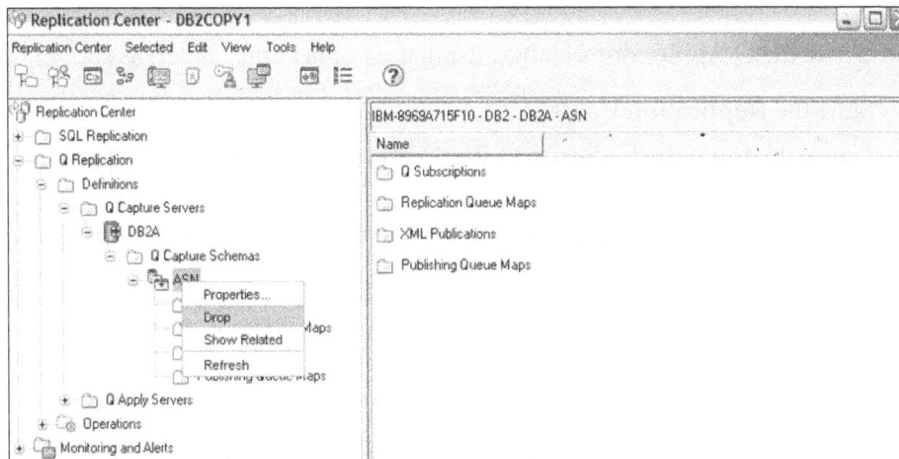

We need to decide if we want to drop the table spaces that are used by these control tables:

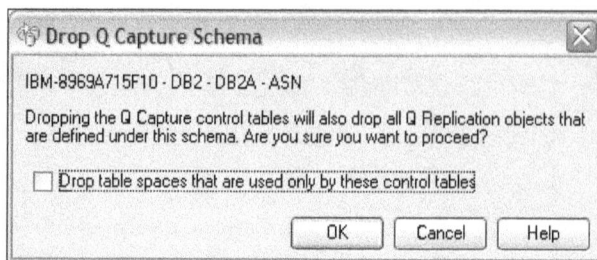

13. And then click **OK**.

To create/drop the Q Capture control tables using an ASNCLP command, see the *Common Q replication tasks – To create/drop Q Capture control tables on DB2A* section of *Chapter 5, The ASNCLP Command Interface*.

Create/drop the Q Apply control tables

To create the Q Apply control tables in database DB2B, we only need to specify the schema (ASN) and a Queue Manager (QMB).

We can create the Q Apply control tables using the Replication Center, as shown next:

1. Start the **Replication Center**.

2. Navigate down the folders to **Q Replication | Definitions | Q Apply Servers**.

3. Right-click on **Q Apply Servers** and select **Create Q Apply Control Tables**.

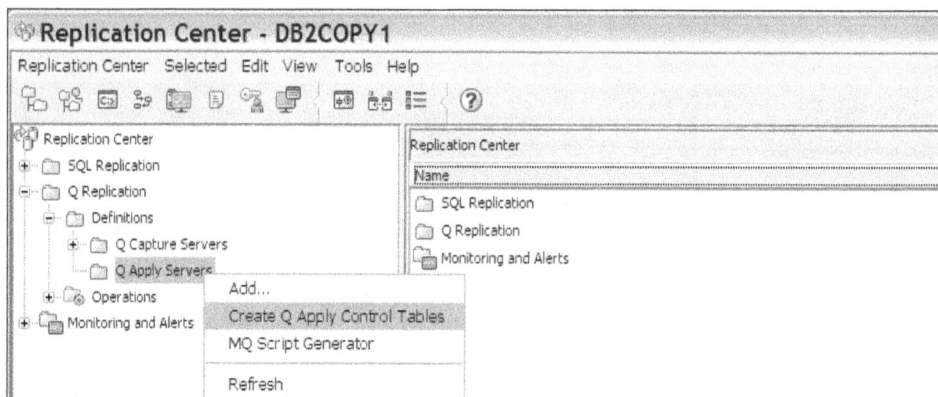

4. Fill in the next screen as shown in the following screenshot. It is on this screen that we decide on which DB2 server we want to create the control tables (DB2B), the **User ID** and **Password** that the **Replication Center** needs to access the database and the **Q Apply schema** (ASN):

5. On the third screen we need to specify the **Queue Manager** (QMB) that resides where the Q Apply control server is:

That is all we have to specify—note that we did not have to specify any queue names.

To drop the Q Apply control tables using the Replication Center, follow the instructions in the previous section about dropping the Q Capture control tables.

To create/drop the Q Apply control tables using ASNCLP commands refer to the *Common Q replication tasks – To create/drop Q Capture control tables on DB2B* section of *Chapter 5*.

Registering a table for Q replication

For a table to participate in replication, it needs to have its DATA CAPTURE CHANGES flag set. Note that one of the effects of setting this flag is that the space required for DB2 logging will increase.

The flag is set automatically when a Q subscription is created or it can be set manually using the ALTER TABLE command shown next:

```
db2 ALTER TABLE <table-name> DATA CAPTURE changes
```

The DATA CAPTURE options are:

```
    +-DATA CAPTURE--+-NONE---------------------------------+---
                    '-CHANGES--+------------------------+-'
                               '-INCLUDE LONGVAR COLUMNS-'
```

The INCLUDE LONGVAR COLUMNS parameter allows data replication utilities to capture changes made to LONG VARCHAR and LONG VARGRAPHIC columns. The clause may be specified for tables that do not have any LONG VARCHAR or LONG VARGRAPHIC columns since it is possible to ALTER the table at a later date to include such columns.

We can check if the flag has been set for a table using the following query:

```
db2 "SELECT SUBSTR(tabschema,1,10) AS tabschema, SUBSTR(tabname,1,20) AS
tabname, datacapture FROM syscat.tables"
```

Where DATACAPTURE can take one of the following values:

> L = Table participates in data replication, including replication of LONG VAR-CHAR and LONG VARGRAPHIC columns.
>
> N = Table does not participate in data replication.
>
> Y = Table participates in data replication, excluding replication of LONG VAR-CHAR and LONG VARGRAPHIC columns.

Managing Queue Maps

In this section, we look at creating, altering, and dropping Replication/Publication Queue Maps.

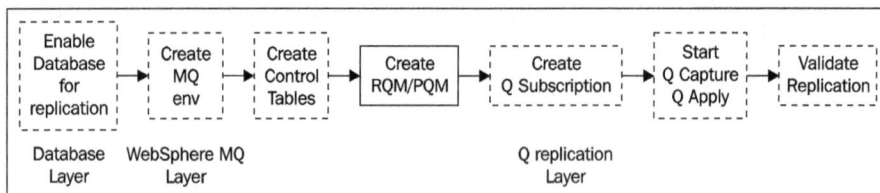

We will show examples using the Replication Center and `ASNCLP` commands.

Creating a Queue Map

The following screenshots show how to create a **Replication Queue Map** using the
Replication Center.

1. From the **Q Capture Schemas** folder, navigate down through the **Q Capture
Schema** (`ASN` in our example), right-click on the **Replication Queue Maps**
folder, and click on **Create**.

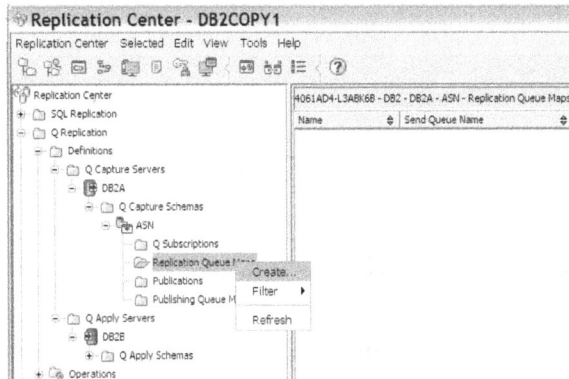

This takes us to the **Create Replication Queue** Map screen, as shown next.

2. Fill out the required information in the **General** tab, namely the Q Apply
server name and schema, the names of the Send, Receive, and Administration
queues, and the name of the Replication Queue Map:

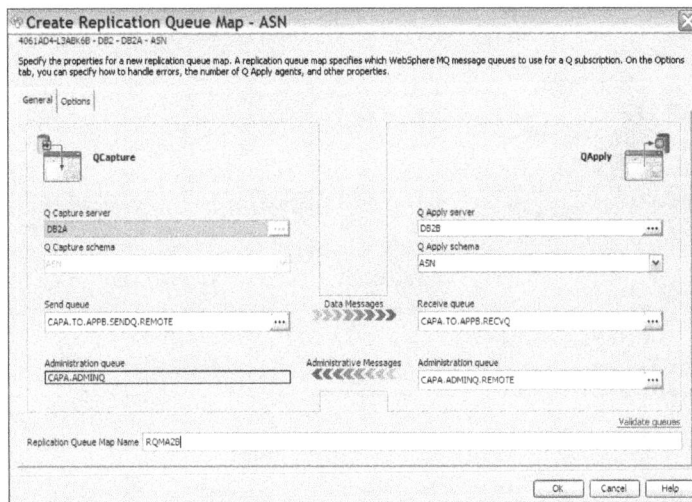

1. The **Options** tab allows us to change the values as shown. Of particular interest is the maximum message length value, and what option we want for handling errors:

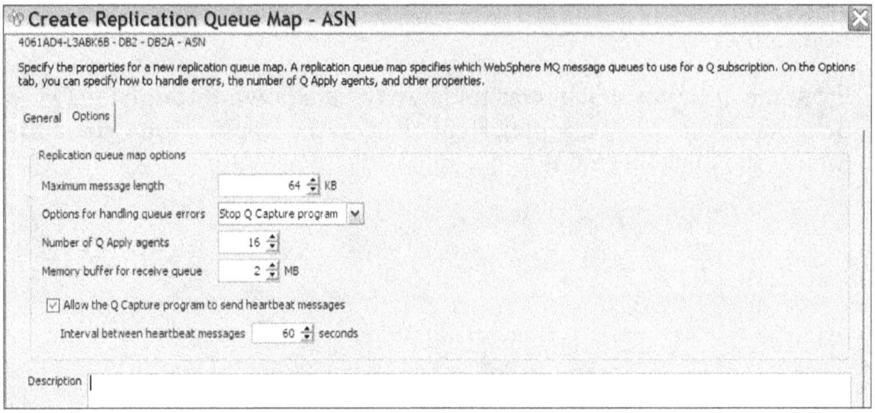

Click on **OK** to generate the SQL script, and then we can decide whether to run the script now or save it.

2. To create a **Publication Queue Map**, navigate to the **Publishing Queue Map** folder, right-click it and select **Create**, as shown next:

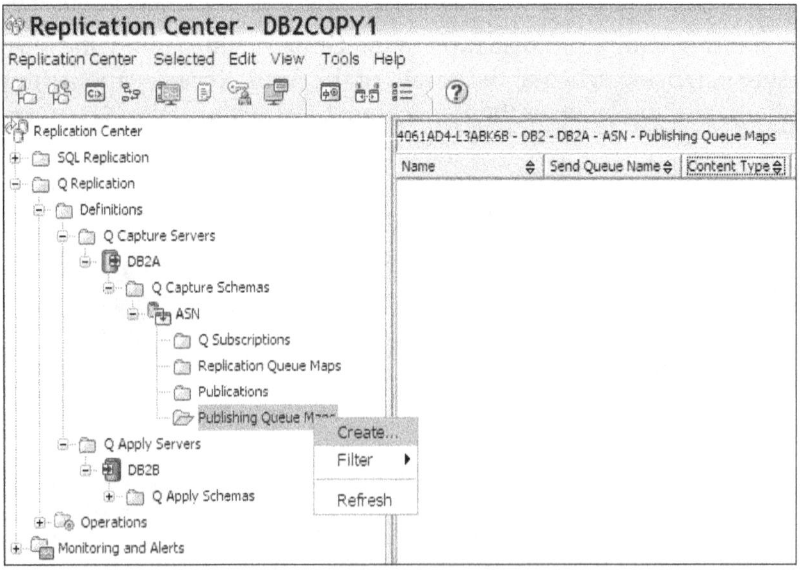

3. The **General** tab is where we give the Publication Queue Map a name, and the **Properties** tab is where we specify the Send Queue name, and the format of the published message:

Click **OK** to generate the SQL script, and then we can decide whether to run the script now or save it.

To create a Replication Queue Map using ASNCLP commands refer to the *Queue Map maintenance – To create a Replication Queue Map* section of *Chapter 5*.

Altering a Replication Queue Map

To alter a Replication Queue Map using the **Replication Center**, right click on it in the **Replication Queue Maps** folder, and click on **Properties**.

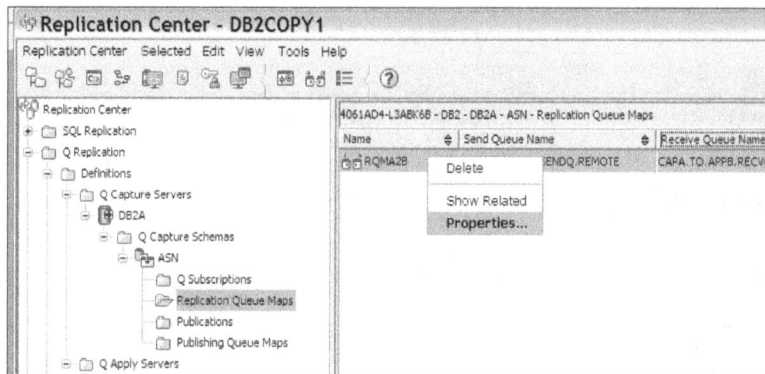

If any values are changed in the **Properties** tab, then an UPDATE SQL statement to the IBMQREP_SENDQUEUES table will be generated, which can be run now or saved for running later.

To alter a Replication Queue Map using ASNCLP commands refer to the *Queue Map maintenance – To alter a Replication Queue Map* section of *Chapter 5*.

Drop/delete a Queue Map

To drop a Replication Queue Map using the **Replication Center**, right-click on the RQM to be dropped in the **Replication Queue Maps** folder, and click on **Delete**.

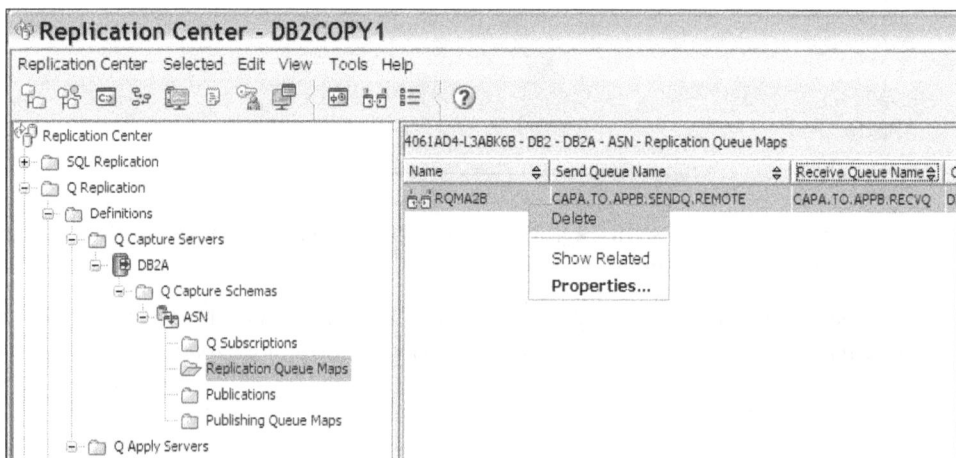

Note that an RQM cannot be dropped if it is being used by a Q subscription.

To drop an RQM using ASNCLP commands see the *Queue Map maintenance – To drop a Queue Map* section of *Chapter 5*.

To drop a Publication Queue Map, follow these instructions, but use the **Publications Queue Maps** folder.

Listing the RQM for a Receive Queue

The Q Apply IBMQREP_RECVQUEUES control table holds information about Receive Queues and Replication Queue Maps. The following query lists the RQMs and Receive Queues:

```
db2 "SELECT SUBSTR(repqmapname,1,20) AS rqm, SUBSTR(recvq,1,20) AS recvq
FROM asn.ibmqrep_recvqueues"
    RQM                     RECVQ
    -------------------- --------------------
    RQMA2B                  CAPA.TO.APPB.RECVQ
```

Q subscription maintenance

In this section, we cover how to create, alter, and drop a Q subscription.

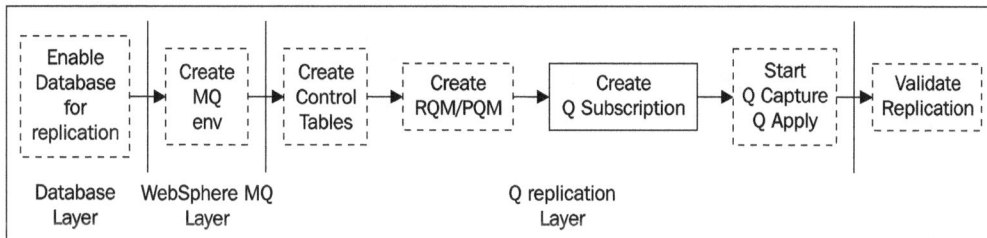

We will show examples using the Replication Center and ASNCLP commands.

Creating a Q subscription

To create a Q subscription using the **Replication Center**, right-click on the **Q Subscriptions** folder and click on **Create**:

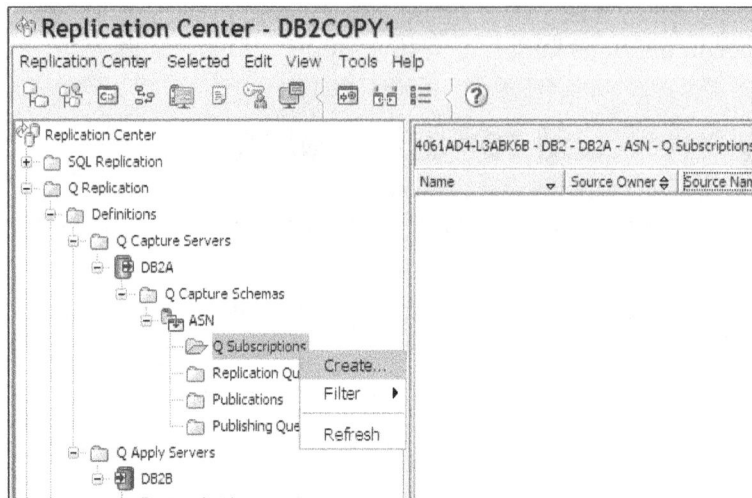

This takes us through a series of 10 screens to create the Q subscription. Here's **Screen 1**, Subscriptions:

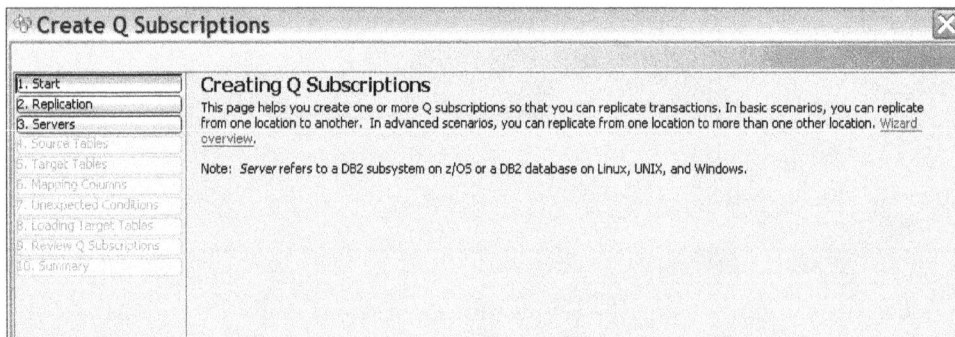

Screen 2, Replication: This is where we decide what type of replication we want to perform (that is, unidirectional, bidirectional, and so on). The GUI is clever, it will only present us with "valid" options—all other options being grayed out. What is meant by a "valid" option? Well, if we have the Q capture control tables defined on one server and the Q Apply control tables defined on a second server then the only type of replication that can be set up between the servers is unidirectional, and the Replication Center will thus only let us select unidirectional as the replication option.

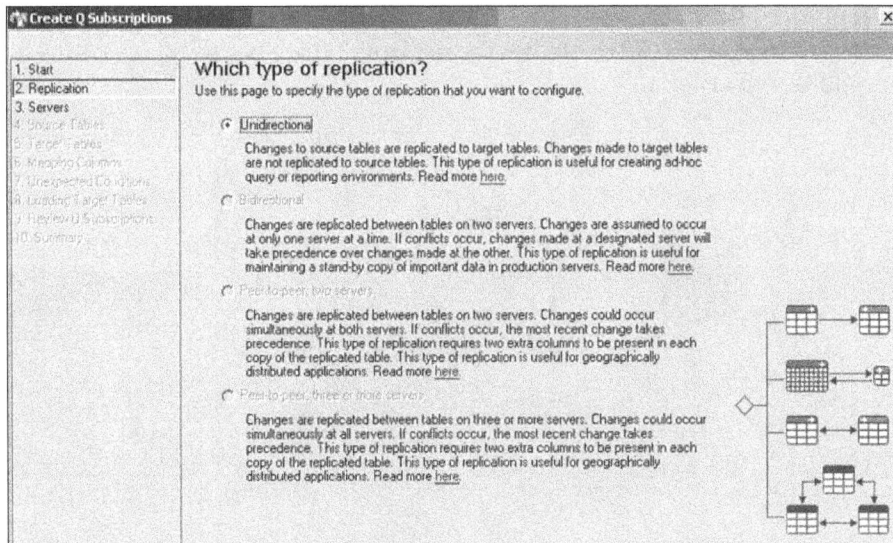

Screen 3, Servers: It is here that we tell the Replication Center what the source and target servers are and we can also specify the Replication Queue Map name. In our example, we have called it RQMA2B. If we have not created a Replication Queue Map before this point, then the Replication Center will take us through that process from this screen.

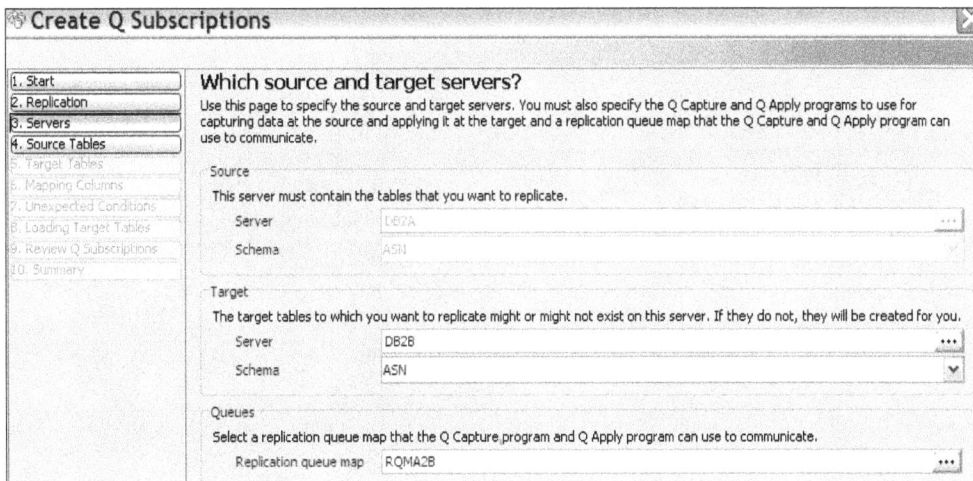

Screen 4, Source tables: This is where we select the source tables to be replicated from a drop-down menu. We can filter the list from which we select by setting appropriate search criteria.

Select Source Tables

Search criteria

Column	Comparison	Values
Schema	NOT LIKE	SYS%
Name	NOT LIKE	IBM%
Schema	LIKE	

⦿ Meet all conditions   ○ Meet any conditions

[Retrieve]   [Count]

Name	Schema	Table space	Comment	In
T1	ERIC	USERSPACE1		
T2	ERIC	USERSPACE1		
T3	ERIC	USERSPACE1		

Screen 5, Target: This is where we specify what type of target we want, for example a table, a stored procedure or a CCD table. If we specify a table as the target, then we can specify if that table already exists or if we want Q Apply to create it, and if so, we can give it a different schema, name, and table space from the source table.

Create Q Subscriptions

1. Start	**Which target?**
2. Replication	Use this page to specify the target for your Q subscription.
3. Servers	
4. Source Tables	⦿ Use a table
5. Target	○ Use a stored procedure
6. Rows and Columns	Use a stored procedure as your target if you want to transform data before applying it to a table. Your stored procedure must be registered with DB2 on the Q Apply server. Learn more about using stored procedures as targets here.
7. Unexpected Conditions	○ Use a consistent-change-data (CCD) table
8. Loading the Target Table	Use a CCD table to store source table changes for auditing or distribution. Learn more about using CCD tables here.
9. Review Q Subscriptions	
10. Summary	

Target properties

⦿ New table   ○ Existing table

Table owner	ERIC
Table name	T1
Table columns	Same as source table ...
Table space	TST1 (New) ...

As this point we can also sub select the columns to be replicated (see next screen).

Screen 6, Rows and columns: It is on this screen that we can filter the columns and rows that we want to replicate. Note that we can only filter in unidirectional replication, see the *Q replication filtering and transformation – Filtering rows/columns* section of *Chapter 1, Q Replication Overview*. The eclipse expansion button on the **Columns** line allows us to select only certain columns to replicate. The expansion button eclipse on the **Rows** line allows us to write a WHERE clause to filter the rows to be replicated. This WHERE clause must contain the keyword WHERE and then the condition, with source table columns prefixed with a colon (:), for example:

```
WHERE :c1 > 1000
```

We can reference columns in other tables in the WHERE clause, in which case we do not have to prefix those columns with a colon. In the following example, the val column of table tab_other is not prefixed with a colon:

```
WHERE :c1 > 1000 AND :c2 > (SELECT SUM(val) FROM tab_other)
```

It is also on this screen that we can specify whether or not to replicate deletes from the source table (the default is YES).

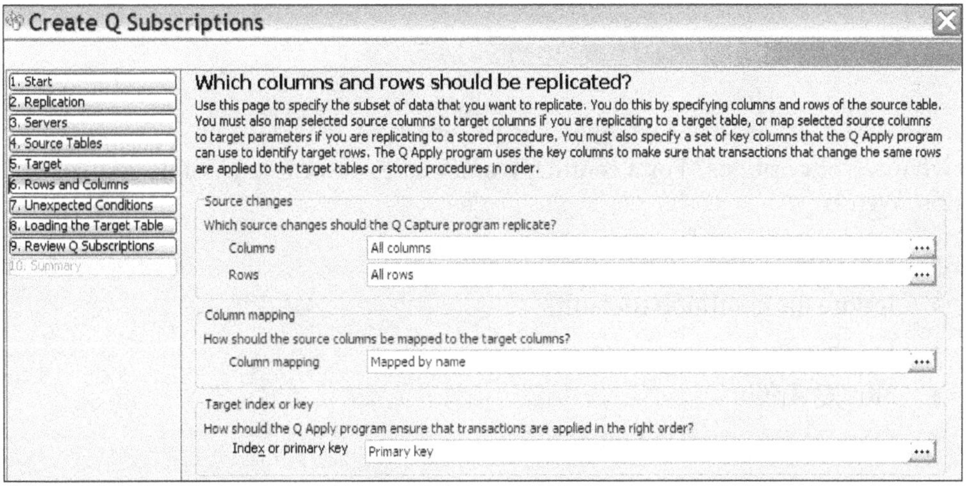

Screen 7, Unexpected conditions: It is on this screen that we tell Q Apply how to react to two different types of unexpected conditions: a conflict and an error. A conflict is a problem with the data in the target table (the row that Q Apply is trying to process does not exist/already exists). An error is basically all other problems.

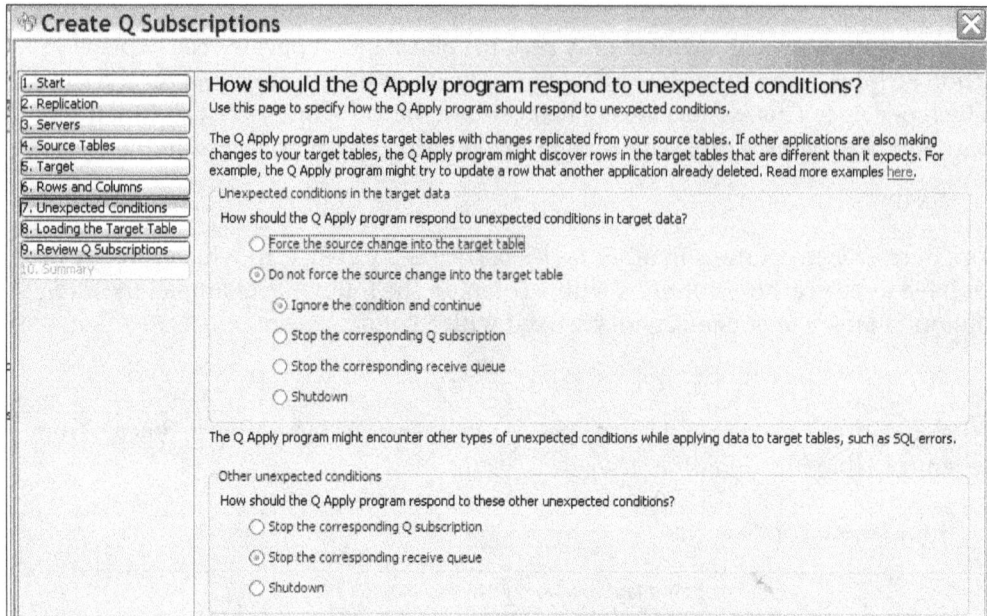

So what are our options? For a conflict, we can take one of five possible courses of action. We can:

- Force the source change into the target table
- Ignore the condition (default)
- Disable the Q subscription
- Stop Q Apply
- Stop reading from the queue

If we choose to force the source change into the target table, then we need to carefully plan for situations when this may happen. The default value does not really let us know that there is a problem. If we stop Q Apply, then that would be the easiest to pick up with any basic monitoring, however this would not be the best option if we have more than one active Q subscription. A similar argument applies to stopping the Receive Queue — we could have other Q subscriptions dependent on that Receive Queue. Stopping the Q subscription will only affect that one source/target table and may be the best option.

For an error we can take one of three possible courses of action. We can:

- Disable the Q subscription and notify Q Capture
- Stop reading from the Receive Queue (default)
- Stop Q Apply without applying the transaction

The default of stopping to read from the Receive Queue might not be the easiest condition to pick up with monitoring. Stopping Q Apply without applying the transaction means that we have to fix the original problem before starting Q Apply again.

Screen 8 — Loading the target table: It is on this screen that we tell Q Apply how we want to deal with loading the target table. We can:

- Let Q Apply choose the best method
- Perform a manual load
- Not perform av load

If we let Q Apply choose the best method, then it will choose between a LOAD FROM CURSOR, an EXPORT/LOAD, and an EXPORT/IMPORT. If we select this option, then we need to create a password file on the Q Apply server (see section *The password file*). We would perform a manual load if the source table was very large and it is quicker to perform an unload/load outside of Q replication (using IBM High Performance Unload). There are also situations where we do not want to perform a load of the target table at all.

Screen 9, Review Q subscriptions: This screen is displayed after the Replication Center has analyzed all the information we have inputted in the previous eight screens, and decides if the Q subscription is valid or not.

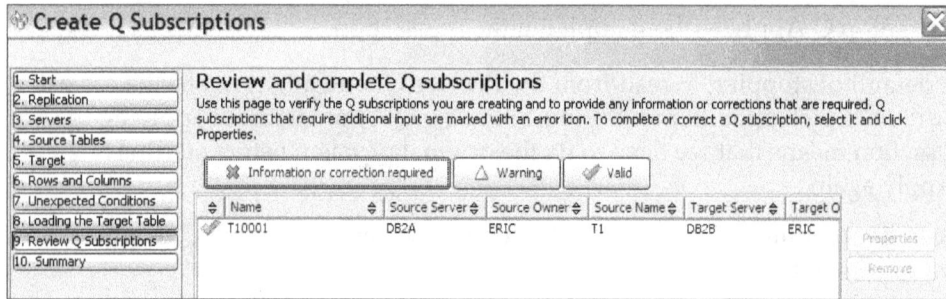

If the Q subscription is valid (green tick), then we can proceed to the final **Summary** screen. If we get a red cross against the Q subscription, then it means that there is a problem with the Q subscription and we can either go back through the screen or highlight the Q subscription and press the **Properties** button to review the information we have supplied. The third option is that we get a yellow triangle, which is a warning (perhaps a unique index has not been defined on the source table).

Click **Next** and then **Finish** to generate the SQL script, and then we can decide whether to run the script now or save it.

To create a Q subscription using ASNCLP commands, see the *Common Q replication tasks – To create Q subscriptions* section of *Chapter 5*.

Altering a Q subscription

To alter a Q subscription using the Replication Center, list out the current Q subscriptions by selecting the **Q subscriptions** folder, then right-clicking on the one to be altered, and selecting **Properties**:

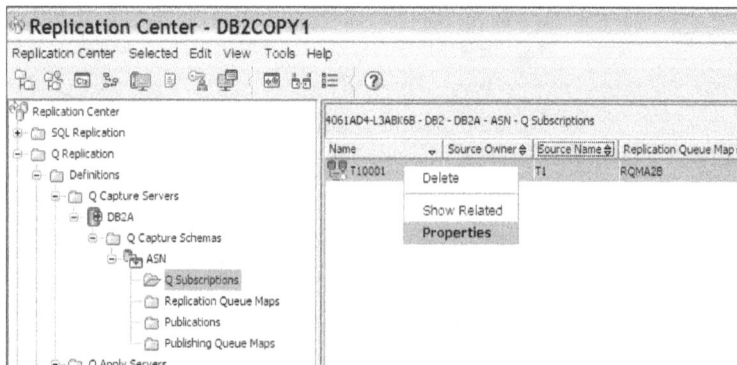

We can either run the script immediately or save it.

There are three possible methods to reinitialize a Q subscription using commands, depending on whether we want to instigate a load of the target table or not. We can:

- **Stop and start Q Capture**: We stop and start Q Capture using the following commands:

  ```
  $ asnqccmd CAPTURE_SERVER=db2a STOP
  
  $ asnqcap CAPTURE_SERVER=db2a STARTMODE=warmsi
  ```

  This will instigate a new load of the target table.

- **Re-initialize Q Capture to pick up the new definitions using the** asnqccmd **command with the reinit option**: We can re-initialize Q Capture to pick up the new definitions using the asnqccmd command with the **reinit** option. This is a useful option if we have changed many Q subscriptions and want all of them picked up at once. This command will not instigate a new load of the target tables.

  ```
  $ asnqccmd CAPTURE_SERVER=db2a REINIT
  ```

- **Issue a** CAPSTART **signal**: You can insert a CAPSTART signal or use an ASNCLP command.

This will instigate a new load of the target table.

From CLP-A, issue:

```
db2 "INSERT INTO asn.ibmqrep_signal(signal_time, signal_type, signal_
subtype, signal_input_in, signal_state) VALUES (current timestamp, 'CMD',
'CAPSTART', 'T10001','P')"
```

Check in the Q Capture log file (DB2.DB2A.ASN.QCAP.log) that the signal has been received and processed:

```
2006-02-13-20.28.01.114000 <subMgr::handleSignal> ASN7019I  "Q
Capture" : "ASN" : "WorkerThread" : "CAPSTART" signal was received and
will be processed.
2006-02-13-20.28.06.632000 <subMgr::handleSignal> ASN7019I  "Q
Capture" : "ASN" : "WorkerThread" : "P2PSPOOLING" signal was received
and will be processed.
2006-02-13-20.28.06.632000 <subMgr::handleP2PSPOOLING> ASN7017I  "Q
Capture" : "ASN" : "WorkerThread" : The target table "HELEN.T3" is
ready to be loaded from source table "HEATHER.T3" for XML publication
or Q subscription "T30001".
```

Checking the status of a Q subscription

We can check whether a Q subscription is active or not, by examining the
IBMQREP_SUBS table.

From CLP-A, issue:

```
db2 "SELECT SUBSTR(subname,1,10) AS subname, state AS s, state_time FROM
asn.ibmqrep_subs"
```

This query will show the state of the Q subscription, which should be A for active
(the different states are explained in the *The control tables – The Q Capture control tables*
section, under the IBMQREP_SUBS table in *Chapter 3, The DB2 Database Layer*).

Stopping a Q subscription

We can stop a Q subscription (that is stop the table data being replicated) using the
Replication Center, as shown in the following screenshot. Navigate through the
Operations folder to the **Q Capture Servers** folder. Right-click on the server name,
and select **Manage | Q subscriptions**:

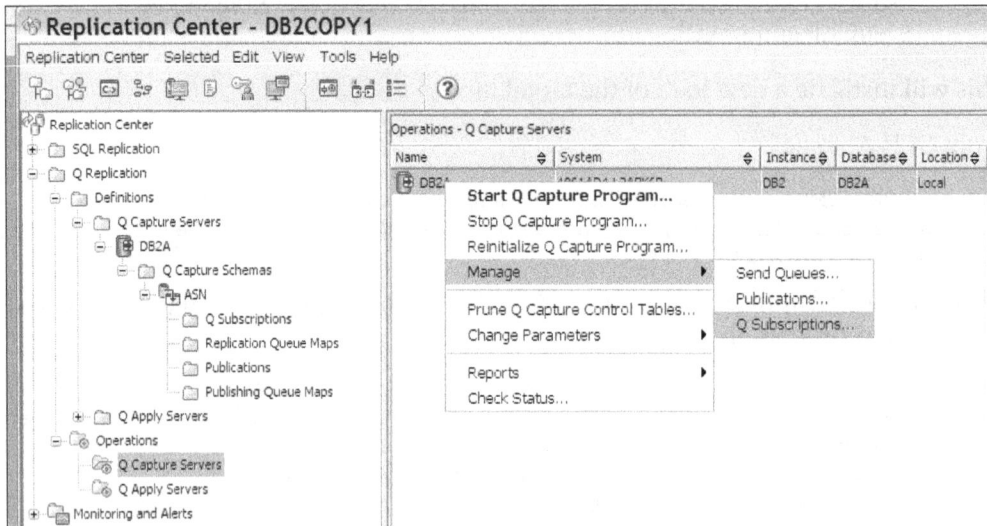

Highlight the Q subscription to be stopped and click the **Stop** button:

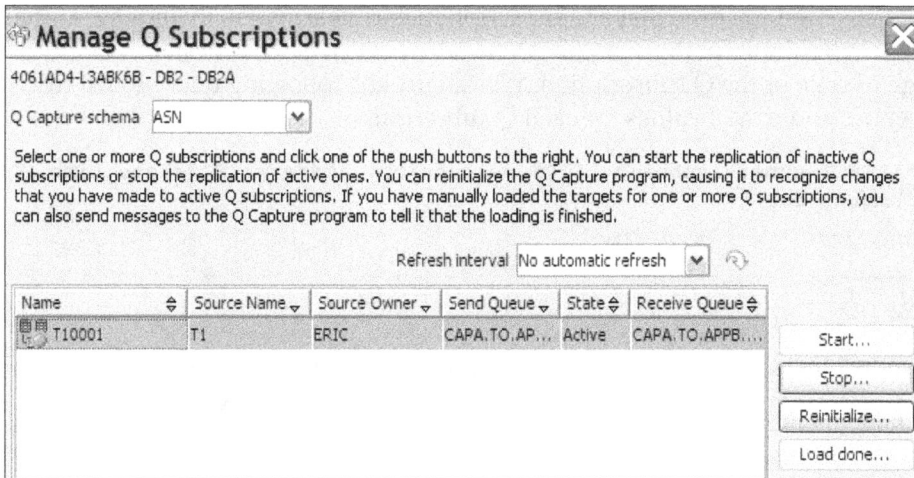

This generates the following SQL script:

```
INSERT INTO ASN.IBMQREP_SIGNAL
  (signal_type, signal_subtype, signal_input_in)
  VALUES ('CMD', 'CAPSTOP', 'T10001');
```

To stop a Q subscription using ASNCLP commands, see the *Q subscription maintenance – To stop a Q subscription* section of *Chapter 5*.

Determining when a Q subscription became inactive

When a Q subscription becomes inactive the fact is recorded in the Q Capture log:

```
2010-01-10-15.59.02.531000 <subMgr::handleSignal> ASN7019I  "Q
Capture" : "ASN" : "WorkerThread" : "CAPSTOP" signal was received and
will be processed.
2010-01-10-15.59.02.546000 <subMgr::handleCAPSTOP> ASN7013I  "Q
Capture" : "ASN" : "WorkerThread" : The publication or Q subscription
"TAB1" was deactivated.
2010-01-10-15.59.02.937000 <updateSubDbState> ASN7133I  "Q Capture"
:"ASN" : "WorkerThread" : The publication or Q subscription "TAB1" was
stopped.
```

We can also find the time that a Q subscription was deactivated by looking at the STATE_TIME column in the IBMQREP_SUBS table, which is the timestamp of the last change of state of the Q subscription. We can use the following query to list the STATETIME and STATE values for each Q subscription:

db2 "SELECT substr(subname,1,10) as subname, state as S, state_time FROM asn.ibmqrep_subs"

```
    SUBNAME     S STATE_TIME
    ---------- - -------------------------
    TAB1        I 2010-01-10-15.59.02.937000
```

This shows that Q subscription TAB1 was inactivated at the timestamp shown.

If we have the Replication Alert Monitor set up, then we could also look at the IBMSNAP_ALERTS table:

db2 "SELECT alert_time, alert_code FROM asn.ibmsnap_alerts"

And look for message ASN5157W.

Listing the attributes of a Q subscription

To list the attributes of a Q subscription use the queries in the *The control tables-The Q Capture control tables* section of *Chapter 3, The DB2 Database Layer,* under the entry for IBMQREP_SUBS.

Listing all Q subscriptions using a RQM

We can list all Q subscriptions and the Replication Queue Maps they use as follows:

db2 "SELECT SUBSTR(a.subname,1,10) AS subname, SUBSTR (b.PUBQMAPNAME,1,20) AS RepQueMap FROM asn.ibmqrep_subs A, asn.ibmqrep_sendqueues B WHERE a.sendq = b.sendq "

```
    SUBNAME     REPQUEMAP
    ---------- --------------------
    TAB1        RQMA2B
```

Specifying a table as the initial load source

In unidirectional replication, the target table will be loaded from the source table.

In multi-directional replication, we need to specify which table will be used to initially load the other table(s). If we are using ASNCLP scripts, then the option is selected when we specify a value for the `has load phase` parameter, which is discussed in the *To create Q subscriptions – Q subscription for bidirectional replication* section of *Chapter 5*.

So consider the situation where we have a table called T1 on DB2A and we want to make this the source for the initial load. This is the scenario we demonstrate in the *Bidirectional replication* section of *Appendix A*, and the content file for the Q subscription is `SYSA_contbidi.txt`. In the `options` section of the content file we have simply specified:

```
set subgroup "TABT1";

set server multidir to db "DB2A";
set server multidir to db "DB2B";

set multidir schema "DB2A".ASN;
set multidir schema "DB2B".ASN;

set connection SOURCE "DB2A".ASN
TARGET "DB2B".ASN replqmap "RQMA2B";

set connection SOURCE "DB2B".ASN
TARGET "DB2A".ASN replqmap "RQMB2A";

set tables("DB2A".ASN.ERIC.T1, "DB2B".ASN.FRED.T1);
create qsub subtype b;
```

This means we will pick up all the defaults:

allchanged rows=n	before values=n	error action=q
changed cols only=y	conflict action=k	
has load phase=i	conflict rule=i	

If we are setting up replication using the Replication Center, then we specify which sever should be used as the source for the initial load on screen 8, as shown next:

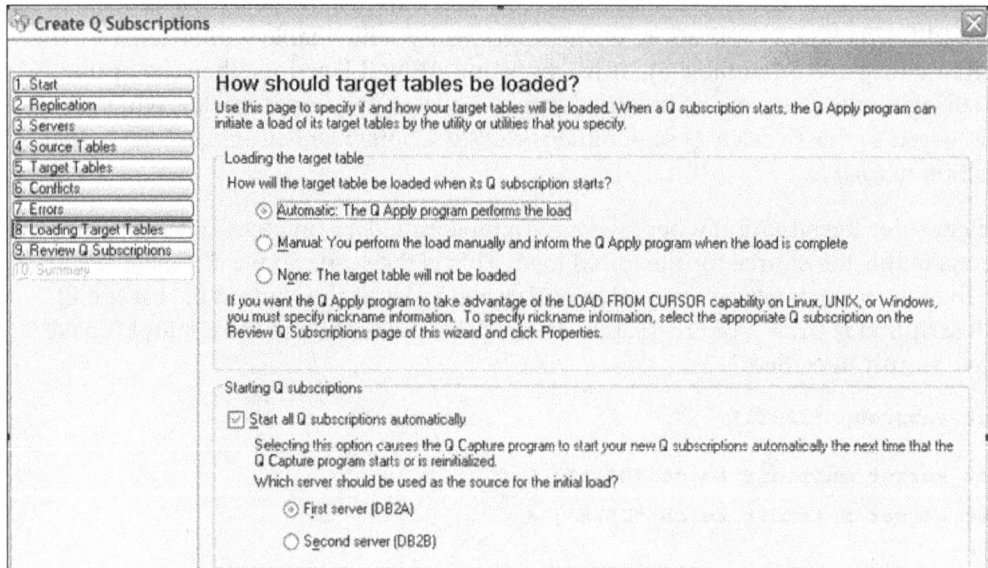

To check what values we have, use the following query, which we run on each system:

```
db2 "SELECT SUBSTR(subname,1,10) AS subname, has_loadphase AS l, state AS
s, SUBSTR(target_server,1,6) AS trgsrv, SUBSTR(source_name,1,10) AS src_
name, SUBSTR(target_name,1,10) AS targ_name, target_type FROM
asn.ibmqrep_subs"
```

For DB2A:

```
SUBNAME     L S TRGSRV SRC_NAME    TARG_NAME  TARGET_TYPE
---------- - - ------ ---------- ---------- -----------
T10001     I N DB2B   T1          T1                   1
```

The Q subscription called T10001 is defined on DB2A. The target server is DB2B — Q Apply on DB2B will do an initial load. The STATE ("S") of the Q subscription is "N" which means that the Q subscription or publication is new. The Q Capture program automatically activates this Q subscription or publication when the program is started or reinitialized.

For DB2B:

```
SUBNAME       L S TRGSRV SRC_NAME    TARG_NAME   TARGET_TYPE
----------    - - ------ ----------  ----------  -----------
T10002        I I DB2A   T1          T1                    1
```

The Q subscription called T10002 is defined on DB2B. The STATE ("S") of the Q subscription is "I" which means that the Q subscription or publication is inactive.

What this tells us is that if we take the defaults in the options section of the content file, then if the source table is populated on DB2A, then when Q Capture and Q Apply are started, the target table on DB2B is populated with the contents of the source table. It goes this way because the STATE ("S") on the Q subscription on DB2A is "N" and on DB2B it is "I".

Let's consider another situation. In the foreign key example, the *Conflict detection examples* section from *Appendix A*, where we have a table called DEPT on DB2A and we want to explicitly make this the source for the initial load. In the options section of the content definition file we would specify:

```
create qsub subtype b
from node db2a.asn

SOURCE
all changed rows y
has load phase I
TARGET
conflict rule A
conflict action I
error action s
load type 0
oksqlstates "000"
from node db2b.asn

SOURCE
all changed rows N
has load phase N
TARGET
conflict rule A
conflict action F
error action s
load type 0
oksqlstates "000";
```

On the second line, we are on DB2A and has load phase refers to DB2B and what will happen there.

For DB2A:

SUBNAME	L	S	TRGSRV	SRC_NAME	TARG_NAME	TARGET_TYPE
DEPT0001	I	N	DB2B	DEPT	DEPT	1
XEMP0001	I	N	DB2B	XEMP	XEMP	1

For DB2B:

SUBNAME	L	S	TRGSRV	SRC_NAME	TARG_NAME	TARGET_TYPE
DEPT0002	N	I	DB2A	DEPT	DEPT	1
XEMP0002	N	I	DB2A	XEMP	XEMP	1

The preceding options file will result in the target table on DB2B being loaded from the source table on DB2A.

If we had switched the has load phase from the aforementioned values of I/N to N/I so that the query returned:

For DB2A:

SUBNAME	L	S	TRGSRV	SRC_NAME	TARG_NAME	TARGET_TYPE
DEPT0001	N	N	DB2B	DEPT	DEPT	1
XEMP0001	N	N	DB2B	XEMP	XEMP	1

For DB2B:

SUBNAME	L	S	TRGSRV	SRC_NAME	TARG_NAME	TARGET_TYPE
DEPT0002	I	I	DB2A	DEPT	DEPT	1
XEMP0002	I	I	DB2A	XEMP	XEMP	1

And redefined our Q subscriptions, then when we start Q Capture and Q Apply, the target tables are not populated, but the source tables are not overwritten either (and this does not depend on the target tables being initially populated or not).

Source table maintenance

This section goes through some of the common Q replication source table maintenance tasks.

The following list summarizes the source table maintenance tasks and whether they are allowed in a Q replication scenario. Can we:

- **Add a column to a Q subscription?**: Yes, see the *To add a column to a Q subscription* section.

- **Remove a column from a replicated source table?**: No, see the *To remove a column from a replicated source table* section.

- **Alter the column attributes of a replicated source table?**: No, see the *To alter the column attributes of a replicated source table* section.

- **Perform an online** REORG **on the source table?**: Yes, see the *Performing a reorganization on the source table* section.

- **Perform a classic reorganization on the source table?**: No, see the *Performing a reorganization on the source table* section.

- **Perform a** RUNSTATS **on the source table?**: Yes, see the *Collecting statistics on the source table* section.

- **Perform a** LOAD **operation?**: It is possible, see the *Performing a load on the source table* section.

- **Perform an** IMPORT **operation?**: Yes, see the *Importing data into the source table* section.

Adding a column to a Q subscription

Why in the title to this section do we say "...to a Q subscription" and not "to a source table"? Remember that when a Q subscription was initially defined for unidirectional replication, we could have specified just a subset of the source columns and now we want to replicate one more column. On the other hand, we could want to add a column to the source table and want to ensure that we replicate that new column as well (in both unidirectional and multi-directional replication).

To demonstrate how to do this, let's use a unidirectional setup, as described in the *Unidirectional replication* section of *Appendix A*. Say we have an original source table called `ERIC.T1`, which is replicated using a Q subscription called `TAB1`, and we want to add a column named `c4` of type `CHAR(1)` to it.

From CLP-A, issue:

```
db2 "ALTER TABLE eric.t1 ADD COLUMN c4 CHAR(1) "
```

At this point, we have added a column to the source table but not the Q subscription. We can insert into the new table without any problems but note that any data added into the new column before the Q subscription is updated will either require a table reload or manual updates of the target table.

To inform Q Apply about the new column we can either use an ASNCLP command or use an SQL command to insert a row into the signal table. The ASNCLP command is of the form shown next:

```
ALTER ADD COLUMN

USING SIGNAL (c4)

QSUB TAB1

USING REPQMAP RQMA2B;
```

We can add more than one column at a time by adding a comma-separated list: `USING SIGNAL (c4,c5)`.

The signal command is of the form shown next (from CLP-A):

```
$ db2 "insert into ASN.IBMQREP_SIGNAL (SIGNAL_TIME, SIGNAL_TYPE, SIGNAL_
SUBTYPE, SIGNAL_INPUT_IN, SIGNAL_STATE ) values (CURRENT TIMESTAMP,
'CMD', 'ADDCOL', 'TAB1;C4', 'P')"
```

The `ADDCOL` parameter needs a Q subscription name and the name of the column we want to add.

> The parameter `'subname;column_name'` is case sensitive—even though double quotation marks are not used.

The new column in the target table will not have a default value—it will be `NULL`. If we want the new column to have a default value, then we need to update the target table manually.

If we are adding a column to a table with an active subscription, then the `ALTER TABLE` and the `ADDCOL` signal should be performed in the same transaction.

Removing a column from a replicated source table

There is no ASNCLP command to remove a column from a Q subscription. The procedure we have to follow is:

1. Stop the Q subscription for the table.
2. Drop the Q subscription for the table.
3. Alter the table on the source/target to remove the column.
4. Create a new Q subscription and perform a load (automatic/manual) onto the target system (if this is performed during a quiesced state, then no reload is required).

Altering the column attributes of a replicated source table

There is no method in Q replication to change the column attributes of a replicated table. The procedure we have to follow is the same as for removing a column, except in step 3 rather than altering the table to remove the column we alter the table to change a column's attribute.

Performing a reorganization on the source table

If we perform an inplace reorganization (`inplace reorg`) of the source table as follows:

```
db2 REORG TABLE eric.t1 INPLACE ALLOW WRITE ACCESS START
```

Then the changes to the table are logged, and will therefore be picked up by Q replication.

If we perform an offline reorganization (`classic reorg`) of the source table as follows:

```
db2 REORG TABLE eric.t1 ALLOW READ ACCESS
```

Then the changes to the table are not logged and will not be replicated.

In a **bidirectional** scenario, any reorganizations should specify ALLOW WRITE ACCESS if reorganizations are performed while tables are being updated, otherwise rows may be rejected if Q Apply cannot insert the record due to the reorganization restricting write access to the table.

Collecting statistics on the source table

Performing a RUNSTATS on the source table has no implications for Q replication.

Performing a load on the source table

This section is split into two—the first part discusses the situation, which existed prior to DB2 9.7 and the second section applies to DB2 9.7 and beyond.

So, prior to DB2 9.7, what happened if a LOAD operation was performed on the source table (not an initial load but a load during normal operations)? Also does it matter if we specified COPY YES or not on the LOAD operation? Here is a typical LOAD command:

```
LOAD FROM "C:\asnclp_qrep\book\SYSA_loaduni.txt"
OF DEL
METHOD P (1, 2, 3)
MESSAGES "C:\asnclp_qrep\book\msg_loaduni.txt"
INSERT INTO ERIC.T1 (C1, C2, C3)
COPY YES TO "c:\temp"
ALLOW READ ACCESS
```

If we perform a LOAD operation on the source table, then the load will complete, but the rows that have been loaded will not be replicated. A LOAD operation will not stop Q Capture or Q Apply, it will not generate any messages in the log files nor will it inactivate the Q subscription. In a multi-directional scenario, the table being loaded will be unavailable for write access while the load is taking place, so any Q Apply inserts will fail and will be written to the IBMQREP_EXCEPTIONS table.

If we have loaded rows into a source table and then at some point do a delete from <table> command, then the command will complete successfully on both sides, but on the non-load side there will be an entry in the IBMQREP_EXCEPTIONS table for each row that was loaded/deleted.

Note that the above discussion is valid irrespective of whether the LOAD was run with the COPY YES or COPY NO option.

Since DB2 9.7, Q replication has been able to handle loads being performed on the source table for the following types of replication: unidirectional, bidirectional, and peer-to-peer two-way (not three-way or above).

There is a new parameter in the create Q subscription command called CAPTURE_LOAD, whose default value is W, which means that Q Capture issues a warning message after the load completes. The other option for the parameter is R, which also forces Q Capture to issue a warning message, but then the Q subscription for the source table is stopped and started, thus prompting a load of the target table if one is specified for the Q subscription. Clearly if the source table is large, then the operational implications of performing such a refresh of the target table should be analyzed.

Importing data into the source table

It is possible to perform an IMPORT into a source table which is being replicated and because the IMPORT operation is logged, Q replication will handle it.

Adding a new source table to Q replication

We can add a new table to Q replication while Q Capture and Q Apply are running:

1. The first step is to create a Q subscription for the new table. See the *To create a Q subscription* section for details on how to create a Q subscription.

2. Once the Q subscription has been created, it needs to be activated. See the *To reinitialize a Q subscription* section for the available options.

3. Check the status of the Q subscription. See the *To check the status of a Q subscription* section.

Stop replicating (remove) a table

We remove a table from Q replication by stopping the Q subscription relating to that table, see the *To stop a Q subscription* section.

Administrative commands/tasks

Let's move on now from the setup phase to administering a running system.

There are a number of administrative commands, which cover tasks such as starting/stopping Q Capture and Q Apply and working with them once they have started. The commands are:

asnqcap	Start Q Capture
asnqccmd	Work with a running Q Capture
asnqapp	Start Q Apply
asnqacmd	Work with a running Q Apply
asnmon	Start a Replication Alert Monitor
asnmcmd	Work with a running Replication Alert Monitor
asnscrt	Create a DB2 replication service to start the replication programs (windows only)
asnslist	List DB2 replication services (windows only)
asnsdrop	Drop DB2 replication services (windows only)
asnpwd	Create and maintain password files
asntrc	Operate the replication trace facility
asntdiff	Compare data in source and target tables
asntrep	Repair differences between source and target tables
asnqmfmt	Format and view Q replication and event publishing messages.

The following tables show a list of common tasks for Q Capture, Q Apply, and monitoring respectively and what command to use:

Common administration tasks—Q Capture

If we want to...	Command
Start Q Capture and specify start up parameters.	asnqcap
Work with a running Q Capture:	asnqccmd
• Check/change parameter values	
• Prune the control tables	
• Check Q Capture status	
• Stop Q Capture	
• Reinitialize one or all Q subscriptions or XML publications	
• Reinitialize one Send Queue	

Common administration tasks — Q Apply

If we want to...	Command
Start Q Apply and specify start up parameters.	asnqapp
Work with a running Q Apply:	asnqacmd
• Check/change parameter values	
• Check Q Apply status	
• Prune the control tables	
• Stop Q Apply	
• Stop Q Apply reading from a queue	
• Start Q Apply reading from a queue	
• Reinitialize one Receive Queue	

Common administration tasks — Monitoring

If we want to...	Command
Start a Replication Alert Monitor and specify start up parameters.	asnmon
Work with a running Replication Alert Monitor:	asnmcmd
• Check/change parameter values	
• Check monitor status	
• Stop a monitor	
• Reinitialize a monitor	
Operate the Q replication Analyzer	asnqanalyze
Operate the replication trace facility	asntrc
Compare data in source and target tables	asntdiff
Repair differences between source and target tables	asntrep
Format and view WebSphere MQ messages that are used in Q replication	asnqmfmt

Before we look at working with Q Capture and Q Apply, let's cover viewing messages and retrieving queue information, because we will use both of these techniques later on when we work with Q Capture and Q Apply.

Viewing messages using asnqmfmt

We can use the asnqmfmt command to format and view messages that are used in Q replication and Event Publishing.

Note that for Event Publishing, we must run the asnqmfmt command from the directory that contains the mqcap.xsd schema definition file (the default location is SQLLIB/samples/repl/q).

The asnqmfmt command has many parameters (shown next), but the two required as a minimum are the queue name we want to view messages for and the Queue Manager name to which the queue belongs:

- queue_name: This parameter specifies the name of a WebSphere MQ queue whose messages we want to format, view, and optionally delete.

- queuemanagername: This parameter specifies the name of the WebSphere MQ Queue Manager where the queue is defined.

- ofilepath_name: This parameter specifies the name of the file that contains the formatted output. If the -o parameter is not specified, the formatted messages will be written to standard output (stdout). By default, the file is created in the directory from which the asnqmfmt command was invoked. We can change the directory by specifying a path with the filename.

- hex: This parameter specifies that the messages are formatted in hexadecimal. If we do not specify this parameter, messages will be displayed according to their message format type, either compact or XML.

- lnumber: This parameter specifies the number of messages that we want to format.

- delmsg: This parameter specifies that the messages will be deleted from the queue after they are formatted.

- mqmd: This parameter specifies that we want to view the WebSphere MQ message descriptor for each message that is formatted.

- oencoutput_encoding_name: This parameter specifies a code page to be used for formatting the messages. If we do not specify this parameter, messages will be formatted in the default code page for the operating system where the command is invoked.

The following sections will look at a couple of examples.

Retrieving Q Capture Restart Queue information

If we are going to start Q Capture from a point in the DB2 log, as described in the *Starting Q Capture from a point in the DB2 log* section, then we need to find the `qRestartMsg.restartLSN` and `qRestartMsg.lastCommitSEQ` values from the Restart Queue. If we use our unidirectional example (*Unidirectional replication* from *Appendix A*), where we have a Restart Queue name of `CAPA.RESTARTQ` and a Queue Manager name of `QMA`, then the command will be:

```
$ asnqmfmt CAPA.RESTARTQ   QMA
```

ASN0585I "AsnQMFmt" : "N/A" : "Initial" : The program successfully loaded the WebSphere MQ library "mqm.dll". Environment variable ASNUSEMQCLIENT is set to "".

**** Message number: 1

**** Message size: 364

  qRestartMsg for MAINLINE log reader.

  qRestartMsg.capServer : DB2A

  qRestartMsg.capSchema : ASN

  qRestartMsg.qRestartsgSize : 364

  qRestartMsg.freeNodeSpace : 0

  Number of partition at restart: 1

  qRestartMsg.nodeId: 0

  qRestartMsg.restartLSN: 0000:0000:0000:023b:35f8

  qRestartMsg.lastCommitSEQ: 4614:f4b1:0000:0001:0000

  qRestartMsg.lastCommitTime: 2007-04-05-14.08.01.000001

  qRestartMsg.reuseSEQ: 0000:0000:0000:0000:0000

  qRestartMsg.reuseTime: 2007-04-05-13.55.31

  Number of send queues at restart: 1

  [0] sendq name: CAPA.TO.APPB.SENDQ.REMOTE

      sendq activation time: 1175777731

      sendq next msg seq no: 0000000000000000000000000000003c3

We can see the values for `qRestartMsg.restartLSN` and `qRestartMsg.lastCommitSEQ`.

If we do not know the Restart Queue name, we can find it by using the following query:

```
db2 "SELECT SUBSTR(qmgr,1,10) AS qmgr, SUBSTR(restartq,1,20) AS restartq
FROM asn.ibmqrep_capparms "
```

```
QMGR          RESTARTQ
----------    --------------------
QMA           CAPA.RESTARTQ
```

Q Capture and Q Apply administration

In this section, we look at Q Capture and Q Apply administration.

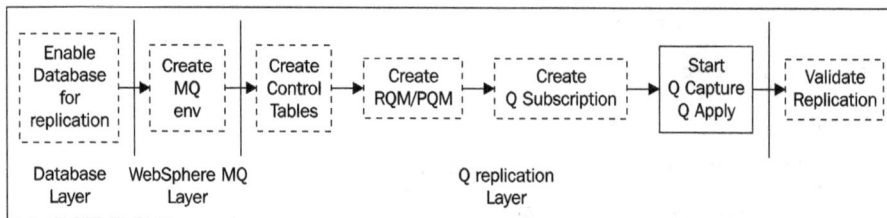

Q Capture and Q Apply can be administered from the Replication Center or from the command line. In this section, we will focus on the latter.

> Because of the asynchronous nature of Q replication, it does not matter in which order we **WARM** start/stop Q Capture and Q Apply. However, in multi-directional replication, if we **COLD** start, then the start order is important. If we are cold starting Q Capture, then all the Q Captures need to be started, up, and running before starting any of the Q Applys.

From the list of commands in the *Administrative commands/tasks* section:

- The two commands used with Q Capture are: asnqcap and asnqccmd.
- The two commands used with Q Apply are: asnqapp and asnqacmd.

Before we look at the commands we need to cover the Q Capture and Q Apply logs.

The Q Capture/Q Apply log names are made up of the following components:

- The instance name
- The Q Capture database server name
- The control table schema
- A label (QCAP.LOG for Q Capture or QAPP.LOG for Q Apply)

So for Q Capture with its control tables in the DB2A database and a schema of ASN in the DB2 instance, the log name will be: db2.DB2A.ASN.QCAP.log. The Q Capture and Q Apply logs get written (as default) to the directory where the programs were started, or to the directory pointed to by the CAPTURE_PATH and APPLY_PATH start up parameters.

The log files do not have to be recreated—if the log files do not exist when Q Capture and Q Apply need to write to them, then they will be created.

To stop these log files becoming too large and unwieldy, a job can be set up to rename the log files at a regular interval, but Q Capture and Q Apply need to be down before the logs can be renamed.

If we are experiencing problems with Q Capture or Q Apply, then we can start both programs in "debug" mode by appending DEBUG=Y to each start command.

Q Capture administration

Let's quickly recap the major tasks that Q Capture performs:

- To "read" the DB2 log, and put committed transactions onto its Send Queue
- To keep track of what has been processed
- Initiates pruning of the control tables

Starting Q Capture

The asnqcap command is used to start Q Capture and has numerous parameters, discussed next. To issue the command we need to be either DBADM or SYSADM for the database and have write authority on the directory where Q Capture will write its log (c:\temp in our scenario). The command is:

```
$ asnqcap [<parameter>=<value> ...]
```

The parameters are:

Parameter	Description
ADD_PARTITION=Y|N	Determines whether Q Capture starts reading the log file for partitions that were added since the last time Q Capture was restarted.
AUTOSTOP=Y|N	Terminate Q Capture after hitting end of log.
CAPTURE_PATH=	Location of Q Capture log files.

Parameter	Description
`CAPTURE_SCHEMA=`	Name of schema used to identify Q Capture.
`CAPTURE_SERVER=`	Name of the Q Capture control server (that is, the source database).
`COMMIT_INTERVAL=n│500`	Milliseconds between commits to WebSphere MQ.
`IGNORE_TRANSID=transaction_ID`	Specifies that Q Capture ignores the transaction that is identified by `transaction_ID`. The transactions are not replicated or published (97).
`LOB_SEND_OPTION=I/S`	Specifies whether Q Capture sends LOB values inlined (`I`) within a transaction message, or in a separate message (`S`) (97).
`LOGRDBUFSZ=n│256`	Specifies the size of the buffer that Q Capture passes to DB2 when Q Capture retrieves log records. DB2 fills the buffer with available log records that Q Capture has not retrieved (97).
`LOGREUSE=Y│N`	Reuse or append messages to the log file.
`LOGSTDOUT=Y│N`	Send messages to standard output.
`LSN=formatted_lsn`	Specifies the log sequence number at which Q Capture starts during a warm restart. When specifying the `LSN` parameter, we must also specify the `MAXCMTSEQ` parameter.
`MAXCMTSEQ=formatted_lsn`	The commit log record position of the last transaction that was successfully sent by Q Capture before shutdown. This log marker is internal to replication, subject to change, and is different for each type of database system. The marker is encoded as a 10-character string (97).
`MEMORY_LIMIT=n│32`	Maximum bytes for rebuilding transactions from log.
`MSG_PERSISTENCE=Y/N`	Specifies whether Q Capture writes persistent (logged) messages to WebSphere MQ queues (97).
`MONITOR_INTERVAL=n│300`	Seconds between inserts into the monitor table.

Parameter	Description
MONITOR_LIMIT=n|10080	Minutes before a monitor table row can be pruned.
PRUNE_INTERVAL=n|300	Seconds before Q Capture tries pruning control tables.
QFULL_NUM_RETRIES (RN)=N|30	Specifies the number of retries to attempt with a maximum of 1,000 retries. A value of 0 instructs Q Capture to stop whenever an MQPUT operation fails.
QFULL_RETRY_DELAY (RD)=N|250	Specifies how long in milliseconds Q Capture waits between MQPUT attempts. The allowed value range is 10 milliseconds to 3,600,000 milliseconds (1 hour). The default delay is 250 milliseconds or the value of the COMMIT_ INTERVAL parameter, whichever is less.
SIGNAL_LIMIT=n|10080	Minutes before a signal table row can be pruned.
SLEEP_INTERVAL=n|5000	Milliseconds to sleep after hitting end of log.
STARTALLQ=Y/N	Specifies whether Q Capture activates all Send Queues during startup. We can use this parameter to keep a disabled Send Queue inactive.
STARTMODE=[COLD|	Start reading at end of log, wait for CAPSTART.
WARMSI|: SI =	Switch Initially to cold start if no restart info.
WARMSA|: SA =	Switch Always to cold start if error.
WARMNS]: NS =	Never Switch to cold start.
TERM=Y|N	Terminate Q Capture if DB2 terminates.
TRACE_LIMIT=n|10080	Minutes before a trace table row can be pruned.

The default value for the SLEEP_TIME variable called is 5,000 milliseconds. Reducing this value to say 1,000 milliseconds may reduce the Q Capture latency.

The minimum information we need to provide to start Q Capture is the location of the Q Capture control tables (DB2A), but usually we also specify the Q Capture schema (which defaults to ASN), the Q Capture path (where the Q Capture logs gets written to) and how we want to start Q Capture. An example of the start command is shown below:

From CLP-A, issue:

```
asnqcap capture_server=DB2A capture_schema=ASN capture_path=c:\temp
startmode=WARMSI
```

The Q Capture startup parameters are stored in the IBMQREP_CAPPARMS control table, which can be queried using the SQL shown in the *The Q Capture control tables* section of *Chapter 3, The DB2 Database Layer*.

The Q Capture startup messages are shown in the *The Q replication layer – Monitoring Q Capture startup* section of *Chapter 7, Monitoring and Reporting*.

If we try and start Q Capture and it does not start and a log file is not created in the appropriate directory, then check that there is a valid InfoSphere Replication Server license, see the *Q replication constituent components* section of *Chapter 1, Q Replication Overview*.

We can start Q Capture from a known point in the DB2 log without having to do a full refresh of the target tables. See section *Starting Q Capture from a point in the DB2 log* for details on how to start Q Capture for a point in the DB2 log.

Now let's turn to the asnqccmd command, which is used to administer a running Q Capture and has numerous parameters and commands:

```
asnqccmd [<parameter>=<value> ...] [command]
```

The possible parameters are:

- CAPTURE_SCHEMA=: Name of schema used to identify Q Capture.
- CAPTURE_SERVER=: Name of the Q Capture control server.
- LOGSTDOUT=Y|N: Send messages to standard output.

The possible commands are:

- CHGPARMS: Change Q Capture's operational parameters.
- PRUNE: Prune Q Capture's control tables.
- QRYPARMS: Query Q Capture's operational parameters.
- REINIT: Reinitialize all Q Capture subscriptions.
- REINITQ: Reinitialize one of Q Capture's Send Queues.

- STATUS: Query the status of Q Capture's threads.
- STATUS SHOW DETAILS: Enhanced display status of Q Capture's threads.
- STOP: Stop Q Capture.

Stopping Q Capture

An example of the command to stop Q Capture is:

```
asnqccmd CAPTURE_SERVER=db2a STOP
```

Querying the status of Q Capture

We have a couple of ways of displaying/checking the status of Q Capture.

Firstly, we can check the parameters that Q Capture was actually started with, by using the qryparms option of the asnqccmd command:

From CLP-A, issue:

```
asnqccmd CAPTURE_SERVER=db2a QRYPARMS
```

Secondly, we can use the STATUS option of the asnqccmd command, which shows the status of the Q Capture threads:

```
asnqccmd CAPTURE_SERVER=db2a STATUS

ASN0600I  "AsnQCcmd" : "" : "Initial" : Program "mqpubcmd 9.7.1" is
starting.

ASN0520I  "AsnQCcmd" : "ASN" : "Initial" : The STATUS command
response: "HoldLThread" thread is in the "is resting" state.

ASN0520I  "AsnQCcmd" : "ASN" : "Initial" : The STATUS command
response: "AdminThread" thread is in the "is resting" state.

ASN0520I  "AsnQCcmd" : "ASN" : "Initial" : The STATUS command
response: "PruneThread" thread is in the "is resting" state.

ASN0520I  "AsnQCcmd" : "ASN" : "Initial" : The STATUS command
response: "WorkerThread" thread is in the "is doing work" state.
```

We can also use the STATUS SHOW DETAILS option. This gives a more detailed report about Q Capture status, with the following information:

- Whether Q Capture is running.
- The time that has elapsed since the program started.

- The location of the Q Capture diagnostic log.
- The number of active Q subscriptions.
- The value of the CURRENT_LOG_TIME and CURRENT_MEMORY. These values may be newer than what is inserted into the IBMQREP_CAPMON control table.
- The logical log sequence number of the last transaction that Q Capture published to a Send Queue.
- The amount of memory in megabytes that Q Capture used during the latest monitor interval to build transactions from log records.

For Linux, UNIX, and Windows only:

- The path to DB2 log files
- The oldest DB2 log file needed for a Q Capture restart
- The oldest DB2 log file captured

The command to check on the status of Q Capture is shown next (which takes a couple of seconds to run):

asnqccmd CAPTURE_SERVER=db2a STATUS SHOW DETAILS

```
2009-11-06-13.27.07.250000 ASN0600I  "AsnQCcmd" : "" : "Initial" :
Program "mqpubcmd 9.7.4" is starting.

2009-11-06-13.27.07.437000 ASN0592I  "AsnQCcmd" : "ASN" : "Initial"
The program attached to the IPC queue with keys "(Global\
OSSEIPC48tempDB2.DB2A.ASN.QCAP.IPC, Global\OSSEIPC49tem

pDB2.DB2A.ASN.QCAP.IPC, Global\OSSEIPC50tempDB2.DB2A.ASN.QCAP.IPC)".

2009-11-06-13.27.07.468000 ASN0594I  "AsnQCcmd" : "ASN" : "Initial"
The program created an IPC queue with keys "(Global\OSSEIPC48tempDB2.
DB2A.ASN.QCAP.IPC.CMD7784, Global\OSSEIPC49

tempDB2.DB2A.ASN.QCAP.IPC.CMD7784, Global\OSSEIPC50tempDB2.DB".

Q Capture program status

Server name                                         (SERVER)
= DB2A

Schema name                                         (SCHEMA)
= ASN

Program status                                      (STATUS)
=  Up

Time since program started             (UP_TIME) =   1d 19h 12m 36s

Log file location                      (LOGFILE) = c:\temp\DB2.DB2A.
ASN.QCAP.log

Number of active Q subscriptions              (ACTIVE_QSUBS) = 1
```

Log reader currency   (CURRENT_LOG_TIME) = 2009-11-05-
09.35.38.000001

Last committed transaction published (LSN) (ALL_PUBLISHED_AS_OF_LSN)
= 0000:5FCA:7A04:0000:0000

Current application memory   (CURRENT_MEMORY)
= 0 MB

Path to DB2 log files   (DB2LOG_PATH) = C:\DB2\NODE0000\
SQL00007\SQLOGDIR\

Oldest DB2 log file needed for Q Capture restart (OLDEST_DB2LOG) =
S0000009.LOG

Current DB2 log file captured   (CURRENT_DB2LOG) =
S0000009.LOG

Note that the output from this command shows the oldest DB2 log file needed for
Q Capture to restart.

Altering a running Q Capture

To alter a running Q Capture is a two step process: we first have to change the
parameter, and then we have to reinitialize Q Capture.

To temporarily alter a parameter of Q Capture, we use the `asnqccmd` command with
the `chgparms` keyword and one of the following parameters:

```
autostop          memory_limit            signal_limit
commit_interval   monitor_interval        sleep_interval
logreuse          monitor_limit           term
logstdout         prune_interval          trace_limit
```

For example, if we want to temporarily alter the `monitor_interval` parameter for a
running Q Capture to 10 seconds, we would issue:

```
asnqccmd CAPTURE_SERVER=db2a CHGPARMS monitor_interval=10
```

If we want to temporarily change the value of two parameters then these are listed in
a space delimited list, not a comma delimited list:

```
asnqccmd capture_server=DB2A chgparms prune_interval=60
sleep_interval=10000
```

Note, that these commands only change the values for the running Q Capture.
If we stop and start Q Capture, it will take the parameter values from the
IBMQREP_CAPPARMS table, so to make the change permanent we need to update the
IBMQREP_CAPPARMS table:

```
db2 "UPDATE asn.ibmqrep_capparms SET monitor_interval=10 WHERE qmgr=
'QMA' "
```

Starting Q Capture from a point in the DB2 log

We can use command line parameters to start Q Capture at a known point in the DB2 log without triggering a load of the target tables, by supplying the following values:

- `lsn`: The log sequence number (LSN) of the oldest uncommitted transaction that we want to capture.

- `maxcmtseq`: The LSN of the most recently committed transaction that was put on the Send Queue.

We can find these values using the `asnqmfmt` command, as described in the *Viewing messages using asnqmfmt* section, or we can look in the Q Capture log for the message `ASN7109I`.

Once we have the `lsn` (`qRestartMsg.restartLSN`) and `maxcmtseq` (`qRestartMsg.lastCommitSEQ`) values we can plug them into the `asnqcap` command, which, using the names in our example would be:

```
asnqcap CAPTURE_SERVER=db2a CAPTURE_SCHEMA=asn
LSN=0000:0000:0000:023b:35f8 MAXCMTSEQ=4614:f4b1:0000:0001:0000
```

> We can also specify the `LSN` and `MAXCMTSEQ` values without colons to save space, for example `LSN=FFFFFFFFFFFFFFFFFFFF`.

We can test the concept of starting Q Capture from a known point in the DB2 log as follows:

- Set up a bidirectional scenario.

- Have an application program insert rows into a table on server `SYA`.

- While the application is running, cancel Q Capture running on server `SYA`.

- Use the `asnqmfmt` command to determine the restart values.

- Check in the Q Capture log to determine the restart values.

- Confirm that the restart values from the `asnqmfmt` command and the Q Capture log are consistent.

- Restart Q Capture using the `asnqcap` command with the appropriate restart values.

Starting Q Capture without triggering a load

To start Q Capture from the end of the log without triggering a load of the target, specify all FFFFs in the asnqcap command:

```
asnqcap CAPTURE_SERVER=db2a CAPTURE_SCHEMA=asn
LSN=FFFF:FFFF:FFFF:FFFF:FFFF MAXCMTSEQ=FFFF:FFFF:FFFF:FFFF:FFFF
```

Taking a Q Capture trace (asntrc)

To take a Q Capture trace using the asntrc command, we need to turn the trace on before starting Q Capture:

```
asntrc on -db db2a -schema asn -qcap
Trace is turned on, with IPC key 'Global\OSSEIPC109tempDB2.DB2A.ASN.QCAP.
TRC'
```

Then start Q Capture:

```
start asnqcap capture_server=DB2A startmode=cold
```

Wait for the problem to occur. Then get the trace format and the trace flow:

```
asntrc fmt -db db2a -schema asn -qcap > trc.fmt
asntrc flw -db db2a -schema asn -qcap > trc.flw
```

Turn off trace:

```
asntrc off -db db2a -schema asn -qcap
Trace is turned off.
Unable to free the trace buffer at this time.
The "QCAP" application will free the trace buffer while it is running or
when it is restarted.
Use the asntrc "kill" option to free the trace buffer, if the "QCAP"
application is stopped.
```

View the trace output using any text editor:

```
notepad trc.flw
```

Q Apply administration

Let's recap the major tasks that Q Apply performs:

- Realizes that a Q subscription is ready to be processed
- Performs a full refresh of the target table (if specified)
- Replicates new changes from its Receive Queues to the target tables

Starting Q Apply

The `asnqapp` command is used to start Q Apply and has numerous parameters, which are discussed next. To start Q Apply we need to be either DBADM or SYSADM and have write authority on the directory where Q Apply will write its log (`c:\temp` in our scenario). If we had specified that Q Apply should do an automatic load, then Q Apply needs SELECT authority on the source tables. The command is:

```
asnqapp [<parameter>=<value> ...]
```

The parameters are shown next (with corresponding column names in the IBMQREP_APPLYPARMS table shown in brackets after each parameter):

Parameter	Description
`APPLY_PATH=`	Location of Q Apply work files (APPLY_PATH).
`APPLY_SCHEMA=ASN`	Name of schema used to identify Q Apply.
`APPLY_SERVER=DB2DBDFT`	Name of the Q Apply control server.
`APPLYUPTO`	Q Apply applies up to a timestamp and then stops (97).
`AUTOSTOP=Y|N`	Terminate Q Apply after all queues are emptied.
`BUFFERED_INSERTS=Y/N`	Specifies whether Q Apply uses buffered inserts, which can improve performance in some partitioned databases.
`CLASSIC_LOAD_FILE_SZ=500,000`	(CLASSIC_LOAD_FILE_SZ) (97).
`COMMIT_COUNT=<n>|1`	Specifies the number of transactions that each Q Apply agent thread applies to the target table within a commit scope (COMMIT_COUNT) (97)
`DEADLOCK_RETRIES=n|3`	Number of retries for SQL deadlock errors (DEADLOCK_RETRIES)
`DFTMODELQ`	Specifies a Model Queue name other than IBMQREP.SPILL.MODELQ that Q Apply will use (97).
`DIAGLOG=Y|N`	Send messages to the log file (deprecated in V9.7.1)
`IGNBADDATA=Y|N`	Federated targets specifies whether Q Apply checks for illegal characters in data from the source if the code page from the source and target are different and continues processing even if it finds illegal characters (97).

Parameter	Description
INSERT_BIDI_SIGNAL=N|Y	Specifies whether Q Capture and Q Apply use P2PNORECAPTURE signal inserts to prevent recapture of transactions in bidirectional replication (INSERT_BIDI_SIGNAL) (**97**).
LOADCOPY_PATH	Use this parameter when the primary server in a HADR configuration is loaded by Q Apply calling the DB2 LOAD utility. Setting this parameter prompts Q Apply to start the LOAD utility with the option to create a copy of the loaded data in the specified path. The secondary server in the HADR configuration then looks for the copied data in this path (LOADCOPY_PATH) (**97**).
LOAD_DATA_BUFF_SZ=n|8	Use with multidimensional clustering (MDC) tables. Specifies the number of 4KB pages for the DB2 LOAD utility to use as buffered space for transferring data within the utility during the initial loading of the target table. This parameter applies only to automatic loads using the DB2 LOAD utility (LOAD_DATA_BUFF_SZ) (**97**).
LOGREUSE=Y|N	Reuse or append messages to the logfile.
LOGSTDOUT=Y|N	Send messages to standard output.
MAX_PARALLEL_LOADS=n|15	Specifies the maximum number of automatic load operations of target tables that Q Apply can start at the same time for a given Receive Queue (MAX_PARALLEL_LOADS) (**97**).
MONITOR_INTERVAL=n|300	Seconds between inserts into to monitor table (MONITOR_INTERVAL).
MONITOR_LIMIT=n|10080	Minutes before a monitor table row can be pruned (MONITOR_LIMIT).
NICKNAME_COMMIT_CT=n|10	Specifies the number of rows after which the import utility commits changes to nicknames that reference the target table during the loading process. This parameter applies only to automatic loads for federated targets, which must use the export and import utilities. (NICKNAME_COMMIT_CT) (**97**).

Parameter	Description
P2P_2NODES= Y|N	This parameter allows Q Apply to optimize for performance in a peer-to-peer configuration with only two active servers by not logging conflicting deletes to the IBMQREP_DELTOMB table. Only use the setting p2p_2nodes = y for peer-to-peer replication with two active servers (**97**).
PRUNE_INTERVAL=n|300	Seconds before Q Apply tries pruning control tables.
PWDFILE=asnpwd.aut	Name of the password file (PWDFILE).
QMGR	Queue Manager name (QMGR) (**97**).
RICHKLVL=0|2|5	Specifies the level of referential integrity checking. By default, Q Apply checks for RI-based dependencies between transactions to ensure that dependent rows are applied in the correct order (**97**).
SKIPTRANS="<tranid>"	Specifies that Q Apply should not apply one or more transactions from one or more Receive Queues based on their transaction ID (**97**).
SPILL_COMMIT_COUNT=n|10	Specifies how many rows are grouped together in a commit scope by the Q Apply spill agents that apply data that was replicated during a load operation (SPILL_COMMIT_COUNT) (**97**).
SQL_CAP_SCHEMA	(SQL_CAP_SCHEMA) (**97**).
TERM=Y|N	Terminate Q Apply if DB2 terminates (TERM).
TRACE_LIMIT=n|10080	Minutes before a trace table row can be pruned (TRACE_LIMIT).

> If we specify a timestamp for the APPLYUPTO parameter, Q Apply stops when it receives a transaction with a source timestamp that is later than the specified timestamp. This timestamp must be specified as a full or partial timestamp in **Greenwich Mean Time** (**GMT**). If we are going to use this parameter, then we should set the heartbeat interval to a value greater than zero so that Q Apply can tell if the APPLYUPTO time has passed.

When starting Q Apply, the minimum information we need to provide is the location of the Q Apply control tables (DB2B), but usually we also specify the Q Apply schema (which defaults to ASN), and the Q Apply log path/password file location. An example of the command required to start Q Apply is:

```
asnqapp APPLY_SERVER=db2b APPLY_PATH="C:\TEMP"
```

There are two ways of displaying the parameters that Q Apply was started with — we can either query the IBMQREP_APPLYPARMS control table or we can issue the asnqacmd command with the qryparms option, both of which are shown next.

To query the IBMQREP_APPLYPARMS control table, use the SQL in the *The control tables – The Q Apply control tables* section of *Chapter 3*.

Before we issue the asnqacmd command with the qryparms option let's look at the command in more detail.

The format of the asnqacmd command is:

```
asnqacmd [<parameter>=<value> ...] [command]
```

The parameter can be:

- APPLY_SCHEMA=: Name of schema used to identify a Q Apply.
- APPLY_SERVER=: Name of the Q Apply control server.
- LOGSTDOUT=Y|N: Send messages to standard output.

The command can be:

- CHGPARMS: Change Q Apply operational parameters.
- PRUNE: Prune Q Apply control tables.
- QRYPARMS: Query Q Apply operational parameters.
- REINITQ: Refresh parameters for a queue if active.
- STATUS: Query the status of Q Apply threads.
- STATUS SHOW DETAILS: Query the enhanced status for Q Apply.
- STARTQ: Start processing messages from a queue.
- STOP: Stop Q Apply.
- STOPQ: Stop processing messages from a queue.
- TRCSTART: Start writing program flow information to the Q Apply trace buffer (deprecated in V9.7).

So, to use the `asnqacmd` command with the `qryparms` option to check the status of Q Apply issue:

```
asnqacmd APPLY_SERVER=db2b APPLY_SCHEMA=asn QRYPARMS
```

Stopping Q Apply

An example of the command required to stop Q Apply is:

```
$ asnqacmd APPLY_SERVER=db2b STOP
```

Querying the status of Q Apply

To query the status of Q Apply use the command shown:

```
asnqacmd APPLY_SERVER=db2b STATUS SHOW DETAILS
```

The STATUS SHOW DETAILS option gives the following information:

- Whether Q Apply is running
- Time since the program started
- Location of the Q Apply diagnostic log
- Number of active Q subscriptions
- Time period used to calculate averages

The following information is also displayed for each active Receive Queue:

- Queue name
- Number of active Q subscriptions
- Values of OLDEST_TRANS and OLDEST_INFLIGHT_TRANS from the IBMQREP_APPLYMON table, which are gathered at the time that we run the command and may be newer than the values in the control table
- Average **end-to-end latency**
- Average **Q Capture latency**
- Average **queue latency**
- Average **Q Apply latency**
- Amount of memory in bytes that the browser thread used for reading transactions from the queue
- Number of messages on the queue (queue depth)
- Logical log sequence number of the oldest transaction that Q Apply committed to the target

Starting a Receive Queue

If the Q Apply log contains message ASN7525I "The receive queue "<queue_
name>" (replication queue map "<queue_map_name>") is not in active
state and is not being processed by the Q Apply program. If the skip
trans parameter was specified, it is ignored because the queue is
inactive", then we should first check the state of the Receive Queue, which is
indicated by the STATE column in the IBMQREP_RECVQUEUES table. If it is marked as
I (inactive), then we need to restart it, using one of the following methods:

- Use the startq parameter of the asnqacmd command, which means we do
  not have to restart Q Apply:

  asnqacmd APPLY_SERVER=db2b STARTQ=CAPA.TO.APPB.RECVQ

- Change the STATE column in the IBMQREP_RECVQUEUES table to A and restart
  Q Apply.

Now let's move on to look at when we need a password file, and what a password
file actually is.

The password file

We need a password file in two situations:

- If we have Q Capture and Q Apply running on different machines, and if we
  are expecting Q Apply to perform an initial load, then Q Apply must be able
  to connect to the remote Q Capture server. We therefore need a password file
  on the Q Apply server.

- If we are using the Replication Alert Monitor, then we need a password file
  on the system that is running the monitor tables.

If Q Capture and Q Apply are running on the same machine (that is, they are both
local databases), then we do not need a password file.

We create a password file using the `asnpwd` command. The password file needs to be in the directory pointed to by the `APPLY_PATH` Q Apply start parameter. The `asnpwd` command has different parameters, depending on the task required, as shown in the following table:

Task	Command
To create/initialize	`asnpwd {INIT} [ENCRYPT {ALL|PASSWORD}]`
	`[{USING} <file-path-name>]`
To add an alias	`asnpwd {ADD ALIAS} <alias-name>`
	`{ID} <user-id> {PASSWORD} <password>`
	`[{USING} <file-path-name>]`
To modify an alias	`asnpwd {MODIFY ALIAS} <alias-name>`
	`{ID} <user-id> {PASSWORD} <password>`
	`[{USING} <file-path-name>]`
To delete an alias	`asnpwd {DELETE ALIAS} <alias-name>`
	`[{USING} <file-path-name>]`
To list the entries	`asnpwd {LIST} [{USING} <file-path-name>]`
To run with trace	`asnpwd -t {INIT|ADD|MODIFY|DELETE|LIST}`

To create a password file with the default name (`asnpwd.aut`) in the directory from where we issued the `asnpwd` command from, issue:

```
asnpwd init encrypt password
```

To create a password file called `passfil.txt` in the `c:\temp` directory issue:

```
asnpwd init encrypt password using c:\temp\passfil.txt
```

Once we have created a password file we can populate it using the `ADD ALIAS` option.

To add an alias for server `DB2A` with a userID of `db2admin` and a password of `fred`:

```
asnpwd ADD ALIAS db2a ID db2admin PASSWORD fred USING c:\temp\passfil.txt
```

We can list all the entries in the password file using the `LIST` option:

```
asnpwd LIST USING c:\temp\passfil.txt
Alias: DB2A  ID: db2admin
Number of Entries: 1
```

We can modify an entry in the password file by using the MODIFY ALIAS option. Say we want to change the password entry for the db2admin user to be heather, we would issue:

```
asnpwd MODIFY ALIAS db2a ID db2admin PASSWORD heather USING c:\temp\
passfil.txt
```

We can delete an entry from the password file by using the DELETE ALIAS option:

```
asnpwd DELETE ALIAS db2a USING c:\temp\passfil.txt
```

Note that if we are using a non standard password file, then we should update the APPLYPARMS table.

Copying (promoting) Q replication environments

What do we mean by *copying* (or *promoting*) environments? Well, suppose we have developed a replication solution on a test machine and now want to build a similar solution on a production machine — we have two choices: if we have built the test solution using ASNCLP scripts, then we can just move these scripts over to the production machine, edit them to reflect the new schema, database names, and so on and then run them there. The point to watch out for with this approach is that the scripts have to be complete — what happens if something has been changed, which has not been reflected in the ASNCLP scripts! The second option is to use the promote functionality of the ASNCLP commands, which we will discuss next.

The ASNCLP PROMOTE procedure

Let's look at promoting a unidirectional setup from a test environment to a production one. We have replication set up between DB2A and DB2B on test and want to move this to DB2C and DB2D on production.

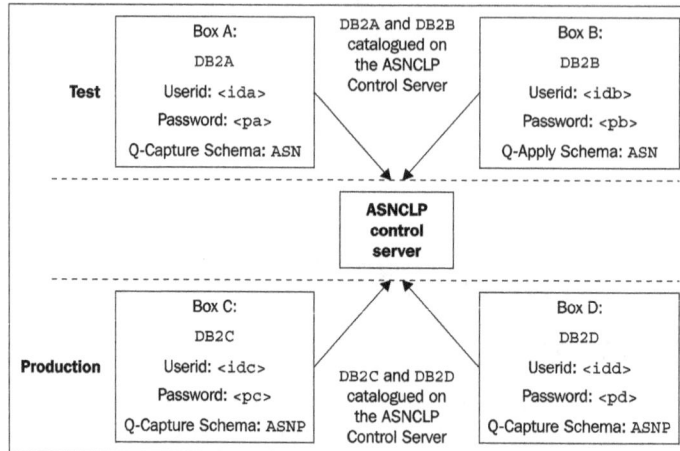

We will issue all commands from our ASNCLP Control Server, which has all the databases catalogued on it as their original names. We have to perform the following steps:

1. Create the Q Capture control tables on DB2C.
2. Create the Q Apply control tables on DB2D.
3. Create the WebSphere MQ environment on DB2C and DB2D.
4. Create an ASNCLP command file promote_uni.asnclp, substituting the values from the preceding diagram into the place holders (leaving the double quotation marks, as they are important!).

```
ASNCLP SESSION SET TO Q REPLICATION;
SET RUN SCRIPT NOW STOP ON SQL ERROR ON;

SET LOG "prom.log";

SET SERVER CAPTURE TO DBALIAS db2a ID "<ida>" PASSWORD "<pa>"
PROMOTE TO DBALIAS db2c ID ""<idc>" PASSWORD "<pc>" SCHEMA asnp;

SET SERVER TARGET TO DBALIAS db2b ID "<idb>" PASSWORD "<pb>"
PROMOTE TO DBALIAS db2d ID "<idd>" PASSWORD "<pd>" SCHEMA asnp;

SET OUTPUT PROMOTE SCRIPT "replqmap_qsub.in";

SET OUTPUT CAPTURE SCRIPT "promote_capture_repqmap.sql";
SET OUTPUT TARGET SCRIPT "promote_target_repqmap.sql";
```

```
PROMOTE REPLQMAP LIKE "%";

PROMOTE QSUB REPLQMAP LIKE "%";
```

It's in the last two lines where we specify which Replication Queue Maps and which Q subscriptions to promote. In this case they say to promote all Replication Queue Maps and all Q subscriptions which use those Replication Queue Maps.

5. Run the ASNCLP command file `promote_uni.asnclp` as:

    ```
    asnclp -f promote_uni.asnclp
    ```

Any error messages are written to the file `prom.log`.

The output file that is created is `replqmap_qsub.in`. If the command executes successfully, then we should see something like:

```
ASNCLP SESSION SET TO Q REPLICATION;

#Current Q Capture definitions are at arch level 0905

#Current Q Apply definitions are at arch level 0905

SET OUTPUT CAPTURE SCRIPT "promote_capture_repqmap.sql";

SET OUTPUT TARGET SCRIPT "promote_target_repqmap.sql";

SET LOG "prom.log";

SET SERVER CAPTURE TO DB DB2C ID db2admin PASSWORD "xxxxxxxx";

 SET CAPTURE SCHEMA SOURCE "ASNP";

SET SERVER TARGET TO DB DB2D ID db2admin PASSWORD "xxxxxxxx";

 SET APPLY SCHEMA "ASNP";

CREATE REPLQMAP "RQMA2B"

 USING ADMINQ "CAPA.ADMINQ.REMOTE" RECVQ "CAPA.TO.APPB.RECVQ" SENDQ
"CAPA.TO.APPB.SENDQ.REMOTE"

 NUM APPLY AGENTS 3 MAX AGENTS CORRELID 0 MEMORY LIMIT 9 ERROR ACTION
S HEARTBEAT INTERVAL 0 MAX MESSAGE SIZE 4;

ASNCLP SESSION SET TO Q REPLICATION;

#Current Q Capture definitions are at arch level 0905

#Current Q Apply definitions are at arch level 0905

SET OUTPUT CAPTURE SCRIPT "promote_capture_repqmap.sql";

SET OUTPUT TARGET SCRIPT "promote_target_repqmap.sql";

SET LOG "prom.log";

SET SERVER CAPTURE TO DB DB2C ID db2admin PASSWORD "xxxxxxxx";

 SET CAPTURE SCHEMA SOURCE "ASNP";

SET SERVER TARGET TO DB DB2D ID db2admin PASSWORD "xxxxxxxx";
```

```
 SET APPLY SCHEMA "ASNP";

SET PROFILE CUSTOMER FOR OBJECT TARGET TABLESPACE OPTIONS UW
BUFFERPOOL IBMDEFAULTBP PAGESIZE 4096;

CREATE QSUB (  SUBNAME "TAB1" REPLQMAP "RQMA2B"

 DB2ADMIN.CUSTOMER OPTIONS ALL CHANGED ROWS N HAS LOAD PHASE I SPILL_
MODELQ IBMQREP.SPILL.MODELQ.0.1.1 SUPPRESS DELETES N

 TARGET NAME FRED.CUSTOMER IN QAASN CREATE USING PROFILE CUSTOMER
TYPE USERTABLE

 TRGCOLS INCLUDE ( CID CID,HISTORY HISTORY,INFO INFO ) KEYS ( CID )

 CONFLICT ACTION F ERROR ACTION Q LOAD TYPE 2);
```

Note that the password is shown in plain text.

This will promote the Replication Queue Map and Q subscription definitions from the test system to the production system.

We have now finished looking at promoting from a test system to a production system.

Summary

This chapter focused on the administrative tasks that we need to perform to set up and administer a Q replication environment. We started by looking at how we define the WebSphere MQ queues and the Q replication control tables. We moved on to look at Q subscription maintenance tasks, such as creating, altering and dropping a Q subscription. We then looked at how we should handle source table maintenance, where we covered adding and removing columns from a Q subscription. Next, we looked at administering the Q Capture and Q Apply programs, and when we need a password file. Finally, we looked at how to promote a Q replication environment from a test system to a production system.

In these six chapters, we have covered the building blocks that are needed for Q replication. We bring this all together in Appendix A, which covers setting up different scenarios from the simplest unidirectional scenario to a scenario involving peer-to-peer four-way replication.

Before we look at the examples, we move on to the final chapter which covers monitoring and reporting.

7
Monitoring and Reporting

This is the last chapter of the book. In this chapter, we discuss:

- How we can monitor our Q replication setup
- The tools available to report on the setup, for documentation, and trouble-shooting purposes

We will start by looking at what we need to monitor at the three different layers (database layer, WebSphere MQ layer, and Q replication layer). We then go on to discuss the Replication Alert Monitor and other tools to monitor the environment. The chapter concludes with some *what if* scenarios, some comments on Q replication performance, and a discussion on some common error messages.

The answer to the question *What do we need to monitor* is almost the same as the answer to the question *How long is a piece of string.* The simple answer is *it depends* — which we are sure, will not come as a big surprise to you. What we hope to do in the following sections is — give you a manageable list of items to monitor to cover most situations.

The database layer

The only thing we need to check in the database layer is that the DB2 instance is running, and that we can connect to the databases involved in replication. There are, of course, things like log usage on the Q Capture server to be considered.

The WebSphere MQ layer

The first thing we need to check is that the Queue Managers are running. We then need to check the Listeners and Channels. Let's look at a unidirectional setup as an example. There are a number of WebSphere MQ, operating system, and DB2 commands that can be issued on each system to check the status of the various components, as shown in the following diagram:

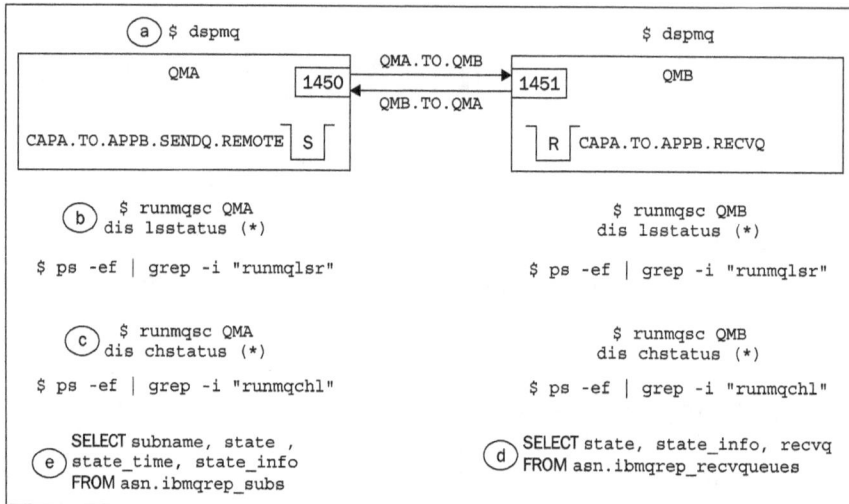

Note that points (d) and (e) are really in the Q replication layer, but are shown here for completeness.

Checking that the Queue Managers are running

Use the following DSPMQ MQ command to display the status of a Queue Manager:

$ dspmq

We will see the following message:

```
QMNAME(QMA)              STATUS(Running)
```

If we see the following message:

```
QMNAME(QMA)              STATUS(Ended unexpectedly)
```

Then the Queue Manager is not active and we need to start it using the STRMQM command, as described in the *Create/start/stop a Queue Manager – Starting a Queue Manager* section of *Chapter 4, WebSphere MQ for the DBA*.

Checking the state of the Listeners

Use the following DISPLAY LSSTATUS MQSC command to check that the Listener is running:

```
$ runmqsc QMA

dis lsstatus(*)

    14 : dis lsstatus(*)

AMQ8631: Display listener status details.

    LISTENER(SYSTEM.LISTENER.TCP.1)    STATUS(RUNNING)

    PID(12912)
```

We can cross check the PID value with the output from the UNIX ps command:

```
$ ps -ef | grep -i "runmqlsr"

Mqm 12912 1 0 Sep1 pts/1 00:00:00 runmqlsr -t tcp -m QMA -p 1450
```

The status should be RUNNING. If it isn't, then we need to start it as described in the *MQ Listener management – Defining/Starting an MQ Listener* section of *Chapter 4*.

Once we have checked the Listener(s), we need to check the Channels.

Checking the state of the Channels

Use the following DISPLAY CHSTATUS MQSC command to check the status of the Channels:

```
$ runmqsc QMA

dis chstatus(*)

    1 : dis chstatus(*)

AMQ8417: Display Channel Status details.

    CHANNEL(QMA.TO.QMB)                    CHLTYPE(SDR)

    CONNAME(192.168.204.128(1451))         CURRENT

    RQMNAME(QMB)                           STATUS(RUNNING)

    SUBSTATE(MQGET)                        XMITQ(QMB.XMITQ)

AMQ8417: Display Channel Status details.

    CHANNEL(QMB.TO.QMA)                    CHLTYPE(RCVR)
```

```
CONNAME(192.168.204.128)                    CURRENT
RQMNAME(QMB)                                 STATUS(RUNNING)
SUBSTATE(RECEIVE)
```

If the Channels are not running, then the following message is displayed:

dis chstatus(*)

```
    3 : dis chstatus(*)
```

AMQ8420: Channel Status not found.

We can also use the operating system `ps` command to check that the Channels are running:

$ ps -ef | grep -i "runmqchl"

```
mqm 8624      1   0 Sep11 pts/0     00:00:00 runmqchl -m QMA -c QMA.
TO.QMB
```

In the DISPLAY CHSTATUS output, we want the STATUS for the channels to have a value of RUNNING. If the status says RETRYING (as shown):

dis chstatus(*)

```
    11 : dis chstatus(*)
```

AMQ8417: Display Channel Status details.

```
    CHANNEL(QMA.TO.QMB)                      XMITQ(QMB.XMITQ)
    CONNAME(127.0.0.1(1451))                 CURRENT
    CHLTYPE(SDR)                             STATUS(RETRYING)
    RQMNAME()
```

Then it could be that the other Queue Manager is not active or that the Listeners have not been started.

To start a Channel see *MQ Channel management – To start a Channel* section of *Chapter 4*.

Checking the state of the Receive Queue

We can use the following query to check the status of the Receive Queue:

$ db2 "SELECT state, state_info, recvq FROM asn.ibmqrep_recvqueues"

```
STATE STATE_INFO RECVQ

----- ---------- -------------------------------------------------

A     ASN7526I   CAPA.TO.APPB.RECVQ
```

If a Receive Queue is not active (A), then it can be activated using the ASNQACMD
STARTQ command, as described in the *Q Apply administration — Starting a Receive
Queue* section of *Chapter 6, Administration Tasks*.

Checking that the Q subscription is active

We can use the following query to check the status of Q subscriptions:

```
$ db2 "SELECT SUBSTR(subname,1,10) AS subname, state AS s, state_time,
state_info FROM asn.ibmqrep_subs"

SUBNAME    S STATE_TIME               STATE_INFO
---------- - ------------------------ ----------

TAB1       A 2009-09-13-10.04.42.089530 -
```

The relevant columns of the table are described in the *The control tables — The Q
Capture control tables* section of *Chapter 3, The DB2 Database Layer*.

The Q replication layer

The basic things we need to monitor are whether Q Capture and Q Apply started
correctly and are active, how far Q Capture is behind the DB2 log, and how far
Q Apply is behind Q Capture.

Monitoring Q Capture start up

To indicate that Q Capture has started successfully, we are looking for two messages
in the Q Capture log:

- ASN0572I: This indicates that Q Capture has started successfully.

- ASN7010I: This indicates that the Q subscription has been
  successfully activated.

```
<subMgr:initAllSubs> ASN7010I  "Q Capture" :  "ASN" : "WorkerThread"
: The program successfully activated  XML publication or Q
subscription "TAB1"  (send queue "CAPA.TO.APPB.SENDQ.REMOTE",
publishing or replication queue map "RQMA2B") for source table
"ERIC.T1".

<subMgr:initAllSubs> ASN7000I  "Q Capture" :  "ASN" : "WorkerThread"
:  "0" subscriptions are active. "0" subscriptions are inactive. "0"
subscriptions that were new and were successfully activated. "0"
subscriptions that were new could not be activated and are
now inactive.
```

```
<handleLogrdInitMsg> ASN7108I  "Q Capture" :  "ASN" : "WorkerThread"
: At program initialization, the highest log sequence number of a
successfully processed transaction is "0000:0000:0000:0000:0000" and
the lowest log sequence number of a transaction still to be committed
is "0000:0000:0000:0180:5125".

<asnqwk> ASN0572I  "Q Capture" :  "ASN" : "WorkerThread" : The
program initialized successfully.

<subMgr::handleSignal> ASN7019I  "Q Capture" :  "ASN" :
"WorkerThread" :  "LOADDONE" signal was received and will be
processed.

<subMgr::handleLOADDONE> ASN7010I  "Q Capture" :  "ASN" :
"WorkerThread" : The program successfully activated  XML publication
or Q subscription "TAB1"  (send queue "CAPA.TO.APPB.SENDQ.REMOTE",
publishing or replication queue map "RQMA2B") for source table "ERIC.
T1".
```

Numerous `ASN0592I` and `ASN0593I` messages.

If Q Capture has started successfully, then we need to check that all the threads are running. We use the following `ASNQCCMD` command with the `STATUS` option to check the threads:

$ asnqccmd CAPTURE_SERVER=db2a STATUS

```
. . . . . . . .

2009-11-26-16.39.46.406000 ASN0520I  "AsnQCcmd" : "ASN" : "Initial"
: The STATUS command response: "HoldLThread" thread is in the "is
resting" state.

2009-11-26-16.39.46.406000 ASN0520I  "AsnQCcmd" : "ASN" : "Initial"
: The STATUS command response: "AdminThread" thread is in the "is
resting" state.

2009-11-26-16.39.46.406000 ASN0520I  "AsnQCcmd" : "ASN" : "Initial"
: The STATUS command response: "PruneThread" thread is in the "is
resting" state.

2009-11-26-16.39.46.406000 ASN0520I  "AsnQCcmd" : "ASN" : "Initial"
: The STATUS command response: "WorkerThread" thread is in the "is
doing work" state.
```

All of the threads need to be running. Refer to the *Q Capture administration – Querying the status of Q Capture* section of *Chapter 6* for a description of the threads. Note that we do not see a Transmission thread.

Monitoring Q Apply start up

To indicate that Q Apply has started successfully, we are looking for two messages in the Q Apply log:

- ASN0572I: This indicates that Q Apply has started.

- ASN7526I: This is for each Receive Queue, to indicate that Q Apply is reading from this queue.

```
<Asnenv:setEnvIpcQRcvHdl> ASN0594I  "Q Apply" :  "ASN" : "Initial"
The program created an IPC queue with keys "(Global\OSSEIPC48tempDB2.
DB2B.ASN.QAPP.IPC, Global\OSSEIPC49tempDB2.DB2B.ASN.QAPP.IPC, Global\
OSSEIPC50tempDB2.DB2B.ASN.QAPP.IPC".

<asnqapp::main> ASN0572I  "Q Apply" :  "ASN" : "Initial" : The
program initialized successfully.

. . . . . .

<brwzMain> ASN7526I  "Q Apply" :  "ASN" : "BR00000" : The Q Apply
program has started processing the receive queue "CAPA.TO.APPB.RECVQ"
for replication queue map "RQMA2B".
```

If Q Apply has started successfully, then we need to check that all the threads are running. We can use the following ASNQCCMD command with the STATUS option to check the threads:

$ asnqacmd APPLY_SERVER=db2b STATUS

```
. . . . . . . . .

2009-11-26-17.08.48.984000 ASN0520I  "AsnQAcmd" : "ASN" : "Initial"
: The STATUS command response: "HoldLThread" thread is in the "is
resting" state.

2009-11-26-17.08.48.984000 ASN0520I  "AsnQAcmd" : "ASN" : "Initial"
: The STATUS command response: "AdminThread" thread is in the "is
resting" state.

2009-11-26-17.08.48.984000 ASN0520I  "AsnQAcmd" : "ASN" : "Initial"
: The STATUS command response: "MonitorThread" thread is in the "is
resting" state.

2009-11-26-17.08.49.000000 ASN0520I  "AsnQAcmd" : "ASN" : "Initial"
: The STATUS command response: "BR00000" thread is in the "is doing
work" state.
```

All of the threads need to be running. Refer to the *Q Apply administration – Querying the status of Q Apply* section of *Chapter 6* for a description of the threads.

Checking that Q Capture and Q Apply are active

Q Capture and Q Apply can maintain a relative level of independence, in other words Q Capture can be up while Q Apply is down, and vise versa. However, if Q Apply is down, then it cannot read from its Receive Queue and the queue depth will increase until it hits it MAXDEPTH value at which time Q Capture will abend because at that point it cannot put any more messages onto its Send Queue.

We can use the Replication Alert Monitor (Refer to the *Monitoring using the Replication Alert Monitor* section of this chapter) or the asnqccmd/asnqacmd commands (as shown previously) to check whether Q Capture and Q Apply are active.

Checking the Q Capture and Q Apply log files

The Q Capture and Q Apply log names and locations were discussed in the *Q Capture and Q Apply administration* section of *Chapter 6*.

When browsing the log files, look out for any messages of the form ASNxxxxE, which indicates an error condition.

Checking the APPLYTRACE and CAPTRACE tables

The two control tables of interest are IBMQREP_APPLYTRACE and IBMQREP_CAPTRACE. The IBMQREP_APPLYTRACE table contains informational, warning, and error messages from Q Apply. The IBMQREP_CAPTRACE table contains informational, warning, and error messages from Q Capture.

We need to select from these tables on a regular basis to check for any errors. If Q Capture is running on DB2A and Q Apply on DB2B then:

A query we can use to interrogate the IBMQREP_CAPTRACE table is:

```
$ db2 "SELECT operation, trace_time, description FROM
asn.ibmqrep_captrace WHERE operation IN ('ERROR', 'WARNING')"
```

A query we can use to interrogate the IBMQREP_APPLYTRACE table is:

```
$ db2 "SELECT operation, trace_time, description,1,100 FROM
asn.ibmqrep_applytrace WHERE operation IN ('ERROR', 'WARNING')"
```

How far is Q Capture behind the DB2 log

To check how far Q Capture is behind the DB2 log, use the `asnqccmd` command described in the *Q Apply administration – Querying the status of Q Apply* section of *Chapter 6*.

How far is Q Apply behind Q Capture

To check how far Q Apply is behind Q Capture, use the `asnqacmd` command described in the *Q Apply administration – Querying the status of Q Apply* section of *Chapter 6*.

Listing Q subscription status

Use the following query to check the state of Q subscriptions:

```
$ db2 "select substr(subname,1,10) as subname, state as S, state_time
from asn.ibmqrep_subs "
```

Listing Receive Queue status

Use the following query to check the state of Receive Queues:

```
$ db2 "SELECT recvq, state FROM ASN.IBMQREP_RECVQUEUES WHERE RECVQ =
'CAPA.TO.APPB.RECVQ' "
```

```
RECVQ                                                STATE
-------------------------------------------------- -----
CAPA.TO.APPB.RECVQ                                   A
```

To start a Receive Queue, use the `ASNQACMD STARTQ` command described in the *Q Capture and Q Apply administration – Q Apply administration* section of *Chapter 6* for details.

Table synchronization

If the system is not generating any errors, then we need to check that the source and target tables are in sync, which is not a trivial task. There are two methods we can use:

1. We can do a SELECT COUNT(*) from both the source and target tables, but at best this will just tell us that the number of rows is the same — if the system is being used, then the number may not be the same. Also, this just reports back on the number of rows, not the contents of the rows.

2. To help with this problem, Q replication has two utilities called `asntdiff` and `asntrepair`. These utilities allow us to detect and repair differences between source and target tables in Q replication without manually comparing the tables or performing a load (full refresh) of the target.

The best time to use the `asntdiff` utility is when the source and target tables are stable. We might want to run the utility when Q Capture and Q Apply have caught up and stopped. For example, we could run the utility when Q Capture reached the end of the DB2 recovery log and all changes are applied at the target. If applications are still updating the source, the comparison might not be accurate.

So to compare the table identified by the Q subscription `TAB1`, we would issue the following command:

```
$ asntdiff DB=db2a SCHEMA=asn WHERE= "WHERE SUBNAME = 'TAB1' "
```

The different latencies

There are three different latencies (stored in the `IBMQREP_APPLYMON` table such as Q Capture latency, Q Apply latency, and MQ latency, which are shown in the following diagram:

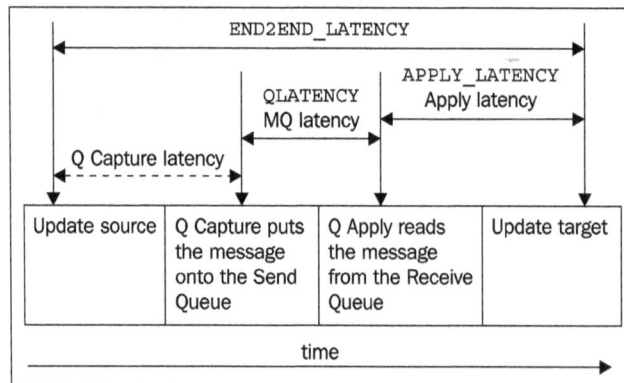

1. Q Apply latency is from the `APPLY_LATENCY` column of `IBMQREP_APPLYMON`. It is the average elapsed milliseconds between the time that Q Apply reads transactions from the Receive Queue and the time that they were committed to the target.

2. MQ latency is from the `QLATENCY` column of `IBMQREP_APPLYMON`. It is the average elapsed milliseconds between the time that Q Capture puts messages on the Send Queue and the time that Q Apply got them from the Receive Queue.

3. Q Capture latency is the `END2END_LATENCY` column minus the `APPLY_LATENCY` and `QLATENCY` columns from `IBMQREP_APPLYMON`. `END2END_LATENCY` is the average elapsed milliseconds between the time that transactions were committed to the source table and the time that they were committed to the target.

What we want to measure is the overall latency (`END2END_LATENCY`) and its constituent components.

In a bidirectional setup, one of the things to check is that the latency values are the same for one direction as the other.

We can use the `asnqacmd` command with the `STATUS SHOW DETAILS` option to report on the latencies:

```
$ asnqacmd APPLY_SERVER=db2b STATUS SHOW DETAILS
ASN0600I  "AsnQAcmd"  :  ""  :  "Initial"  :  Program "asnqacmd 9.1.0" is
starting.
 Q Apply program status
    Server name                               (SERVER) = DB2B
    Schema name                               (SCHEMA) = ASN
    Program status                            (STATUS) =  Up
    Time since program started        (UP_TIME) =     0d  0h  2m 26s
    Log file location        (LOGFILE) = C:\TEMP\DB2.DB2B.ASN.QAPP.log
    Number of active Q subscriptions          (ACTIVE_QSUBS) = 1
    Time period used to calculate average (INTERVAL_LENGTH) =   0h  2m
18.266s

    Receive queue : CAPA.TO.APPB.RECVQ
        Number of active Q subscriptions                  (ACTIVE_QSUBS) =
1
 All transactions applied as of (time)        (OLDEST_TRANS) = 2007-
04-06-09.36.03.000000
 All transactions applied as of (LSN) (ALL_APPLIED_AS_OF_LSN) =
0000:0000:0000:0000:0000
 Oldest in-progress transaction           (OLDEST_INFLT_TRANS) = 1900-
01-01-00.00.00.000        Average end-to-end latency        (END2END
LATENCY) =  0h  0m  0.0s
        Average Q Capture latency     (CAPTURE_LATENCY) =  0h  0m  0.0s
        Average WSMQ latency                 (QLATENCY) =  0h  0m  0.0s
        Average Q Apply latency        (APPLY_LATENCY) =  0h  0m  0.0s
        Current memory                 (CURRENT_MEMORY ) = 0 MB
        Current queue depth                    (QDEPTH) = 0
```

The following lines match the labels in the preceding latency diagram:

```
Average end-to-end latency (END2END LATENCY)
Average Q Capture latency (CAPTURE_LATENCY)
Average WSMQ latency (QLATENCY)
Average Q Apply latency (APPLY_LATENCY)
```

The Q Capture latency is for the number of records in a transaction.

The DB2 log latency is the time that Q Capture is behind the DB2 log. It is calculated as `monitor_time-current_log_time` from the `IBMQREP_CAPMON` table:

```
$ db2 "SELECT monitor_time, monitor_time-current_log_time AS
DB2_log_latency_sec FROM asn.ibmqrep_capmon ORDER BY monitor_time DESC
FETCH FIRST 5 ROWS ONLY "
```

MONITOR_TIME	DB2_LOG_LATENCY_SEC
2006-02-18-17.52.08.562000	4.596000
2006-02-18-17.51.38.519000	4.587000
2006-02-18-17.51.08.466000	4.577000
2006-02-18-17.50.38.383000	4.527000
2006-02-18-17.50.08.339000	4.516000

We could have found the `current_log_time` using the `asnqccmd`
`CAPTURE_SERVER=db2a CAPTURE_SCHEMA=asn STATUS SHOW DETAILS` command,
but it does not give us the monitor time:

```
2007-04-06-10.13.24.187000 ASN0600I  "AsnQCcmd" :  "" : "Initial" :
Program "mqpubcmd 9.1.0" is starting.
  Q Capture program status
    Server name                                    (SERVER) = DB2A
    Schema name                                    (SCHEMA) =
    Program status                                 (STATUS) =  Up
    Time since program started     (UP_TIME) =   0d  0h 39m 47s
    Log file location      (LOGFILE) = C:\TEMP\DB2.DB2A.ASN.QCAP.log
    Number of active Q subscriptions           (ACTIVE_QSUBS) = 1
    Log reader currency  (CURRENT_LOG_TIME) = 2007-04-06-
09.38.47.000001
     Last committed transaction published (LSN) (ALL_PUBLISHED_AS_OF_
LSN) = 0000:0000:0000:0241:0879
    Current application memory             (CURRENT_MEMORY ) = 0 MB
```

```
    Path to DB2 log files (DB2LOG_PATH) = C:\DB2\NODE0000\SQL00002\
SQLOGDIR\

    Oldest DB2 log file needed for Q Capture restart      (OLDEST_
DB2LOG) = S0000004.LOG

    Current DB2 log file captured                         (CURRENT_
DB2LOG) = S0000004.LOG
```

The base monitor tables

What we mean by *base* are the tables that are available outside of the Replication Alert Monitor, namely for Q Capture its IBMQREP_CAPMON and IBMQREP_CAPQMON, and for Q Apply it is IBMQREP_APPLYMON.

The Q Capture tables

The columns of IBMQREP_CAPMON and IBMQREP_CAPQMON are shown in the *The control tables – The Q Capture control tables* section of *Chapter 3*. The difference between the two tables is that IBMQREP_CAPMON contains statistics about the whole of Q Capture whereas IBMQREP_CAPQMON contains statistics for each Send Queue.

The ROWS_PROCESSED column of the IBMQREP_CAPMON table shows all the rows that Q Capture has read from the DB2 log irrespective of whether the rows are for a subscribed table or not.

The ROWS_PUBLISHED column of the IBMQREP_CAPQMON table shows the number of rows Q Capture has sent to the Send Queue.

The Q Apply tables

The table of interest is IBMQREP_APPLYMON. Check the MEM_FULL_TIME column, which tells us if we have enough agents defined.

Collection of data for historical analysis

All of the strategies discussed so far have been real time strategies. What about collecting information for historical analysis. All of the information that we need is in the xxxMON control tables where xxx is CAP and APPLY for Q Capture and Q Apply respectively.

The tables of interest for Q Capture are IBMQREP.CAPMON and IBMQREP.CAPQMON, and for Q Apply it is IBMQREP.APPLYMON, and these tables were discussed in the previous section.

What we will collect is the hourly-rolled up information for the parameters shown in the following tables.

Historical monitoring of Q Capture

In this section, we create a table to contain historical Q Capture information and then issue some SQL to populate it. The history table will contain the following columns (Note that the pruning of the control tables may affect your results):

RUNDATE (mm/dd/yyyy)	The date for the entry.
hour (int)	End hour for the totals.
COUNT (bigint)	The number of rows from the IBMQREP_CAPMON table that make up this combined entry.
ROWS_PROCESSED (sum) (bigint)	The number of rows (individual insert, update, or delete operations) that Q Capture reads from the log.
TRANS_SKIPPED (sum) (bigint)	The number of transactions (containing changed rows) that were not put on queues because the changes were to columns that are not part of a Q subscription or XML publication (the ALL_CHANGED_ROWS parameter in the IBMQREP_SUBS table was set to No, the default).
TRANS_PROCESSED (sum) (bigint)	The number of transactions that Q Capture processed.
TRANS_SPILLED (sum) (bigint)	The number of transactions that Q Capture spilled to a file after exceeding the MEMORY_LIMIT threshold.
MAX_TRANS_SIZE (max/min) (int)	The largest transaction, in megabytes, that Q Capture processed.
QUEUES_IN_ERROR (sum) (int)	The number of queues that were not accepting messages.

Create a history table as follows:

```
$ db2 "create table db2admin.hist_capmon (rundate date not null, hour
int, count int, sum_rows_processed bigint, sum_trans_skipped bigint,
sum_trans_processed bigint, sum_trans_spilled bigint, max_max_trans_size
int, min_max_trans_size int, max_queues_in_error int, min_queues_in_error
int) "

$ db2 "alter table db2admin.hist_capmon add constraint prid primary key
(rundate) "
```

Populate the Q Capture history table using the following SQL:

```
$ db2 "INSERT INTO db2admin.hist_capmon SELECT '02/15/2006',
HOUR(monitor_time)+1, count(*), SUM(rows_processed), SUM(trans_skipped),
SUM(trans_processed), SUM(trans_spilled), MAX(max_trans_size), MIN(
min_trans_size), MAX(queues_in_error), MIN(queues_in_error) FROM
asn.ibmqrep_capmon WHERE DATE(monitor_time) = '02/15/2006' GROUP
BY(hour(monitor_time)"
```

We would change the date fields to the date we want to collect data for.

Historical monitoring of Q Apply

In this section, we create a table to contain historical Q Apply information and then issue some SQL to populate it. The history table will contain the following columns:

RUNDATE (mm/dd/yyyy)	The date for the entry.
HOUR (int)	End hour for the totals.
COUNT (bigint)	The number of rows from the IBMQREP_APPLYMON table that make up this combined entry.
CURRENT_MEMORY (max/min) (int)	The amount of memory in bytes that the Q Apply browser thread used for reading transactions from this queue.
QDEPTH (max/min) (int)	The queue depth (number of messages on the queue).
END2END_LATENCY (max/min) (int)	The average elapsed milliseconds between the time that transactions were committed to the source table and the time that they were committed to the target.
QLATENCY (max/min) (int)	The average elapsed milliseconds between the time that Q Capture put messages on the Send Queue and the time that Q Apply got them from the Receive Queue.
APPLY_LATENCY (max/min) (int)	The average elapsed milliseconds between the time that Q Apply read transactions from the Receive Queue and the time that they were committed to the target.
TRANS_APPLIED (sum) (bigint)	The total number of transactions from this Receive Queue that the Q Apply committed to the target.

ROWS_APPLIED (sum) (bigint)	The total number of inserts, updates, and deletes from this Receive Queue that Q Apply applied to the target.
TRANS_SERIALIZED (sum) (bigint)	The total number of transactions that conflicted with another transaction (either because of a row conflict or a referential integrity conflict). In these cases, Q Apply suspends parallel processing and applies the row changes within the transaction in the order they were committed at the source.
RI_DEPENDENCIES (sum) (bigint)	The total number of referential integrity conflicts that were detected, forcing transactions to be serialized.
RI_RETRIES (sum) (bigint)	The number of times that Q Apply had to re-apply row changes because of referential integrity conflicts when the transactions that they were part of were executed in parallel.
DEADLOCK_RETRIES (sum) (bigint)	The number of times that Q Apply re-applied row changes because of lock timeouts and deadlocks.
ROWS_NOT_APPLIED (sum) (bigint)	The number of rows that could not be applied, and were entered in the IBMQREP_EXCEPTIONS table.
MONSTER_TRANS (sum) (bigint)	The number of transactions that exceeded the MEMORY_LIMIT for the receive queue set in the IBMQREP_RECVQUEUES table.
MEM_FULL_TIME (sum) (bigint)	The total number of seconds that Q Apply could not build transactions from this Receive Queue because its agents were using all available memory to apply transactions.
OKSQLSTATE_ERRORS (sum) (bigint)	The number of row changes that caused an SQL error that is defined as acceptable in the OKSQLSTATES field of the IBMQREP_TARGETS table. Q Apply ignores these errors.
KEY_DEPENDENCIES (sum) (bigint)	The total number of replication key constraints that were detected, forcing transactions to be serialized.
UNIQ_DEPENDENCIES (sum) (bigint)	The total number of unique index constraints that were detected, forcing transactions to be serialized.
UNIQ_RETRIES (sum) (bigint)	The number of times that Q Apply tried to re-apply rows that were not applied in parallel because of unique index constraints.

Create the Q Apply history table using the following SQL:

```
$ db2 "create table db2admin.hist_appmon (rundate date, hour int, count
int, max_current_memory int, min_current_memory int, max_qdepth int,
min_qdepth int, max_end2end_latency int, min_end2end_latency int, max_
qlatency int, min_qlatency int, sum_trans_applied bigint, sum_rows_
applied bigint, sum_trans_serialized bigint, sum_ri_dependencies bigint,
sum_ri_retries bigint, sum_deadlock_retries bigint, sum_rows_not_applied
bigint, sum_monster_trans bigint, sum_mem_full_time bigint) "
```

Populate the Q Apply history table using the following SQL:

```
$ db2 "INSERT INTO db2admin.hist_appmon SELECT '02/15/2006',
HOUR(monitor_time)+1, COUNT(*),MAX(current_memory), MIN(current_
memory), MAX(qdepth), MIN(qdepth), MAX(end2end_latency), MIN(end2end_
latency), MAX(qlatency), MIN(qlatency), SUM(trans_applied), SUM(rows_
applied), SUM(trans_serialized), SUM(ri_dependencies), SUM(ri_retries),
SUM(deadlock_retries), SUM(rows_not_applied), SUM(monster_trans),
SUM(mem_full_time) FROM asn.ibmqrep_applymon WHERE DATE(monitor_time) =
'02/16/2006' GROUP BY (HOUR(monitor_time)) "
```

We would change the date fields to the date we want to collect data for.

To determine the row throughput

We want to determine the row throughput over the past 10 minutes, 5 minutes, 1 minute, and the latest value.

```
C:\asnclp> db2 -tvf quer01.sql

with t1(num) as (select count(*) from asn.ibmqrep_capmon where
monitor_time > current timestamp - 10 minutes), t2(rowsp) as (select
sum(rows_processed) from asn.ibmqrep_capmon where monitor_time > current
timestamp - 10 minutes) select rowsp/num from t1,t2

1
-----------

          0
```

We could write a stored procedure as follows:

Create a file called sp02.sql containing:

```
create procedure get_thru (in timeval int, out v1 int, out v2 int, out
v3 int)
language SQL
P1: begin
select count(*) into v1 from asn.ibmqrep_capmon where monitor_time >
current timestamp - timeval minutes;
```

```
select sum(rows_processed) into v2 from asn.ibmqrep_capmon where
monitor_time > current timestamp - timeval minutes;

set v3 = v2/v1;
end P1 @
```

Compile this file as:

C:\asnclp> db2 -td@ -vf sp02.sql

And run the procedure as:

C:\asnclp> db2 call get_thru(10,?,?,?)

```
Value of output parameters
--------------------------
Parameter Name   : V1
Parameter Value  : 0
Parameter Name   : V2
Parameter Value  : -
Parameter Name   : V3
Parameter Value  : -
Return Status = 0
```

Or, we could create a file called sp01.sql containing:

```
create procedure get_thru2 (in timeval int)
language SQL
begin
declare c1 cursor with return for
with t1(num) as
(select count(*) from asn.ibmqrep_capmon where monitor_time > current
timestamp - timeval minutes),
t2(rowsp) as
(select sum(rows_processed) from asn.ibmqrep_capmon where monitor_time
> current timestamp - timeval minutes)
select rowsp/num from t1,t2;

open c1;

end @
```

Compile this file as:

C:\asnclp> db2 -td@ -vf sp01.sql

And run the procedure as:

C:\asnclp> db2 call get_thru2(10)

```
Result set 1
-------------

1
-----------

          -

1 record(s) selected.
Return Status = 0
```

Manual monitoring

We can of course monitor manually — what we mean by this, is that, we can write programs and scripts to mimic the function of the Replication Alert Monitor, but why would we want to do this?

- To check if Q Capture is running for our Q Capture with a control table schema of ASN running on the db2a server, we would issue:

  `$ asnqccmd CAPTURE_SERVER=db2a STATUS SHOW DETAILS`

- To check if Q Apply is running with a control table schema of ASN running on the db2b server, we would issue:

  `$ asnqacmd APPLY_SERVER=db2b STATUS SHOW DETAILS`

- To check the depth of a Receive Queue on Queue Manager QMB we would issue:

  `$ runmqsc QMB`

  `:dis ql(CAPA.TO.APPB.RECVQ) CURDEPTH`

Monitoring using the Replication Alert Monitor

We can use the **Replication Alert Monitor (RAM)** to monitor the state of our replication environment.

The Replication Alert Monitor is a program, which comes bundled with the replication code which checks the status of various replication objects and reports on these.

The Replication Alert Monitor control tables are described in the *The control tables – The Replication Alert Monitor control tables* section of *Chapter 3*, but the question that we need to answer is, *where do these control tables go*. We can put them on the same server on which Q Capture is running, or the same server on which Q Apply is running, or they can be placed on a totally different server, as shown in the following diagram. Here we have a monitoring server called MONDB and two monitored servers called DB2A and DB2B.

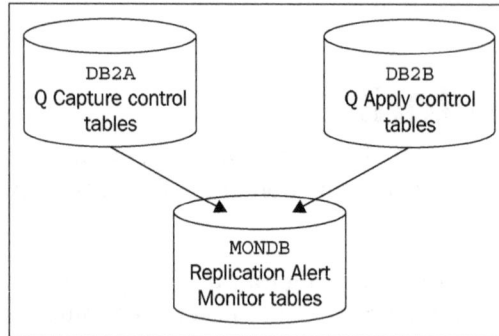

Before we look at setting up the Replication Alert Monitor, let's first look at the Q Capture and Q Apply conditions that we can monitor.

Running Alert Monitoring is a two step process—first we need to create the Alert Monitor and then we need to start it using the asnmon command described in the Starting the Replication Alert Monitor section of this chapter.

Q Capture alert conditions

There are seven Q Capture alert conditions:

- QCAPTURE_STATUS: The Replication Alert Monitor sends an alert when Q Capture is not running.

- QCAPTURE_ERRORS: The Replication Alert Monitor sends an alert when it finds a row with the value of ERROR in the OPERATION column of the IBMQREP_CAPTRACE table.

- QCAPTURE_WARNINGS: The Replication Alert Monitor sends an alert when it finds a row with the value of WARNING in the OPERATION column in the IBMQREP_CAPTRACE table.

- `QCAPTURE_LATENCY`: Q Capture latency measures the difference between the time that data was written to the database and the time that Q Capture passes it on. The Replication Alert Monitor sends an alert when the Q Capture latency exceeds a specified threshold. Q Capture latency is measured in seconds.

- `QCAPTURE_MEMORY`: The Replication Alert Monitor sends an alert when Q Capture uses more memory than a specified threshold. Memory is measured in megabytes.

- `QCAPTURE_TRANSIZE`: The Replication Alert Monitor sends an alert when a transaction that Q Capture is processing uses more memory than a specified threshold. Memory is measured in megabytes.

- `QCAPTURE_SUBSINACT`: The Replication Alert Monitor sends an alert when Q Capture deactivates a Q subscription.

Q Apply alert conditions

There are nine Q Apply alert conditions:

- `QAPPLY_STATUS`: The Replication Alert Monitor sends an alert when Q Apply is not running.

- `QAPPLY_ERRORS`: The Replication Alert Monitor sends an alert when it finds a row with the value of ERROR in the OPERATION column in the IBMQREP_APPLYTRACE table.

- `QAPPLY_WARNINGS`: The Replication Alert Monitor sends an alert when it finds a row with the value of WARNING in the OPERATION column in the IBMQREP_APPLYTRACE table.

- `QAPPLY_LATENCY`: Q Apply latency measures the time it takes for a transaction to be applied to a target table after Q Apply gets the transaction from a Receive Queue. The Replication Alert Monitor sends an alert when the Q Apply latency exceeds the threshold that we specify. Q Apply latency is measured in milliseconds.

- `QAPPLY_EELATENCY`: Q Apply end-to-end latency measures the total time that replication requires to capture changes and apply those changes to a target database. The Replication Alert Monitor sends an alert when the Q Apply end-to-end latency exceeds the threshold that we specify. Q Apply end-to-end latency is measured in seconds.

- `QAPPLY_MEMORY`: The Replication Alert Monitor sends an alert when Q Apply uses more memory than the threshold that we specify. Memory is measured in megabytes.

- QAPPLY_EXCEPTIONS: The Replication Alert Monitor sends an alert when a row is inserted in the IBMQREP_EXCEPTIONS table because of a conflict or SQL error at a target.

- QAPPLY_SPILLQDEPTH: The Replication Alert Monitor sends an alert when the fullness of the spill queue exceeds the threshold that we specify. Fullness is expressed as a percentage.

- QAPPLY_QDEPTH: The Replication Alert Monitor sends an alert when the fullness of any queue exceeds the threshold that we specify. Fullness is expressed as a percentage.

Creating the RAM control tables

In the following examples, we are storing our Replication Alert Monitor control tables in a database called MONDB. We will put the monitor tables in their own table space, which we first have to create:

```
$ db2 connect to mondb
```

```
$ db2 "CREATE REGULAR TABLESPACE TSPACEMON PAGESIZE 4 K MANAGED BY SYSTEM
USING ('C:\tspacemon.txt' ) EXTENTSIZE 16 OVERHEAD 10.5 PREFETCHSIZE 16
TRANSFERRATE 0.14 BUFFERPOOL IBMDEFAULTBP DROPPED TABLE RECOVERY ON"
```

Now we can create the monitor tables by running the following ASNCLP script:

> This is an SQL Replication command and not a Q replication command – therefore we do not set ASNCLP SESSION SET TO to Q REPLICATION but to SQL REPLICATION.

The following shows an example ASNCLP script for creating the monitor control tables in MONDB_crt_control.asnclp:

```
ASNCLP SESSION SET TO SQL REPLICATION;
SET RUN SCRIPT NOW STOP ON SQL ERROR ON;

SET SERVER MONITOR TO DB mondb;

CREATE CONTROL TABLES FOR MONITOR CONTROL SERVER
IN UW OTHERS tspacemon;
```

Check that the tables have been created successfully:

```
$ db2 CONNECT TO mondb
$ db2 list tables for schema asn
```

Setting up e-mail notification

Setting up e-mail notification requires the following steps:

1. create a contact.
2. create a monitor alert.

The contacts that we create are unique to the Replication Alert Monitor — we cannot use contacts created in other GUIs, for example in the Health Center.

The following is the ASNCLP script (`MONDB_create_contact.asnclp`) to create the contact information:

```
ASNCLP SESSION SET TO SQL REPLICATION;
SET RUN SCRIPT NOW STOP ON SQL ERROR ON;

set server monitor to db mondb;

CREATE CONTACT oncalldba EMAIL "kumarp3@uk.ibm.com";
```

For us to be able to use notification the **DB2 Administration Server (DAS)** needs to be active, and we need to have registered an **SMTP (Simple Mail Transfer Protocol)** server with the DAS.

There is no command to check if the DAS is running, all we can do is try and start it again using the `db2admin` command:

```
$ db2admin start
```

```
SQL4409W  The DB2 Administration Server is already active.
```

If we enter the command with the `start` option and the DAS is already active, we will get back the `SQL4409W` message.

We can get the administration information using:

```
$ db2 get admin cfg
```

```
          Admin Server Configuration
 Authentication Type DAS                 (AUTHENTICATION) = SERVER_
ENCRYPT
 DAS Administration Authority Group Name  (DASADM_GROUP) =
 DAS Discovery Mode                          (DISCOVER) = SEARCH
 Name of the DB2 Server System             (DB2SYSTEM) = IBM-
8969A715F10
 Java Development Kit Installation Path DAS   (JDK_PATH) = AUTOMATIC
(C:\Program Files\IBM\SQLLIB\java\jdk)
 Java Development Kit Installation Path DAS   (JDK_64_PATH) =
AUTOMATIC (C:\Program Files\IBM\SQLLIB\java\jdk)
```

```
DAS Code Page                          (DAS_CODEPAGE) = 0
DAS Territory                          (DAS_TERRITORY) = 0
Location of Contact List               (CONTACT_HOST) =
Execute Expired Tasks                  (EXEC_EXP_TASK) = NO
Scheduler Mode                         (SCHED_ENABLE) = ON
SMTP Server                            (SMTP_SERVER) =
Tools Catalog Database                 (TOOLSCAT_DB) = TOOLSDB
Tools Catalog Database Instance        (TOOLSCAT_INST) = DB2
Tools Catalog Database Schema          (TOOLSCAT_SCHEMA) = SYSTOOLS
Scheduler User ID                                      =
Diagnostic error capture level         (DIAGLEVEL) = 3
```

In the preceding output, the SMTP_SERVER value is blank—we have to make sure we have specified a suitable value. The following shows an example of updating the configuration file with a suitable value:

```
$ db2 UPDATE ADMIN CFG USING SMTP_SERVER relay.uk.ibm.com
```

Note that the DAS has been deprecated in DB2 9.7.

Monitoring Q Capture

Let's look at monitoring Q Capture. What we want to check for is:

- If Capture is running
- If any errors and warnings have been generated
- If the latency gets greater than 30 seconds
- If any Q subscriptions become inactive

We can define one monitor to monitor all of the preceding conditions using an ASNCLP script.

For Q Capture running on DB2A, we can use the ASNCLP commands in the MONDB_crt_alert_capture.asnclp file. Note that this is a Q replication command and not an SQL Replication command:

```
ASNCLP SESSION SET TO Q REPLICATION;
SET RUN SCRIPT NOW STOP ON SQL ERROR ON;

SET SERVER MONITOR TO DB mondb;
SET SERVER CAPTURE TO DB db2a;

CREATE ALERT CONDITIONS FOR QCAPTURE SCHEMA ASN
MONITOR QUALIFIER MONAC1
```

```
Notify contact oncalldba (status down, errors, warnings, latency 30,
subscriptions inactive);
```

- The monitor name is MONAC1, which is made up of three parts:

  ```
  MON<DB2-where-program-is-running><type-of-prog><monitor-number>
  ```

  So in this particular case, we are running Q Capture (C) against DB2A (A) and this is the first monitor (1) we are setting up, so the monitor name will be MONAC1.

  We can of course call the monitor anything we like, but it's a good idea to come up with a naming convention.

- The contact name (dbaoncall) is the name that we defined in our contacts list in *Monitoring using the Replication Alert Monitor – Setting up e-mail notification* section of this chapter. The contact needs to exist before we can run the ASNCLP command.

- For each condition that we have specified we get a row in the IBMSNAP_CONDITIONS table. We also get a row written to the IBMSNAP_MONPARMS table.

  Do not forget that the monitor needs to be started after it has been created.

Monitoring Q Apply

What we want to check for when monitoring Q Apply is:

- Whether Q Apply is running
- Whether any errors and warnings are generated
- Whether any exceptions are generated
- Whether the Receive Queue depth is greater than 75%

We can define one monitor to monitor all of these conditions using an ASNCLP script.

For Q Apply running on DB2B:

```
ASNCLP SESSION SET TO Q REPLICATION;
SET RUN SCRIPT NOW STOP ON SQL ERROR ON;

SET SERVER MONITOR TO DB mondb;
SET SERVER APPLY   TO DB db2b;

CREATE ALERT CONDITIONS FOR QAPPLY SCHEMA TST
MONITOR QUALIFIER MONBA1
Notify contact oncalldba (status down, errors, warnings, exceptions,
queue depth 75);
```

It is of course possible to monitor both Q Capture and Q Apply from one monitor qualifier, using the following ASNCLP script:

```
ASNCLP SESSION SET TO Q REPLICATION;
SET RUN SCRIPT NOW STOP ON SQL ERROR ON;

SET SERVER MONITOR TO DB mondb;
SET SERVER CAPTURE TO DB db2a;

CREATE ALERT CONDITIONS FOR QCAPTURE SCHEMA ASN
MONITOR QUALIFIER MONACBA
Notify contact oncalldba (status down, errors, warnings, latency 30,
subscriptions inactive);

SET SERVER MONITOR TO DB mondb;
SET SERVER APPLY   TO DB db2b;

CREATE ALERT CONDITIONS FOR QAPPLY SCHEMA ASN
MONITOR QUALIFIER MONACBA
Notify contact oncalldba (status down, errors, warnings, latency 30,
subscriptions inactive);
```

Note how we have *concatenated* what the monitor qualifier MONACBA should monitor—Q Capture on DB2A and Q Apply on DB2B. We have been able to do this by re-specifying the SET SERVER commands before the second definition—remember that ASNCLP is context specific (that is, it does not save context). We do not need to include the second SET SERVER MONITOR TO DB mondb line for the script to run, but it is included for clarity.

The monitor qualifier name stands for Q Capture running on DB2A and Q Apply running on DB2B—it is a different naming scheme from before. We have to decide on whether we want to create a single monitor qualifier for each component (Q Capture and Q Apply running against respective databases) or whether we want combined monitor qualifiers.

Starting the Replication Alert Monitor

Once we have created our monitors, we need to start them—we do this using the asnmon command, the following shows the parameters:

- monitor_server=<server>: This specifies the name of the Monitor control server where the Replication Alert Monitor runs and the monitor control tables reside. If entered this must be the first parameter.

- monitor_qual=<mon_qual>: This specifies the monitor qualifier that the Replication Alert Monitor program uses. The monitor qualifier identifies the server to be monitored and the associated monitoring conditions. We must specify a monitor qualifier. The monitor qualifier name is case sensitive and can be a maximum of 18 characters.

- `monitor_interval=<n>`: This specifies how frequently (in seconds) the Replication Alert Monitor runs for this monitor qualifier. The default is 300 seconds. This parameter is ignored by the Replication Alert Monitor if you set the `runonce` parameter to `y`.

- `runonce=[n/y]`: This specifies whether the Replication Alert Monitor runs only one time for this monitor qualifier:
    - ○ n: This is the default value. The Replication Alert Monitor runs at the frequency indicated by the `monitor_interval` parameter.
    - ○ y: The Replication Alert Monitor runs only one monitor cycle.

- `autoprune=[y/n]`: This specifies whether automatic pruning of the rows in the Replication Alert Monitor alerts (`IBMSNAP_ALERTS`) table is enabled:
    - ○ y: This is the default value. The Replication Alert Monitor program automatically prunes the rows in the `IBMSNAP_ALERTS` table that are older than the value of the `alert_prune_limit` parameter.
    - ○ n: Automatic pruning is disabled.

- `logreuse=[n/y]`: This specifies whether the Replication Alert Monitor reuses or appends messages to its diagnostic log file (`<db2instance>.<monitor_server>.<mon_qual>.MON.log`):
    - ○ n: This is the default value. The Replication Alert Monitor appends messages to the log file.
    - ○ y: The Replication Alert Monitor reuses the log file by deleting it and then recreating it when it is restarted.

- `logstdout=[n/y]`: This specifies where messages are sent by the Replication Alert Monitor:
    - ○ n: This is the default value. The Replication Alert Monitor program sends messages to the log file only.
    - ○ y: The Replication Alert Monitor program sends messages to both the log file and the standard output (`stdout`).

- `term=[y/n]`: This specifies whether a monitor program keeps running when DB2 is quiesced:
    - ○ y: This is the default value. The monitor program stops when DB2 is quiesced.

- ○ n: The monitor program keeps running while DB2 is in quiesce mode and has forced all applications to disconnect (including the monitor program). When DB2 is taken out of quiesce mode, the monitor program goes back to monitoring replication.

- `alert_prune_limit=<n>`: This specifies how long (in minutes) rows are kept in the Replication Alert Monitor alerts (`IBMSNAP_ALERTS`) table. Any rows older than this value are pruned. The default is 10,080 minutes (seven days).

- `trace_limit=<n>`: This specifies how long (in minutes) a row can remain in the Replication Alert Monitor trace (`IBMSNAP_MONTRACE`) table before it becomes eligible for pruning. All `IBMSNAP_MONTRACE` rows that are older than the value of this `trace_limit` parameter are pruned at the next pruning cycle. The default is 10,080 minutes (seven days).

- `max_notifications_per_alert=<n>`: This specifies the maximum number of the same alerts that are sent to a user, when the alerts occurred during the time period specified by the `max_notifications_minutes` parameter value. Use this parameter to avoid re-sending the same alerts to a user. The default is 3.

- `max_notifications_minutes=<n>`: This parameter works with the `max_notifications_per_alert` parameter to indicate the time period when alert conditions occurred. The default is 60 minutes.

- `pwdfile=<filepath>`: This specifies the fully qualified name of the password file. You define this file using the `asnpwd` command. The default file name is `asnpwd.aut`.

- `monitor_path=<path>`: This specifies the location of the log files used by the Replication Alert Monitor program. The default is the directory where the `asnmon` command was invoked.

- `monitor_errors=<address>`: This specifies the e-mail address to which notifications are sent if a fatal error is detected before the alert monitor connects to the Monitor control server. Use this parameter to send a notification that the Monitor control server connection failed because of invalid start parameters, an incorrect monitor qualifier, an inaccessible database, or other error. Type double quotation marks around the e-mail address text. You can enter multiple e-mail addresses, separated with commas. You can type spaces before or after the commas.

- `email_server=<servername>`: This specifies the e-mail server address. Enter this parameter only if you use the `ASNMAIL` exit routine with SMTP.

- `console=[n/y]`: This specifies whether the Replication Alert Monitor sends alert notifications to the z/OS console. If we set this parameter to Y (yes) and an e-mail server was already configured, alerts are sent to both the z/OS console and the e-mail server:
  - ◦ n: This is the default value. The Replication Alert Monitor does not send alert notifications to the z/OS console.
  - ◦ y: The Replication Alert Monitor sends alert notifications to the z/OS console.

Summarizing the default values:

Parameter	Default	Parameter	Default	Parameter	Default
autoprune	Y	monitor_ errors	None	runonce	N
email_server	None	monitor_ interval	300 secs	trace_limit	10080 minutes
max_ notification_ minutes	60 mins	monitor_ limit	10080 mins		

We can query the IBMSNAP_MONPARMS table to see these values:

```
$ db2 "select substr(monitor_qual,1,10) as monqual, alert_prune_limit as
APL, autoprune as AP, substr(email_server,1,20) as emailserver, logreuse
as R, notif_per_alert as NPA, notif_minutes as NM FROM
asn.ibmsnap_monparms "

$ db2 "select substr(monitor_qual,1,10) as monqual, substr(monitor_
errors,1,10) as ME, monitor_interval as MI, substr(monitor_path,1,20) as
monpath, runonce as R, term as T, trace_limit as TL FROM
asn.ibmsnap_monparms "
```

MONQUAL	APL	AP	EMAILSERVER	R	NPA	NM
----------	-----------	--	--------------------	-	-----------	--------
MONAC1	10080	Y	-	N	3	60

ME	MI	MONPATH	R	T	TL
----------	-----------	--------------------	-	-	-----------
-	300000	-	N	N	10080

So to start the Replication Alert Monitor for the monitor (monac1) we defined for Q Capture, we would issue:

```
$ asnmon MONITOR_SERVER=mondb MONITOR_QUAL=monac1 EMAIL_SERVER=relay.
uk.ibm.com
```

ASN0600I   "Asnmon" :   "" : "Initial" : Program "monitor 9.1.0" is starting.

ASN5101I   MONITOR "MONAC1" : "Initial". The Replication Alert Monitor program started successfully.

If we do not specify an email_server value, then we get the following message:

ASN0600I   "Asnmon" :   "" : "Initial" : Program "monitor 9.1.0" is starting.

ASN5108W   MONITOR "MONAC1" : "Initial". The EMAIL_SERVER parameter was not set so e-mail notification cannot be sent.

ASN5101I   MONITOR "MONAC1" : "Initial". The Replication Alert Monitor program started successfully.z

Issuing the asnmon command without prefixing it with start will lock out the screen on which the command was issued.

Monitor management

We use the ASNMCMD command to manage a running RAM monitor.

When we issue the asnmcmd command, we need to specify:

- The monitor server name
- The monitor name

And then one of the following keywords:

chgparms <parameters>, reinit, status, stop, qryparms, suspend, resume.

Where <parameters> can be:

monitor_interval=<n>, autoprune= [y|n], alert_prune_limit=<n>, trace_limit=<n>, max_notifications_per_alert=<n>, max_notifications_minutes=<n>

We can issue this command from a different screen from which the monitor was started.

Checking which monitors are active

To check which monitors are active, we can use the ASNMCMD command with the STATUS parameter. So to check the status of the monac1 monitor on mondb, we would issue:

```
$ asnmcmd MONITOR_SERVER=mondb MONITOR_QUAL=monac1 STATUS
ASN0600I   "AsnMcmd" :   ""  : "Initial" : Program "asnmcmd 9.1.0" is
starting.
ASN0520I   "AsnMcmd" :   "MONAC1" : "Initial" : The STATUS command
response: "HoldLThread" thread is in the "is resting" state.
ASN0520I   "AsnMcmd" :   "MONAC1" : "Initial" : The STATUS command
response: "AdminThread" thread is in the "is resting" state.
ASN0520I   "AsnMcmd" :   "MONAC1" : "Initial" : The STATUS command
response: "WorkerThread" thread is in the "is resting" state.
```

If there is nothing running, then we get the following messages:

```
ASN0600I   "AsnMcmd" :   ""  : "Initial" : Program "asnmcmd 9.1.0" is
starting.
ASN0506E   "AsnMcmd" :   "ASN" : "Initial" : The command was not
processed. The "Monitor" program is presumed down.
```

Note that there is a slight delay of a few seconds between the ASN0600I message and the ASN0506E message.

We can check when a monitor last ran using the following query:

```
$ db2 "SELECT SUBSTR(monitor_qual,1,10) AS monqual, last_monitor_time,
start_monitor_time, end_monitor_time, lastrun, lastsuccess, status FROM
asn.ibmsnap_monservers"
```

```
MONQUAL     LAST_MONITOR_TIME           START_MONITOR_TIME
MONAC1      2007-03-16-10.18.57.750000 2007-03-16-10.18.57.750000

END_MONITOR_TIME
2007-03-16-10.18.59.765000

LASTRUN                      LASTSUCCESS                 STATUS
2007-03-16-10.18.57.750000 2007-03-16-10.18.57.750000 0
```

Changing or reinitializing a monitor

If we change any of the following while the monitor is running such as contact information, alert conditions, or parameter values:

```
$ asnmcmd MONITOR_SERVER=mondb MONITOR_QUAL=monac1 CHGPARMS
MONITOR_INTERVAL=10
```

Then we do not have to stop and start the monitor, we can just reinitialize it as follows:

```
$ asnmcmd MONITOR_SERVER=mondb MONITOR_QUAL=monac1 REINIT
```

Stopping a monitor

To stop a monitor called monac1, we would issue the following command:

```
$ asnmcmd MONITOR_SERVER=mondb MONITOR_QUAL=monac1 STOP
```

Suspending or resuming a monitor

We cannot suspend a monitor from the Replication Center, we can only use ASNCLP scripts.

We can stop checking Q Capture and Q Apply for all defined alert conditions using the ASNMCMD SUSPEND command. When we want to resume monitoring again, then we issue the ASNMCMD RESUME command. Note that using the ANSMCMD command is an all or nothing approach. The SUSPEND option will suspend all monitoring qualifiers.

So what happens if we just want to suspend monitoring one monitored sever (DB2A or DB2B)? In this case, we would have to create a monitor suspension. We can suspend a monitor once only or on a repeatable basis. If we want to suspend a monitor on a repeatable basis, then it's best to first create a suspension template and then create a monitor suspension. If we want to suspend a monitor server once only, then we just need to create a monitor suspension.

> All dates and times for monitor suspensions are based on the clock at the system where the monitor is running (MONDB). The time format is HH:MM:SS and the date format is YYYY-MM-DD.

The ASNCLP command to create a monitor suspension template is:

```
CREATE MONITOR SUSPENSION TEMPLATE <template_name>
START TIME <starting_time>
REPEATS occ-clause
```

Where `occ_clause` can be:

DAILY FOR DURATION <n> [HOURS | MINUTES]

Or:

WEEKLY DAY OF WEEK <day>

FOR DURATION <n> [HOURS/MINUTES/DAYS]

Where <day> can be Sunday, Monday, Tuesday, Wednesday, Thursday, Friday, or Saturday.

The ASNCLP command to create a monitor suspension is:

```
CREATE MONITOR SUSPENSION <name>
[FOR SERVER <server_name> | ALIAS <server_alias>]
STARTING DATE <date>
[USING TEMPLATE <template_name> | STARTING TIME <starting_time>]
ENDING DATE <date>
ENDING TIME <ending_time>
```

So when should we use templates? We should use them:

- If we want to suspend more than one monitor at the same date or time.
- If we want to suspend a monitor on anything but a daily basis. Note that, we can specify a day of week when we create a monitor suspension template, which is not possible in the monitor suspension definition.

There are eight ASNCLP commands which deal with monitor suspensions:

ASNCLP command:	Description:
LIST MONITOR SUSPENSION	Generates a list of suspensions on a monitor control server.
ALTER MONITOR SUSPENSION	Allows us to change the following properties of a monitor suspension: • The template that is used • The start or end date for using a template • The start or end date for suspending the monitor program one time
DROP MONITOR SUSPENSION	Deletes a monitor suspension from the monitor control tables.
LIST MONITOR SUSPENSION TEMPLATE	Generates a list of monitor suspension templates on a monitor control server.
ALTER MONITOR SUSPENSION TEMPLATE	Allows us to change the frequency and length of monitor suspensions as defined in a suspension template.
DROP MONITOR SUSPENSION TEMPLATE	Deletes a monitor suspension template from the monitor control tables.
CREATE MONITOR SUSPENSION TEMPLATE	Creates a monitor suspension template.
CREATE MONITOR SUSPENSION	Creates a monitor suspension.

Even though we want to monitor Q replication, we need to specify SQL replication in the ASNCLP SESSION line.

So let's look at the ASNCLP command to create a monitor suspension template called LUNCH which starts daily at 12:00 and lasts for one hour:

```
ASNCLP SESSION SET TO SQL REPLICATION;
SET RUN SCRIPT NOW STOP ON SQL ERROR ON;

SET SERVER MONITOR TO DB mondb;

CREATE MONITOR SUSPENSION TEMPLATE lunch
START TIME 12:00:00
REPEATS DAILY
FOR DURATION 1 HOURS;
```

In the preceding command, we have not specified a server on which to apply the suspension — we have only defined the monitor server where to store the metadata. We have also not specified a start and end date — only a start and end time.

Once we have created a monitor suspension template, we can define a monitor suspension for a specific server (that is, source or target) and a specific date range, which uses the template we defined previously.

```
ASNCLP SESSION SET TO SQL REPLICATION;
SET RUN SCRIPT NOW STOP ON SQL ERROR ON;

SET SERVER MONITOR TO DB mondb;
SET SERVER TARGET  TO DB db2b;

CREATE MONITOR SUSPENSION NAME s1
FOR SERVER db2b
STARTING DATE 2007-03-20
USING TEMPLATE lunch
ENDING DATE 2007-12-31;
```

In the above monitor suspension code, we do not have to specify a time value, because the time value is specified in the template definition. Note that now we have to specify a server for the template to work against.

We can also define a monitor suspension without making reference to a template by specifying all the information that we need (this would be the once only processing model):

```
CREATE MONITOR SUSPENSION NAME s2
FOR SERVER db2a
STARTING DATE 2007-03-20
STARTING TIME 12:00:00
ENDING DATE 2007-12-31
ENDING TIME 13:00:00
```

In the above monitor suspension definition we have not specified a template, so we have included the start and end dates and times.

We can list our monitor suspension templates and monitor suspensions using the following ASNCLP command:

```
ASNCLP SESSION SET TO SQL REPLICATION;
SET RUN SCRIPT NOW STOP ON SQL ERROR ON;

SET SERVER MONITOR TO DB mondb;

LIST MONITOR SUSPENSION TEMPLATE;
LIST MONITOR SUSPENSION;
```

This produces the following output:

```
====
CMD: LIST MONITOR SUSPENSION TEMPLATE;
====
TEMPLATE NAME        START TIME FREQUENCY DURATION UNITS
-------------------- ---------- --------- -------- -------
LUNCH                12:00:00   SUNDAY    1.0      HOURS
1 Template(s) found.
====
CMD: LIST MONITOR SUSPENSION;
====
SUSPENSION NAME      SERVER NAME        TEMPLATE NAME      FREQUENCY
DURATION
-------------------- ------------------ ------------------ ---------
S1                   TARGET             LUNCH              SUNDAY
1.0
SUSPENDUNITS   FIRST SUSPENSION    STOP
-------- ------- ------------------- -------------------
HOURS    2007-03-20-12:00:00 2007-12-31-00:00:00
1 Suspension(s) found.
```

We can see the monitor suspension template called LUNCH, which we created and the monitor suspension S1.

We can alter a monitor suspension template by using the ASNCLP command ALTER MONITOR SUSPENSION. Suppose we want to change the suspension day from Sunday to Monday, then the ASNCLP command would be:

```
ASNCLP SESSION SET TO SQL REPLICATION;
SET RUN SCRIPT NOW STOP ON SQL ERROR ON;

SET SERVER MONITOR TO DB mondb;

ALTER MONITOR SUSPENSION TEMPLATE lunch;
LIST MONITOR SUSPENSION TEMPLATE;
```

To drop a monitor suspension, we would use the DROP MONITOR SUSPENSION ASNCLP command:

```
ASNCLP SESSION SET TO SQL REPLICATION;
SET RUN SCRIPT NOW STOP ON SQL ERROR ON;

SET SERVER MONITOR TO DB mondb;
SET SERVER TARGET  TO DB db2b;
DROP MONITOR SUSPENSION s1;
```

Dropping a monitor suspension involves running the following SQL:

```
DELETE FROM ASN.IBMSNAP_SUSPENDS WHERE SUSPENSION_NAME = 'S1'
```

To drop a monitor suspension template, we would use the DROP MONITOR SUSPENSION TEMPLATE ASNCLP command:

```
ASNCLP SESSION SET TO SQL REPLICATION;
SET RUN SCRIPT NOW STOP ON SQL ERROR ON;

SET SERVER MONITOR TO DB mondb;

DROP MONITOR SUSPENSION TEMPLATE lunch;
```

Dropping a monitor suspension template involves running the following SQL:

```
    DELETE FROM ASN.IBMSNAP_TEMPLATES WHERE TEMPLATE_NAME = 'LUNCH'
```

So let's look at an example in a bidirectional scenario as shown in the following diagram:

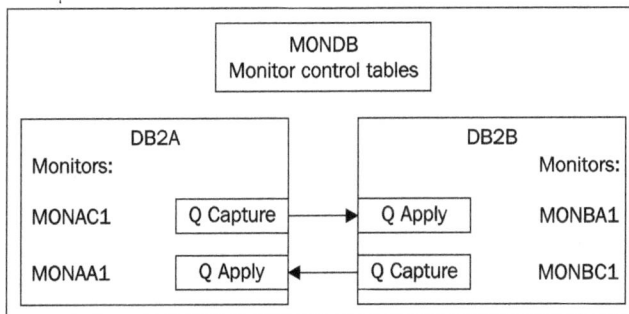

In this example, we have created four monitors to monitor Q Capture and Q Apply on each of the two servers. The monitor_qual are MONAC1, MONAA1, MONBA1, and MONBC1. The monitor_server is MONDB.

If we want to perform maintenance on the DB2B database every Sunday afternoon at 16:00 for one hour, we would create a monitor suspension template as follows:

```
ASNCLP SESSION SET TO SQL REPLICATION;
SET RUN SCRIPT NOW STOP ON SQL ERROR ON;

SET SERVER MONITOR TO DB mondb;

CREATE MONITOR SUSPENSION TEMPLATE tmaintbaft
START TIME 16:00:00
REPEATS WEEKLY DAY OF WEEK SUNDAY
FOR DURATION 1 HOURS;
```

And then, we would create a monitor suspension as follows:

```
ASNCLP SESSION SET TO SQL REPLICATION;
SET RUN SCRIPT NOW STOP ON SQL ERROR ON;

SET SERVER MONITOR TO DB mondb;
SET SERVER TARGET  TO DB db2b;

CREATE MONITOR SUSPENSION NAME maintbaft
FOR SERVER DB2B
STARTING DATE 2007-03-20
USING TEMPLATE tmaintbaft
ENDING DATE 2007-12-31;
```

The ibmsnap_alerts table

The IBMSNAP_ALERTS table contains a record of all the alerts issued by the Replication Alert Monitor. The table records what alert condition occurred, at which server, and when they were detected.

Some common errors in the ALERT_CODE column are:

```
ASN5153W MONITOR "<monitor_qualifier>". The latency exceeds
the threshold value for program "<program_name>". The server
is  "<server_name>". The schema is "<schema>". The   latency is
"<latency>" seconds. The threshold is  "<threshold>"   seconds.
```

```
ASN5157W MONITOR "<monitor_qualifier>". The Q subscription
"<subscription_name>" is inactive. The  server is "<server_name>".
The schema is "<schema>". State information: "<stateinfo>".
```

Other tools available to monitor Q replication

There are a few non replication tools and tasks available to help with monitoring Q replication.

The database layer

The tools available in the DB2 layer are described next.

Optim Data Studio

Optim Data Studio (or the DB2 Control Center main screen) can be used to check that there are connections to the source and target databases.

The DB2 Health Center

The Health Center can be used to raise alerts if the instances containing the source and target databases become inactive.

The WebSphere MQ layer

The tools available in the WebSphere MQ layer are described next.

The WebSphere MQ Explorer

If the MQ layer is not functioning correctly, then Q replication will not work. This GUI is a good way to quickly check if the Listeners and Channels for each Queue Manager are running.

The WebSphere MQSC interface (runmqsc)

If we cannot use a GUI like the WebSphere MQ Explorer, then we need to use the WebSphere MQSC interface. *The WebSphere MQ layer* section of this chapter goes thru the MQSC commands needed to check that everything on the MQ side is functioning correctly.

The rfhutil utility

The rfhutil utility is a free download and comes as part of the WebSphere MQ support pack. It is a GUI which allows us to look at the contents of WebSphere MQ queues—both destructively and non-destructively.

To get to the download site simply search for rfhutil on the Web. Documentation on how to use the utility is available from the download site.

The Q replication layer

The tools available in the Q replication layer are described next.

The Replication Dashboard

The Replication Dashboard is a free down from IBM. It can be used to monitor the latency of the replication environment.

Tivoli Monitoring

Tivoli monitoring of Q replication is outside the scope of this book, but there is an article on the IBM DeveloperWorks website, which describes how to set up Tivoli Monitoring for Q replication:

```
http://www.ibm.com/developerworks/db2/library/techarticle/dm-
0606martin/.
```

The asnqanalyze command

The ASNQANALYZE command is used to gather information about the state of a Q replication or Event Publishing environment. The command produces a formatted HTML report about Q Capture or Q Apply control tables, the DB2 catalog, diagnostic log files for the replication programs, and WebSphere MQ Queue Managers. It needs to connect to the MQ port for the Queue Manager associated with the database, so the Queue Manager must be running and the Listeners started.

The command syntax is:

```
ASNQANALYZE GATHER DATABASE=<Database>
  [INSTANCE=<DB2 Instance -Workstation only.>(DB2)]
  [SUBSYSTEM=<DB2 Subsystem name -z/OS only.>(DSN1)]
  [USERID=<User ID>]
  [PASSFILE=<password file>]
  [SCHEMA=<Capture/Apply Schema>(ASN)]
  [CAPLOGDIR=<Directory of Capture Log>]
  [APPLOGDIR=<Directory of Apply Log>]
  [PORT=<Queue Manager Listener Port>(1414)]
  [CHANNEL=<Server Connection Channel>(SYSTEM.DEF.SVRCONN)]
  [HOSTNAME=<Queue Manager server IP or Hostname>(LOCALHOST)]
  [WARNERRSONLY=<OFF, ON>]
  [GETCOLS=<ON, OFF>]
  [GETMONITOR=<ON, OFF>]
  [LOGDAYS=<number of days to retrieve records>(3)]
  [ZIP=<ON, OFF>]
  -o <fileoutputname>
  Report <XML file1> <XML file2> ...
```

Note what the defaults are. Unless we have used all default values when setting up the environment, we need to specify some parameters. So an example of the command to obtain a detailed level of analysis about the control tables on DB2A is:

```
$ asnqanalyze GATHER INSTANCE=db2 DATABASE=db2a HOSTNAME=127.0.0.1
PORT=1450 SCHEMA=asn CAPLOGDIR=c:\temp
```

Note that, we are specifying the instance name, the IP address, and Listener port number of QMA, where the Q Capture logs are written to, and the schema for the Q Capture control tables. And if we check in the directory from where we issued the command from, we see two files: DB2A.ASN.zip and qanalyzer.log.

The report is contained within the .zip file. To view the report, simply unzip the file. If we do not want to produce a .zip file we could specify ZIP=OFF.

> If we do not enter the GATHER parameter, then the commands runs, but nothing is written to the output directory (that is, the directory we are in).

It is a good idea to run the asnqanalyze command on a regular basis (say weekly), and before or after any changes are made to the replication environment, so that we have an audit trail of such changes.

Some what happens if ... scenarios

What we look at in the following sections are some common *what if* questions. For each scenario, the repercussions are examined for an active Q subscription when a record is inserted.

If MQ is stopped on each server

What we will test in this section is what happens if the Queue Manager is stopped. We will test this using unidirectional replication (Refer to *Appendix A* for details on how to set up unidirectional replication).

1. First let's make sure that replication is working. From CLP-A, issue:

   ```
   $ db2 "insert into eric.t1 values (5,5,'H')"
   ```

   From CLP-B, issue:

   ```
   $ db2 "select * from fred.t1"
   C1          C2          C3
   ----------- ----------- ----------
             5           5 H
     1 record(s) selected.
   ```

   We should see one record in FRED.T1 on DB2B.

   We can see that the unidirectional Q replication setup is working.

2. Now we can continue with our test. Stop the WebSphere MQ on the source server.

```
$ endmqm -p QMA
```

WebSphere MQ queue manager 'QMA' ending.

WebSphere MQ queue manager 'QMA' ended.

Is the Q subscription still active?

```
$ db2 "SELECT SUBSTR(subname,1,10) AS subname, state AS s,
state_time FROM asn.ibmqrep_subs "

SUBNAME     S STATE_TIME
----------  - -------------------------

TAB1        A 2007-04-03-11.23.07.968000
```

We can see that the Q subscription is still in Active state (A), but what does this mean? Let's check Q Capture:

```
$ asnqccmd capture_server=db2a status

2007-04-03-11.50.38.578000 ASN0600I  "AsnQCcmd" :   "" : "Initial"
: Program "mqpubcmd 9.1.0" is starting.
2007-04-03-11.50.46.593000 ASN0506E  "AsnQCcmd" :   "ASN" :
"Initial" : The command was not processed. The "Q Capture" program
is presumed down.
```

3. Now if we check the Q Capture log, we see the entry:

```
<sendQueue::putControlMsg> ASN0574E  "Q Capture" :   "ASN" :
"WorkerThread" : The WebSphere MQ queue manager "QMA" is not
available or it was not started. The program will terminate.
```

The Q subscription may still be in active state, but Q Capture has stopped.

4. Let's insert another row into the source table. From CLP-A, issue:

```
$ db2 "INSERT INTO eric.t1 VALUES(6,6,'H')"
```

Clearly, this row will not get replicated at the current time because Q Capture is stopped, but as the Q subscription is active, it will get replicated as soon as Q Capture is started.

5. So start the source Queue Manager again: From CLP-A, issue:

```
$ strmqm QMA
```

We will, of course, also need to start the Listener for QMA and start the Channel.

The Listener for QMA can be started using the SYSA_QMA_START_RUNMQLSR.BAT batch file. From CLP-A, run the file as:

```
$ SYSA_QMA_START_RUNMQLSR.BAT
```

The Channel from QMA to QMB can be started by executing the contents of the SYSA_QMA_START_RUNMQCHL_AB.BAT file. From CLP-A, run the file as:

```
$ SYSA_QMA_START_RUNMQCHL_AB.BAT
```

The Channel from QMB to QMA can be started by executing the contents of the SYSB_QMB_START_RUNMQCHL_BA.BAT file. From CLP-B, run the file as:

```
$ SYSB_QMB_START_RUNMQCHL_BA.BAT
```

And we need to restart Q Capture. Note that we will use a startmode setting of WARMSI. From CLP-A, issue:

```
$ start ASNQCAP CAPTURE_SERVER=db2a STARTMODE=warmsi

$ db2 "SELECT SUBSTR(subname,1,10) AS subname, state AS s, state_
time FROM asn.ibmqrep_subs"

SUBNAME     S STATE_TIME
----------- - -------------------------
TAB1        A 2007-04-03-11.23.07.968000
```

And if we select from the target table. From CLP-B, issue:

```
$ db2 "select * from fred.t1"

C1          C2          C3
----------- ----------- ----------
          5           5 H
          6           6 H
```

We should see two records in FRED.T1 on DB2B.

Replication has picked up from where it left off.

So if the Queue Manager on the source server is stopped and restarted, then what we have to do is:

- Start the Listener for the Queue Manager
- Ensure all the Channels on all Queue Managers are started
- Start Q Capture

Note that we do not have to do anything to the Q subscription. We have now finished looking at what happens if the Queue Manager on the source server is stopped.

If the Receive Queue is stopped

We will test this using unidirectional replication.

1. First let's make sure that replication is working. From CLP-A, issue:

   ```
   $ db2 "insert into eric.t1 values (7,7,'H')"
   ```

   From CLP-B, issue:

   ```
   $ db2 "select * from fred.t1"
   ```

   ```
   C1              C2              C3
   ----------- ----------- ----------
             7               7 H
      1 record(s) selected.
   ```

   We should see one record in FRED.T1 on DB2B.

   We can see that the unidirectional Q replication setup is working.

2. Now we can continue with our test. Check the status of the Receive Queue. From CLP-B, issue:

   ```
   $ db2 "SELECT recvq, state FROM asn.ibmqrep_recvqueues WHERE recvq
   = 'CAPA.TO.APPB.RECVQ' "
   ```

3. Now stop the Receive Queue:

   ```
   $ asnqacmd APPLY_SERVER=db2b STOPQ='CAPA.TO.APPB.RECVQ'
   ```

   And check the status again using the previous command.

4. Let's insert another row into the source table:

   ```
   $ db2 "insert into eric.t1 values (8,8,'H') "
   ```

   Clearly this row will not get replicated at the current time because the Receive Queue is stopped.

5. Let's restart the Receive Queue:

   ```
   $ asnqacmd APPLY_SERVER=db2b STARTQ='CAPA.TO.APPB.RECVQ'
   ```

   Check the status again using the previous command, and check if the row has been replicated:

   ```
   $ db2 "select * from fred.t1"
   ```

   ```
   C1              C2              C3
   ----------- ----------- ----------
             7               7 H
             8               8 H
      1 record(s) selected.
   ```

   We should see two records in FRED.T1 on DB2B.

If Q Apply is not running

This section looks at what happens if Q Apply is not running and a row is captured on the source server. What happens to the message?

One of the things we have to consider if Q Apply is stopped, is that Q Capture sends a heart beat message through its Send Queue (`CAPA.TO.APPB.SENDQ.REMOTE`) telling Q Apply that it is still up and running, but has no transactions to replicate. The frequency of this heart beat message is set when we create a Replication Queue Map and is the `heartbeat interval` parameter (with a default value of five seconds). The sending of the message can be disabled by setting the value to zero.

Let's use the unidirectional setup as our test system, but with the following change— change the `heartbeat interval` parameter to have a value of zero and reinitialize Q Capture, otherwise the change will not take effect. Then perform the following test:

1. To stop Q Apply. From CLP-B, issue:

   ```
   $ asnqacmd APPLY_SERVER=db2b STOP
   ```

2. To insert a record into the source table. From CLP-A, issue:

   ```
   $ db2 "insert into eric.t1 values (2,2,'H') "
   ```

3. Now check the message depth of the Receive Queue on QMB. From CLP-B, issue:

   ```
   $ runmqsc QMB
   dis ql(CAPA.TO.APPB.RECVQ) curdepth
       QUEUE(CAPA.TO.APPB.RECVQ)                TYPE(QLOCAL)
       CURDEPTH(1)
   : end
   ```

We can see that the queue depth for the Receive Queue is one. If we try and browse the queue with the `rfhutil` utility, then all we will see is the compressed message, which is machine readable, as shown in the following screenshot:

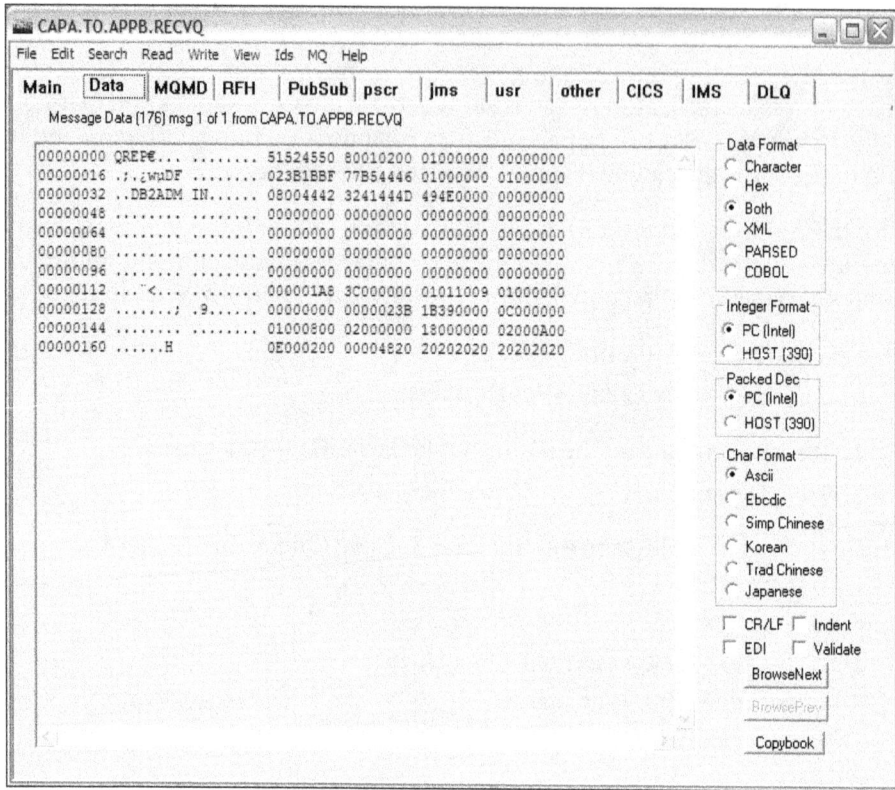

4. Now start Q Apply again. From CLP-B, issue:

```
$ start asnqapp APPLY_SERVER=db2b
```

And if we display the current depth of the queue again. From CLP-B, issue:

```
$ runmqsc QMB
: dis ql(CAPA.TO.APPB.RECVQ) curdepth
   QUEUE(CAPA.TO.APPB.RECVQ)                 TYPE(QLOCAL)
   CURDEPTH(0)
```

We can see that the current queue depth (CURDEPTH) is back to zero.

So the answer to the question *what happens to a message if Q Apply is not running* is that it stays on the local Receive Queue on QMB, which in our setup is called CAPA.TO.APPB.RECVQ.

If the Q Apply Queue Manager is not running

In our examples, the Queue Manager where Q Apply is running is called QMB. What we will do is stop this Queue Manager, which will also stop Q Apply. We will see the following message in the Q Apply log:

```
ASN0574E  "Q Apply" :  "ASN" : "BR00000" : The WebSphere MQ queue manager
"QMB" is not available or it was not started. The program will terminate.
```

1. To stop the Queue Manager for Q Apply. From CLP-B, issue:

   ```
   $ endmqm -p QMB
   ```

2. To insert a record into the source table. From CLP-A, issue:

   ```
   $ db2 "insert into eric.t1 values (3,3,'H') "
   ```

3. Now check the message depth of the Transmission Queue on QMA. From CLP-A, issue:

   ```
   $ runmqsc QMA
   : display ql(QMB.XMITQ) curdepth
       QUEUE(QMB.XMITQ)                        TYPE(QLOCAL)
       CURDEPTH(1): end
   ```

   We can see that we have one message on the Transmission Queue.

4. If we now start the Queue Manager and Listener again and then start Q Apply. From CLP-B, issue:

   ```
   $ strmqm QMB
   $ start asnqapp apply_server=DB2B
   ```

   Now check our target table. From CLP-B, issue:

   ```
   $ db2 "select * from fred.t1"
   C1           C2           C3
   ------------ ------------ ----------
             1            1 H
             2            2 H
             3            3 H
   ```

   We can see on DB2B the row we inserted on DB2A, so replication is working again.

So, the answer to the question *If the Queue Manager where Q Apply is running (QMB) is stopped, where does Q replication store its messages* is that it stores the messages in the Transmission Queue on QMA, which in our setup is called QMB.XMITQ.

If the Receive Queue fills up

We will look at what happens when the Receive Queue on the Apply side becomes full (that is, it has reached its MAXDPETH limit). We will test this using unidirectional replication.

A queue becomes full when the number of messages being held in the queue reaches the maximum number of messages allowed in the queue (MAXDEPTH). This is a configurable parameter and is set at queue creation time, refer to the *MQ Queue management – To define a Local Queue* section of *Chapter 4, WebSphere MQ for the DBA.*

To test what happens when the Receive Queue is full, we will change its MAXDEPTH value to two.

1. From CLP-B, issue:

   ```
   $ runmqsc QMB
   : alter ql(CAPA.TO.APPB.RECVQ) maxdepth(2)
   : dis ql(CAPA.TO.APPB.RECVQ) curdepth,maxdepth
      QUEUE(CAPA.TO.APPB.RECVQ)                 TYPE(QLOCAL)
      CURDEPTH(0)                               MAXDEPTH(2)
   : end
   ```

2. Confirm that the MAXDEPTH value is two. On QMB stop the Receive Queue. This means Q Apply will not read from the queue and messages will build up in the queue. From CLP-B, issue:

   ```
   $ asnqacmd apply_server=DB2B apply_schema=ASN stopq=CAPA.TO.APPB.RECVQ

   ASN0600I  "AsnQAcmd" :   ""  : "Initial" : Program "asnqacmd 9.1.0"
   is starting.
   ASN0522I  "AsnQAcmd" :  "ASN" : "Initial" : The program received
   the "STOPQ" command.
   ```

3. Check the state of the queue. From CLP-B, issue:

   ```
   $ db2 "SELECT recvq, state FROM asn.ibmqrep_recvqueues "
   RECVQ                                                STATE
   -------------------------------------------------- -----
   CAPA.TO.APPB.RECVQ                                    I
   ```

   We can see that the state of the queue is now Inactive (I). Now insert three rows into our source table on DB2A. From CLP-A, issue:

   ```
   $ db2 "insert into eric.t1 values (4,4,'H')"
   $ db2 "insert into eric.t1 values (5,5,'T')"
   $ db2 "insert into eric.t1 values (6,6,'C')"
   ```

And display the queue depths again. From CLP-B, issue:

```
$ runmqsc QMB
: dis ql(CAPA.TO.APPB.RECVQ) curdepth,maxdepth
    QUEUE(CAPA.TO.APPB.RECVQ)                TYPE(QLOCAL)
    CURDEPTH(2)                              MAXDEPTH(2)
: dis ql(DEAD.LETTER.QUEUE.QMB) curdepth,maxdepth
    QUEUE(DEAD.LETTER.QUEUE.QMB)             TYPE(QLOCAL)
    CURDEPTH(1)                              MAXDEPTH(5000)
: end
```

We can see that the Receive Queue (CAPA.TO.APPB.RECVQ) current queue depth has reached its maximum value and that messages are now being placed into the **Dead Letter Queue (DLQ)**, because its current depth is one.

4. Start the Receive Queue. From CLP-B, issue:

```
$ asnqacmd apply_server=DB2B apply_schema=ASN startq=CAPA.TO.APPB.
RECVQ
```

Display the queue depths again. From CLP-B, issue:

```
$ runmqsc QMB
: dis ql(CAPA.TO.APPB.RECVQ) curdepth,maxdepth
    QUEUE(CAPA.TO.APPB.RECVQ)                TYPE(QLOCAL)
    CURDEPTH(0)                              MAXDEPTH(2)
: dis ql(DEAD.LETTER.QUEUE.QMB) curdepth,maxdepth
    QUEUE(DEAD.LETTER.QUEUE.QMB)             TYPE(QLOCAL)
    CURDEPTH(1)                              MAXDEPTH(5000)
: end
```

We can see that the Receive Queue depth is now back to zero, but we still have one message on the DLQ.

5. Insert another row into the source test table. From CLP-A, issue:

```
$ db2 "insert into eric.t1 values (7,7,'M')"
```

And check the Receive Queue current queue depth again. From CLP-B, issue:

```
$ runmqsc QMB
: dis ql(CAPA.TO.APPB.RECVQ) curdepth,maxdepth
    QUEUE(CAPA.TO.APPB.RECVQ)                TYPE(QLOCAL)
    CURDEPTH(1)                              MAXDEPTH(2)
: end
```

We can see that the message is being held in the Receive Queue, because before Q Apply can process this message, it is expecting the message that is currently in the DLQ. No message gets written to the IBMQREP_EXCEPTIONS table or to the Q Apply log for this event.

6. As mentioned in the *Dead Letter Queue handler(runmqdlq)* section of *Chapter 4*, to handle messages in the DLQ, we use a WebSphere MQ utility called runmqdlq—which is the DLQ message handler. We will use the DLQ handler discussed in this section, which is located in the c:\temp directory, and contains the following:

```
REASON(MQRC_Q_FULL) ACTION(RETRY) RETRY(5) WAIT(NO)

$ runmqdlq DEAD.LETTER.QUEUE.QMB QMB < c:\temp\dlqrule.txt
```

7. Now check the depth of the DLQ. From CLP-B, issue:

```
$ runmqsc QMB

: dis ql(DEAD.LETTER.QUEUE.QMB) curdepth,maxdepth

   QUEUE(DEAD.LETTER.QUEUE.QMB)              TYPE(QLOCAL)

   CURDEPTH(0)                               MAXDEPTH(5000)

: end
```

We can see that the depth of the DLQ is now back to zero, and if we check our target table. From CLP-B, issue:

```
$ db2 "select * from fred.t1"
```

```
C1            C2            C3
-----------   -----------   ----------
          1             1 H
          2             2 H
          3             3 H
          4             4 H
          5             5 H
          6             6 H
          7             7 M
```

We can see all rows which we inserted into our source table.

So, the answer to the question *If the Receive Queue for Q Apply fills up where does Q replication store its messages,* is that it stores them in the Dead Letter Queue on QMB, which in our setup is called DEAD.LETTER.QUEUE.QMB.

If the Q Apply Dead Letter Queue fills up

We will look at what happens when both the Receive Queue and the Dead Letter Queue (DLQ) for Q Apply become full.

The steps we will follow are:

1. Set up unidirectional replication.
2. Test the replication with one record.
3. Change the `maxdepth` value of the Receive Queue to two.
4. Change the `maxdepth` value of the Dead Letter Queue to one.
5. Stop Q Apply reading from the Receive Queue.
6. Insert three rows into the source table.
7. See where the messages end up.

Continuing our previous example, the first step is to change the maximum depth of the DLQ to one.

1. From CLP-B, issue:

   ```
   $ runmqsc QMB
   : alter ql(DEAD.LETTER.QUEUE.QMB) maxdepth(1)
   : dis ql(DEAD.LETTER.QUEUE.QMB) curdepth,maxdepth
      QUEUE(CAPA.TO.APPB.RECVQ)              TYPE(QLOCAL)
      CURDEPTH(0)                            MAXDEPTH(1)
   ```

2. Confirm that the MAXDEPTH value is one. And also check the maximum depth for the Receive Queue:

   ```
   : dis ql(CAPA.TO.APPB.RECVQ) curdepth,maxdepth
      QUEUE(CAPA.TO.APPB.RECVQ)              TYPE(QLOCAL)
      CURDEPTH(0)                            MAXDEPTH(2)
   ```

   Confirm that the MAXDEPTH value is two.

   ```
   : end
   ```

3. Now on QMB, stop the Receive Queue. This means Q Apply will not read from the queue and messages will build up in the queue. From CLP-B, issue:

   ```
   $ asnqacmd apply_server=DB2B apply_schema=ASN stopq=CAPA.TO.APPB.
   RECVQ

   ASN0600I  "AsnQAcmd" :   "" : "Initial" : Program "asnqacmd 9.1.0"
   is starting.
   ASN0522I  "AsnQAcmd" :  "ASN" : "Initial" : The program received
   the "STOPQ" command.
   ```

4. Check the state of the queue. From CLP-B, issue:

```
$ db2 "SELECT recvq, state FROM asn.ibmqrep_recvqueues"

RECVQ                                                      STATE
-----------------------------------------------------------------

CAPA.TO.APPB.RECVQ                                         I
```

We can see that the queue is now Inactive (I). Now insert four rows into our source table on DB2A. From CLP-A, issue:

```
$ db2 "insert into eric.t1 values (8,4,'H')"

$ db2 "insert into eric.t1 values (9,4,'T')"

$ db2 "insert into eric.t1 values (10,4,'T')"

$ db2 "insert into eric.t1 values (11,4,'T')"
```

5. Check the state of the Channels. From CLP-A, issue:

```
$ runmqsc QMA

dis chstatus(QMA.TO.QMB)

: end
```

We can see that the status of the Channel is RUNNING. From CLP-B, issue:

```
$ runmqsc QMB

dis chstatus(QMB.TO.QMA)

: end
```

We can see that the status of the Channel is PENDING.

At this point Q Capture and Q Apply are still running, but the Channel QMA.TO.QMB has stopped. Why is this? The following description is paraphrased from http://www-1.ibm.com/support/docview.wss?uid=swg21166048:

A message is sent over a channel, and arrives at the remote end. The amqcrsta (listener process) attempts to deliver the message to the destination queue. If the queue is full, it tries MRTRY (message retry) times to put the message waiting MRTMR (message retry timer) milliseconds between each attempt. If this does not work (because the queue is full on each attempted put) it closes the destination queue, opens the QMGR object and inquires the QMGR object to check for a dead letter queue. It then closes the QMGR object. If a dead letter queue exists the amqcrsta process then repeats the process of attempting to put the message a number of times. During this time the channel is in PAUSED status and the remote end of the channel (that started the conversation) is in RUNNING status. If the put failed (because the dead letter queue is also full) the amqcrsta process sends a message to the conversation initiator to say that the put failed and the channel should be retried. The amqcrsta then ends.

Where `dlqrule.txt` contains:

```
WAIT (NO)
REASON(MQRC_Q_FULL) ACTION (RETRY) RETRY (5)
```

16. Now check the depth of the DLQ. From CLP-B, issue:

    ```
    $ runmqsc QMB
    : dis ql(DEAD.LETTER.QUEUE.QMB) curdepth,maxdepth
       QUEUE(DEAD.LETTER.QUEUE.QMB)                  TYPE(QLOCAL)
       CURDEPTH(0)                                   MAXDEPTH(2)
    : end
    ```

17. We can see that the depth of the DLQ is now back to zero, and if we check
    our target table:

    ```
    $ db2 "select * from fred.t1"

    C1            C2            C3
    -----------   -----------   ----------
              1             1 H
              8             4 H
              9             4 H
             10             4 H
             11             4 H
    ```

    We can see that all the rows that were inserted into the source table have
    been replicated to the target table.

18. Now start Q Capture:

    ```
    $ asnqcap capture_server=DB2A startmode=WARMSI
    ```

We should be up and running again.

The series of events is:

- When the Receive Queue becomes full messages are routed to the DLQ.
- When the DLQ becomes full the Channel from QMA to QMB stops. We cannot
  restart it again until we have dealt with the message on the target server.
- Deal with the messages on the target server in both the Receive Queue and
  the DLQ. Make sure the current queue depth in both queues is zero before
  starting the Channel from QMA to QMB.

If a Dead Letter Queue has not been defined

When we defined our Queue Manager on the target server, we specified a Dead Letter Queue ($ crtmqm –u DEAD.LETTER.QUEUE.QMB QMB) — *what happens if we define a Queue Manager without specifying a Dead Letter Queue.*

This situation is the same as what happens if we had defined a Dead Letter Queue and it fills up. Refer to the *If the Q Apply Dead Letter Queue fills up* section for more information.

What happens if—summary diagram

The following diagram shows in which queue messages are held when various events occur:

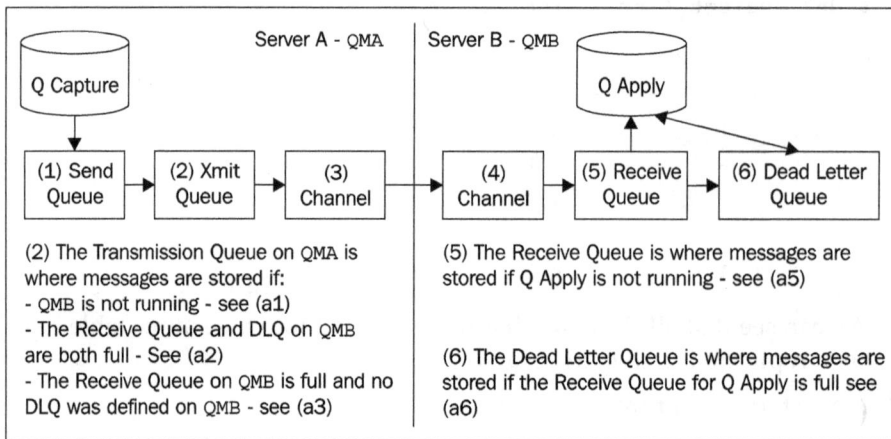

References (all in this *Some what happens if ... scenarios* section):

- **a1**: *If the Q Apply Queue Manager is not running.*
- **a2**: *If the Q Apply Dead Letter Queue fills up.*
- **a3**: *If the Dead Letter Queue has not been defined.*
- **a4**: *If the Q Apply Queue Manager is not running.*
- **a5**: *If Q Apply is not running.*
- **a6**: *If the Receive Queue fills up.*

The following table shows the commands we need to issue to monitor each queue

---

(1) To check the status of the Send Queue. From CLP-A, issue:

   `$ db2 "SELECT sendq, state FROM asn.ibmqrep_sendqueues"`

(2) Transmission Queue: check the depth of the queue. From CLP-A, issue:

   `: dis ql(QMB.XMITQ) curdepth,maxdepth`

(3) Channel: to check the state of the Channel. From CLP-A, issue:

   `: dis chstatus(QMA.TO.QMB)`

(4) Channel: to check the state of the Channel. From CLP-B, issue:

   `: dis chstatus(QMA.TO.QMB)`

(5) To check the status of the Receive Queue. From CLP-B, issue:

   `$ db2 "SELECT recvq, state FROM asn.ibmqrep_recvqueues"`

(6) DLQ: check the depth of the queue. From CLP-B, issue:

   `: dis ql(DEAD.LETTER.QUEUE.QMB) curdepth,maxdepth`

The following shows the queue and Channel definitions:

```
(C1) DEFINE QREMOTE(CAPA.TO.APPB.SENDQ.REMOTE) REPLACE +
PUT(ENABLED) XMITQ(QMB.XMITQ) RNAME(CAPA.TO.APPB.RECVQ) +
RQMNAME(QMB) DEFPSIST(YES)

(C2) DEFINE QLOCAL(QMB.XMITQ) REPLACE +
USAGE(XMITQ) PUT(ENABLED) GET(ENABLED) TRIGGER +
TRIGTYPE(FIRST) TRIGDATA(QMA.TO.QMB) INITQ SYSTEM.CHANNEL.INITQ)

(C3) DEFINE CHANNEL(QMA.TO.QMB) CHLTYPE(SDR) REPLACE +
TRPTYPE(TCP) DISCINT(0) XMITQ(QMB.XMITQ) +
CONNAME('127.0.0.1(1451)')

(C4) DEFINE CHANNEL(QMA.TO.QMB) CHLTYPE(RCVR) REPLACE +
TRPTYPE(TCP)

(C5) DEFINE QLOCAL(CAPA.TO.APPB.RECVQ) REPLACE +
PUT(ENABLED) GET(ENABLED) DEFSOPT(SHARED) DEFPSIST(YES)

(C6) DEFINE QLOCAL(DEAD.LETTER.QUEUE.QMB) REPLACE +
PUT(ENABLED) GET(ENABLED) SHARE DEFSOPT(SHARED) DEFPSIST(YES)
```

Q replication performance considerations

Now let's move on to look at some Q replication performance considerations. Our Q replication environment is made up of four components:

- The DB2 database layer comprising the source and target databases
- WebSphere MQ
- Q Capture
- Q Apply

Let's look at tuning each of these components.

The DB2 database layer

The DB2 source or target databases: The tuning that should be performed for the DB2 databases is normal tuning that we would do for any database. The only point to bear in mind is that the amount of DB2 log space required may increase due to DATA CAPTURE CHANGES being set. There are no other special considerations if the databases are involved in Q replication.

We may need to run RUNSTATS and REORGS on the replication control tables—these tables should be treated as any other application table.

The WebSphere MQ layer

We have mentioned the MAXDEPTH parameter for queues (Refer to the *MQ Queue management – To define a Local Queue* section of *Chapter 4*), and if we increase this value, then we should ensure that WebSphere MQ has been allocated sufficient disk space to handle this number of messages.

One of the Queue Manager parameters mentioned is MAXUMSGS, which is the maximum number of uncommitted messages that can be put on or retrieved from queues (Refer to the *Create/start/stop a Queue Manager* section of *Chapter 4*). If we change the commit_interval parameter (how often, in milliseconds, Q Capture commits transactions to WebSphere MQ) of Q Capture, then we may need to increase the MAXUMSGS value. If we hit this limit, then when Q Capture tries to put a transaction on the Send Queue the MQPUT will fail with reason code 2024 Syncpoint Limit Reached. At that point Q Capture can decide to commit what it's done so far or back out. This is what we will see in the Q Capture log:

```
<qConnMgr::putRestartMsg> ASN0575E   "Q Capture" : "ASN" :
"WorkerThread" : The program encountered a WebSphere MQ error "2024"
while issuing the WebSphere MQ command "MQPUT" on queue "CAPA.
RESTARTQ".
```

```
<handleLogrdInitMsg> ASN0589I  "Q Capture" : "ASN" : "WorkerThread"
The program received an unexpected return code "503" from routine
"mqConnMgr::putRestartMsg".

<qCapStartLogrdThread> ASN0589I  "Q Capture" : "ASN" : "WorkerThread"
The program received an unexpected return code "503" from routine
"waitForLogrdInit".

<asnqwk> ASN7109I  "Q Capture" : "ASN" : "WorkerThread" : At program
termination, the highest log sequence number of a successfully
processed transaction is "0000:0000:0000:0000:0000" and the lowest
log sequence number of a transaction still to be committed is
"0000:0000:0000:023B:0FDA".

<asnThread::stop> ASN0590I  "Q Capture" : "ASN" : "Initial" The
thread "Initial" received return code "503" from the exiting thread
"WorkerThread".

<asnThread::stop> ASN0590I  "Q Capture" : "ASN" : "Initial" The
thread "Initial" received return code "2011" from the exiting thread
"HoldLThread".

<asnThread::stop> ASN0590I  "Q Capture" : "ASN" : "Initial" The
thread "Initial" received return code "2001" from the exiting thread
"AdminThread".

<asnThread::stop> ASN0590I  "Q Capture" : "ASN" : "Initial" The
thread "Initial" received return code "2011" from the exiting thread
"PruneThread".

<Asnenv:delEnvIpcQRcvHdl> ASN0595I  "Q Capture" : "ASN" : "Initial"
The program removed an IPC queue with keys "(Global\OSSEIPC48tempDB2.
DB2A.ASN.QCAP.IPC, Global\OSSEIPC49tempDB2.DB2A.ASN.QCAP.IPC, Global\
OSSEIPC50tempDB2.DB2A.ASN.QCAP.IPC".

<asnqcap::main> ASN0573I  "Q Capture" : "ASN" : "Initial" : The
program was stopped.
```

We can see the replication error message ASN0575E, which points to the WebSphere MQ error 2024.

> The explanation for the replication ASN7109I message is: The Q Capture program terminates and records the values of the restart message. During the next run, Q Capture will start reading the log from the restart log sequence number (the lowest LSN of a transaction still to be committed) and will ignore any transactions whose commit is before the maximum commit sequence number (the highest LSN of a successful transaction). In a partitioned database, these log indicators come from the partition where the Q Capture program is running.

Q Capture

The parameters that we can tune for Q Capture performance are the
`commit_interval`, `memory_limit`, `sleep_interval`, and `max_msg_size` parameters.

- `commit_interval`: This specifies how often, in milliseconds, Q Capture
  commits transactions to WebSphere MQ.

    - `memory_limit`: This specifies the amount of memory that
      Q Capture can use to build DB2 transactions in memory.
      The default value of 32 MB is sufficient for most workloads.
      We might need to increase the memory limit if Q Capture is
      spilling transactions to disk. Ideally, Q Capture should never
      need to spill transactions. If the `TRANS_SPILLED` column in
      the `IBMQREP_CAPMON` table has a value greater than zero, try
      increasing the memory limit.

    - `sleep_interval`: This specifies the number of milliseconds
      that Q Capture waits after reaching the end of the active log
      and assembling any transactions that remain in memory.
      By default Q Capture sleeps for 5,000 milliseconds (five
      seconds) and after this interval, it starts reading the log again.
      A smaller `sleep_interval` can improve performance by
      lowering latency (the time that it takes for a transaction to
      go from source to target), reducing idle time, and increasing
      throughput in a high-volume transaction environment.

    - `max_msg_size`: This determines the size of the memory
      buffer that Q Capture uses for each Send Queue. We set this
      parameter for the Publishing Queue Map or Replication
      Queue Map that contains the Send Queue. After a transaction
      is built in memory, Q Capture uses the `max_msg_size`
      parameter to determine the size of the message to publish.
      If the transaction size in bytes is larger than the maximum
      message size, then the transaction will be split into smaller
      messages. The parameter also determines the largest message
      size that Q Apply will see. For LOB data, a small maximum
      message size can slow Q Apply performance by requiring
      more frequent updates to the target table to replicate an entire
      LOB value.

The `monitor_interval` and `pruning_interval` parameters should be looked at if
the system is CPU constrained.

Q Apply

If we are letting Q Apply handle the initial loads of tables, then it will hold all transactions while the load is being performed in spill files on disk, so we need to ensure that we have enough disk space. To size this we need to know how many rows will be stored while the load is being performed, which is not an easy calculation to make.

The `num_apply_agents` parameter is assigned on a per Receive Queue basis, and is set when we create the Replication Queue Map. It is the number of agent threads that Q Apply uses to concurrently apply transactions from a Receive Queue. A value of one requests that the transactions are executed in the order they were received from the source table, and the default is 16.

Some error messages

This section looks at some error messages generated by Q Capture and Q Apply.

Q Capture: ASN0569E on starting

If we get an `ASN0569E` startup error `SIGSEGV`, it means that we have not started the Queue Manager (`$ strmqm <QMname>`).

Q Capture: ASN7094E

The following is an extract from the Q Capture log showing the error:

```
2006-02-15-08.52.43.441000 ASN7094E  "Q Capture" : "ASN" :
"WorkerThread" : The "P2PSUBSTOPPING" signal failed because the XML
publication or Q subscription "T10001" has an invalid  subtype "B" or
an invalid state "G".

2006-02-15-08.52.43.481000 ASN7094E  "Q Capture" : "ASN" :
"WorkerThread" : The "P2PSUBSTOPPING" signal failed because the XML
publication or Q subscription "T30001" has an invalid  subtype "B" or
an invalid state "G".

2006-02-15-08.52.48.959000 ASN7094E  "Q Capture" : "ASN" :
"WorkerThread" : The "P2PREADYTOSTOP" signal failed because the XML
publication or Q subscription "T10001" has an invalid  subtype "B" or
an invalid state "I".

2006-02-15-08.52.48.969000 ASN7094E  "Q Capture" : "ASN" :
"WorkerThread" : The "P2PREADYTOSTOP" signal failed because the XML
publication or Q subscription "T30001" has an invalid  subtype "B" or
an invalid state "I".
```

What we did was update the ASN.IBMQREP_SUBS column STATE to N for the Q subscriptions:

```
$ db2 connect to db2a

$ db2 "UPDATE asn.ibmqrep_subs SET state = 'N' WHERE subname = 'T10001'"

$ db2 "update asn.ibmqrep_subs set state = 'N' where subname = 'T30001'"

$ db2 connect to db2b

$ db2 "UPDATE asn.ibmqrep_subs SET state = 'N' WHERE subname = 'T30002'"

$ db2 "update asn.ibmqrep_subs set state = 'N' where subname = 'T10002'"
```

Q Apply: hangs when starting

When we start Q Apply as follows:

```
$ asnqapp APPLY_SERVER=db2b APPLY_PATH="C:\TEMP"
```

Then what we expect to see is:

```
ASN0600I  "Q Apply" :  "" : "Initial" : Program "mqapply 9.1.0" is
starting.
ASN7526I  "Q Apply" :  "ASN" : "BR00000" : The Q Apply program has
started processing the receive queue

 "TGT.RECVQ" for replication queue map "RQMSRC2TGT".
```

We are looking for the ASN7526I to tell us that Q Apply has started processing the Receive Queue, which means that Q Apply is now ready.

But what happens if we only see the following message:

```
ASN0600I  "Q Apply" :  "" : "Initial" : Program "mqapply 9.1.0" is
starting.
```

It could mean that the Receive Queue which Q Apply needs to read from is inactive. We can check the STATE of each Receive Queue as follows:

```
$ db2 "SELECT SUBSTR(repqmapname,1,12) AS rqm, SUBSTR(recvq,1,20)
AS recvq, SUBSTR(sendq,1,20) AS sendq, SUBSTR(adminq,1,20) AS
adminq, SUBSTR(capture_server,1,5) AS caps, capture_alias AS capal,
SUBSTR(capture_schema,1,10) AS capschema, state FROM asn.ibmqrep_
recvqueues "
```

RQM CAPS	RECVQ	SENDQ	ADMINQ
RQMSRC2TGT SRCDB	TGT.RECVQ	TGT.RECVQ	TGT.ADMINQ

```
CAPAL    CAPSCHEMA   STATE
SRCDB    ASN         A
```

If the `STATE` column has a value of `I`, which means inactive, we can start the Receive Queue using the following command:

```
$ asnqacmd APPLY_SERVER=tgtdb STARTQ='TGT.RECVQ'
```

The Receive Queue will be stopped if Q Apply cannot process a message on the queue and we specified *stop reading from the Receive Queue* when we set up the Q subscription, which is done as follows. If we are using the Replication Center, then the action is chosen in Step 7, as shown in the following screenshot:

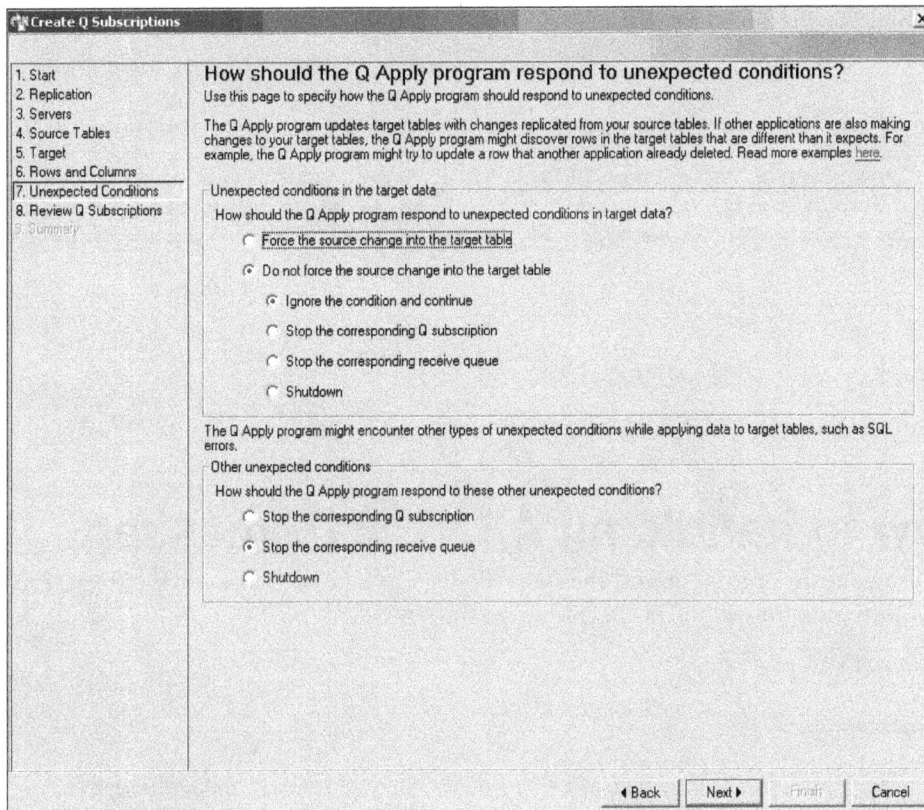

If we are using ASNCLP commands, then the action is chosen when we assign a value to the `ERROR ACTION` parameter:

```
CREATE QSUB
USING REPLQMAP RQMSRC2TGT
(SUBNAME DT01 DT.EMPL
```

```
OPTIONS
HAS LOAD PHASE N
EXIST TARGET
NAME DT.EMPL_CCD_SP
TYPE STOREDPROC
CONFLICT ACTION F
ERROR ACTION Q
LOAD TYPE 0);
```

Let's quickly recap what the possible values for ERROR ACTION can be:

- S: Stop Q Apply without applying the transaction
- D: Disable subscription and notify Q Capture
- Q: Stop reading from the Receive Queue

We can check the value of the ERROR ACTION parameter using the following query:

```
$ db2 "select SUBSTR(subname,1,20) AS subname, SUBSTR(recvq,1,30) AS
recvq, conflict_rule AS r, conflict_action AS a, error_action AS e, has_
loadphase AS l, CAST(load_type AS CHAR) AS t FROM asn.ibmqrep_targets"
```

SUBNAME	RECVQ	R	A	E	L	T
DT01	TGT.RECVQ	K	F	Q	N	0

We can see that the ERROR ACTION parameter has a value of Q.

How to handle an ASN7551E message

This is a common problem and the help file lists five tasks that we have to perform. The commands for each of these steps are shown next.

The help display says:

Explanation:

The Q Apply program cannot replicate any further changes until it finds the expected message. It will apply all changes that belong to messages that it already received.

User Response:

Look for the message with the expected message ID on all the Dead Letter Queues of all the WebSphere MQ queue managers that are used to transmit messages between the Q Capture and Q Apply programs. If we recover the message, put it on the receive queue, preserving the WebSphere MQ message header information (especially the message ID).

If the message cannot be recovered, follow these steps:

1. Use the `stopq` command to stop Q Apply from reading from the receive queue (this command was covered in the *Some what happens if ... scenarios – If the Receive Queue is stopped* section of this chapter).

   ```
   $ asnqacmd APPLY_SERVER=db2b STOPQ='CAPA.TO.APPB.RECVQ'
   ```

2. Deactivate all of the Q subscriptions for this Replication Queue Map.

   ° Get the RQM name using the Receive Queue from step 1.

   ° We can use the query in the *To manage Queue Maps – To list the RQM for a Receive Queue* section of *Chapter 6, Administration Tasks*, to get the RQM for a particular Receive Queue.

   ° We can use the query in the *Q subscription maintenance – To list all Q subscriptions using a RQM* section of *Chapter 6*, to get a list of the Q subscriptions using the RQM from the previous step.

3. Empty the Send Queue and the Receive Queue.

   Refer to the *MQ Queue management – To empty a Local Queue* section of *Chapter 4, WebSphere MQ for the DBA*, for details of how to empty the Send and Receive Queues.

4. Use the `startq` command so that Q Apply resumes reading from the Receive Queue.

   Refer to the *Q Apply administration – Starting a Receive Queue* section of *Chapter 6*, for details of how to do this.

5. Activate all the Q subscriptions for this Replication Queue Map.

   Refer to the *Q subscription maintenance – To start a Q subscription* section of *Chapter 5, The ASNCLP Command Interface*, for details of how to do this.

Q Apply: ASN7094E

We got this error when we tried to issue a signal which was not appropriate for the Q subscription or publication.

```
2005-04-02-02.37.43.821590 ASN7094E  "Q Capture" : "ASN" :
"WorkerThread" : The "P2PREADYTOSTOP" signal failed because the XML
publication or Q subscription "TAB010002" has an invalid  subtype "B"
or an invalid state "I".
```

We updated the ASN.IBMQREP_SUBS column STATE to "N" for Q subscription TAB010002 and restarted Q Apply.

Q Apply: ASN7505E

We got this error when we set up the target table incorrectly.

```
2005-04-02-19.05.20.544083 <QAsub::loadUniqConstrs> ASN7505E  "Q
Apply" : "ASN" : "BR00000" : The attributes of target columns are not
set up correctly for Q subscription "TAB010002" (receive queue "CAPA.
TO.APPB.RECVQ", replication queue map "RQMA2B"). Reason code: "6".
```

We declared a unique index.

Summary

In this chapter, we looked at how to monitor and report on the Q replication setup. We showed how to monitor that Q Capture and Q Apply were running, how far Q Capture is behind the DB2 log, and how far Q Apply is behind Q Capture. We then went on to describe the Replication Alert Monitor and how to use monitors. We also looked at other available tools to monitor the Q replication setup, and covered the asnqanalyze command to report on the system. We then covered seven *what if* scenarios, and drew all of these into a summary diagram. We finally covered some performance considerations and some common Q replication error messages.

This brings us to the end of our Q replication journey. We have shown you how to plan and set up a Q replication scenario and how to monitor it. We hope that you have found the book useful and wish you every success on your Q replication journey.

The Appendix (available online) will take you through numerous examples of setting up Q replication and Event Publishing scenarios, from unidirectional replication to peer-to-peer 4-way replication.

Index

L

M

V

W

WHERE clause 150
WHERE condition 149
worker thread, Q Capture 42

X

XML control message
  about 46
  activate subscription 46
  deactivate subscription 46
  invalidate send queue 46
  load done 46
XML data types, replicating 22
XML expressions 22

Z

z/OS 11, 20 , 53

[PACKT] enterprise PUBLISHING

professional expertise distilled

Thank you for buying
IBM InfoSphere Replication Server and Data Event Publisher

About Packt Publishing

Packt, pronounced 'packed', published its first book "Mastering phpMyAdmin for Effective MySQL Management" in April 2004 and subsequently continued to specialize in publishing highly focused books on specific technologies and solutions.

Our books and publications share the experiences of your fellow IT professionals in adapting and customizing today's systems, applications, and frameworks. Our solution based books give you the knowledge and power to customize the software and technologies you're using to get the job done. Packt books are more specific and less general than the IT books you have seen in the past. Our unique business model allows us to bring you more focused information, giving you more of what you need to know, and less of what you don't.

Packt is a modern, yet unique publishing company, which focuses on producing quality, cutting-edge books for communities of developers, administrators, and newbies alike. For more information, please visit our website: www.packtpub.com.

About Packt Enterprise

In 2010, Packt launched two new brands, Packt Enterprise and Packt Open Source, in order to continue its focus on specialization. This book is part of the Packt Enterprise brand, home to books published on enterprise software – software created by major vendors, including (but not limited to) IBM, Microsoft and Oracle, often for use in other corporations. Its titles will offer information relevant to a range of users of this software, including administrators, developers, architects, and end users.

Writing for Packt

We welcome all inquiries from people who are interested in authoring. Book proposals should be sent to author@packtpub.com. If your book idea is still at an early stage and you would like to discuss it first before writing a formal book proposal, contact us; one of our commissioning editors will get in touch with you.

We're not just looking for published authors; if you have strong technical skills but no writing experience, our experienced editors can help you develop a writing career, or simply get some additional reward for your expertise.

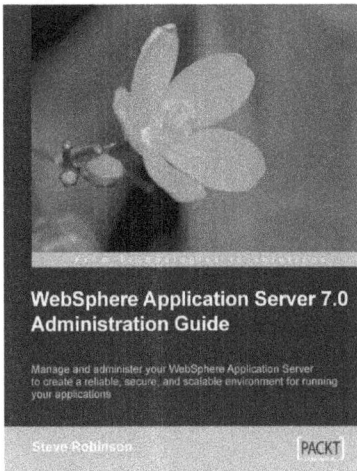

www.ingramcontent.com/pod-product-compliance
Lightning Source LLC
Chambersburg PA
CBHW080915220326

41598CB00034B/5580